Don't kid yourself!
Business is tough!
so this will be a tough read

because there are no short-cuts in business.
Many business books are written entertainingly to
make it seem easy. This is not that kind of book.
This is the real world of business. This is reality.
Sure, an inspirational guru can give you a kick in the
pants that inspires you to have a great business idea.
But then what? Then you need this book. If you find it a
hard slog, fine. Leave it and come back to it. That's how
we intended you to use it. As a constant reference guide.
A support. A help when the going gets tough. And it will.
Business doesn't make things easy for you. Business just
throws obstacles at you. You need weapons. This is a big
book of weapons, with two street-smart guys who explain
how to use them, in plain words, not business school style.
This is street-smart style. A whole different kind of school.
This is straight talk. This is not theory. This is execution.

john & mark

Library of Congress Control Number: 2011918006
CreateSpace, North Charleston, SC

Street Smart Disciplines

Printed in the United States of America.

ISBN: 1466335696
ISBN 13: 9781466335691

STREET SMART
DISCIPLINES
OF SUCCESSFUL PEOPLE

**7 Indispensable Disciplines
For Breakout Business Success**

John A. Kuhn & Mark K. Mullins

Praise For Street Smart Disciplines

"If you read only one business book this year make it this one."

Dan Weil, Partner-Cofounder, Village Associates Real Estate

"This is the book I wish I had when I first started my travel business, which became one of the largest internet companies in Asia. Following the disciplines in this practical, street savvy guide will help you work smart, save time and money and most importantly achieve success in business. Keep this book close by. You will want to refer to it time and again."

Michael Kenny, Founder/CEO, Agoda.com, subsidiary of Priceline.com

"A smart, valuable and much needed business book."　　**Douglas Mo, Attorney at Law**

"It captures the essence of good business practices and distills the most important disciplines. These pages are packed with clear thinking, sound advice and lots of street smart common sense that success demands".

Frank Caufield, Cofounder, Kleiner, Perkins, Caufield & Byers

"A must read for anyone who wants to experience breakout success in business. Kuhn and Mullins share the lessons of their exceptional thirty-plus years of experience in a step-by-step tutorial of habits, skills, and critical knowledge (real "from the street") that the reader can immediately put into practice. Their enthusiastic style reflects their own drive, focus, and strategic success in business. Each chapter provides valuable "put into practice" strategies for success, accessible and to the point."

Judy Lamb,　Sr. Lecturer of Education, Washington University, St. Louis

"Our company has successfully integrated the Street Smart Disciplines into our daily operations and have seen a profound effect. We're dramatically more effective; our sales efforts are more focused, our communication incredibly more productive. In the last 2 years, revenue has doubled and our profit has increased by over 15 percent. This book changed the way we do business, and we will never go back to our old methods. We have been in business over 20 years, but by integrating these disciplines, we have seen results beyond our wildest expectations".

Jerry Koch, President, Chemtron/River Bend Labs

"We have taken a leadership position in our industry by executing the Street Smart Disciplines. John and Mark have provided the go-to reference for every situation! The disciplines helped shape our mission statement, strategy, what we do, and how we do it. The results have been outstanding. We increased our revenue over 100 percent in one year, and profits are going through the roof".

Tony Genovese, President & CEO, Enhance Medical Systems

A Word from John and Mark

Why do you need this book? How is it different? Why do people like it? What's all the buzz about? And what are "street smarts," anyway?

Street smarts are what you get from *doing it,* not from reading about it. Yes, we had college educations so we're reasonably book smart but we're also street smart. Our success was much more a result of what we learned on the street *creating and running businesses.* Way more important. Way more useful. And, we're two guys who *actually did* it.

We started one of our first companies with $1,000 and a good idea, nothing brilliant – it was in the magazine publishing business. You'll learn more about that experience as the book unfolds. We think you'll enjoy it because we're regular guys you can relate to.

Very soon we realized that this business could be big if we played it right. We then had to figure out how to not screw it up and how to make it as successful as we could, hoping to sell it eventually and make some serious money.

Which is exactly what we did.

We built the company into a multi-million dollar business and then sold it debt-free to the Meredith Corporation, a large media company. But that's not the point.

The point is we identified and followed seven specific disciplines to get there. Our success in this business and the continuing success in our lives have been the result of the flawless execution of *every* discipline in this book.

This is the first book that explains the how and why of disciplines.

We knew that our next career would be to pass on this knowledge and experience to people like you who have the ideas and ambition – but maybe not all the tools and techniques – to succeed. In simple, straight talk we give you an honest look at how things *really* get done and what it *really* takes to succeed in business and, yes, life.

So, this is the book we have to give you, and it's priceless. We share it with those who have a burning desire to realize their dreams of success and everything it represents: independence, security, freedom, wealth, happiness, and maybe even fame.

When we finalized the manuscript we sent it to a bunch of people – MBAs, academics, corporate executives, and successful street smart guys like us – who just tell it like it is. They all said essentially the same thing: *this is the book that has been missing all these years – a distillation of indispensable business disciplines for success.*

The good news is that all the stuff we share with you works. The bad news is that it's not easy. There are no short-cuts, no overnight successes. It took us years to figure out exactly what the disciplines are and to isolate and distill *the seven most vital ones that true success demands.*

With this book you can succeed pretty fast because you won't waste any time learning how. We know it works and we're going to show you, step-by-step. All you have to do is follow these seven disciplines all the time, no matter what. We still do.

Remember, lots of obstacles will be thrown in your way so you need real world weapons to break through. You're going to war. Understand these disciplines, and most important, apply and master them, and you'll be ready.

Successfully yours,
John and Mark

Foreword by Frank Caufield

It's very clear that the current business environment is rapidly and constantly changing. Speed, flexibility, creativity, and constant adaptation are the mantras of this new playing field. Successful business people work smart and stand ready to reinvent their business strategies, or, if necessary, themselves. Regardless of your age, education, or skill set, reinvention can be achieved with the right attitude and commitment to practice certain disciplines.

When John and Mark first asked me to write the foreword for this book, I thought back to the specific disciplines that guided me through my own life. Working in venture capital for over 35 years I analyzed and helped fund hundreds of companies. That led me to think about the disciplines displayed by the successful leaders at those companies. Everyone who achieved breakout success had one thing in common: a set of disciplines they rigorously followed and, most importantly, executed with great commitment.

I have known John and Mark for over twenty years, and they have raised the bar in isolating the most essential disciplines that true success demands. I've seen brilliant people who operate without these disciplines simply fail, and conversely, I've seen people of average talent who execute with these disciplines become incredibly successful.

The Street Smart Disciplines can be learned, practiced, and perfected. John and Mark have packed these pages with clear thinking, sound advice, and street-smart common sense. Achieving extraordinary success is never easy, but the rewards of unrelenting discipline can be monumental.

Frank Caufield, Cofounder, Kleiner, Perkins, Caufield & Byers

Frank Caufield has been active in the venture capital field since the early 1970s. He is a cofounder of Kleiner, Perkins, Caufield, and Byers (KPCB), one of the largest and most prominent venture capital firms in the USA. Frank has served on the board of Quantum Corporation, Caremark, Inc., Megabios, Verifone, Inc., Wyse Technology, Quickturn Corporation, AOL, the Council on Foreign Relations and many other private and public companies. He is currently the lead independent director of Time Warner. He also serves as a director of The U.S. Russia Investment Fund and The U.S. Russia Foundation, He is a past president of the Western Association of Venture Capitalists and the National Venture Capital Association. A graduate of the US Military Academy, he holds an MBA from the Harvard Business School.

Table of Contents

Introduction

What if one book gave you access to more than fifty combined years of real world, street smart business experience and best practices mined from successful people and businesses encapsulated into seven easy to understand and executable action plans for Breakout Success?

What if you could immediately start applying this vast storehouse of knowledge that combines the winning perspectives of successful entrepreneurial as well as corporate and academic experts? With this book it's no longer a question of *if* but *when*. *Street Smart Disciplines of Successful People* provides the seven indispensable disciplines that will help you pave your way to Breakout Success.

For decades, the authors worked on isolating the essential and vital disciplines that people must incorporate into their playbook to reach the pinnacle of success. They used the very same street smart disciplines in this book to start and build one of their earlier companies on a shoestring, achieve extraordinary success and eventually sell the company to a large, diversified media company and make millions. They still use the disciplines in their careers to achieve continued financial and personal fulfillment.

They demystify the process of achieving Breakout Success in straightforward, no-nonsense language. There is no convoluted jargon or complex theory—just concise, street-proven and practical, yet memorable, inspiring, and powerful lessons.

These are not theories. These are indispensable disciplines drawn from real people, real experiences, real problems, and real solutions. They are time-tested and proven on the street by the authors, successful companies, and successful people from Wall Street to Main Street, and include a success-creating compilation of advice, tactics, techniques, and strategies.

The Street Smart Disciplines' eye-opening insights and practical wisdom will inspire and guide go-getters who want to climb the corporate ladder, aspiring entrepreneurs looking to launch new businesses, and established business owners who want to take their organizations to the next level. In short, this book is for all success-driven individuals in any career or business.

This book of disciplines is not just words on paper; it is like having a business consultant and career coach right at your desk, there whenever you need to recharge and regroup on your way to Breakout Success. The great news is you can learn and integrate all seven Disciplines into your life and be on your way to achieving more success and personal fulfillment than you ever dreamed possible.

About the Authors

John A. Kuhn has decades of successful corporate, entrepreneurial, and academic experience.

John worked as a sales and marketing executive for the 3M Company and as Chief Operating Officer at a publishing division of Meredith Corporation. Additionally he was cofounder and president of the American Park Network, the largest publisher of national and state park magazines in the United States and also was the founder and CEO of Buenos Aires Metropolis, a city-lifestyle magazine in Buenos Aires, Argentina. Presently, he is president of Devenoge Highland Properties, a real estate company in San Francisco, and Punta del Este, Uruguay.

A former high school business teacher, he currently is a university business lecturer and has a consulting firm, Street Smart Advisory Group, with Mark Mullins, his good friend and coauthor.

John resides in San Francisco and Buenos Aires.

Mark K. Mullins has years of successful corporate executive experience and is a serial entrepreneur with a long history of accomplishments. He is an innovative business builder with over thirty years of success in startups and corporations.

Mark was an executive and partner of the American Park Network (APN) with John. After APN was acquired by the Meredith Corporation, he became a publisher and built a division creating magazines for the California Department of Commerce and the California Ski Industry Association. Additionally, Mark was founder of Mountain Sports Publishing in Aspen, Colorado, publishing visitor guides for ski resorts and official publications for World Cup Skiing. He also served as an executive for Zoom Systems in San Francisco.

Mark is actively involved with consulting, executive coaching, and writing.

He and his wife, Loretta (married 31 years), reside in Lake Tahoe and Clayton, Missouri. Their son, Trevor, lives in Venice Beach, California, and works for UBS in Los Angeles, and their daughter, Haley, is an entrepreneur living in Clayton, Missouri.

Street Smart Advisory Group

We are an international consulting firm that works with clients across a wide array of industries.

Our seasoned advisory team has decades of corporate and entrepreneurial experience, and specializes in working with startups and medium-size companies to maximize their growth, revenue, and value.

We help our clients develop a clear vision, direction, and results with agility and speed. We build high-performance companies and create smart organizations by preparing them for a changing marketplace in an ever-changing world.

We work to optimize all operations through the implementation of disciplined processes and provide specific strategic and tactical advice to help clients achieve their goals.

Our core consulting strengths lie in the planning and execution of value creation and optimization programs designed to achieve revenue and profit growth.

- Goals/targets: Strategic deep-drill review to achieve corporate objectives
- Customer attraction/retention: Sales and marketing analysis
- Team assessment and analysis
- Systems and process optimization
- Increasing speed of execution
- Industry/market competitive assessment
- Understanding and managing complexity
- Operational/managerial efficiency
- Revenue/productivity/profit assessment
- Growth and value development

John A. Kuhn and Mark K. Mullins

For more information regarding our services or to explore how we may be able to help your organization, please visit our website at

www.streetsmartdisciplines.com

"BUSINESS IS A COMBINATION OF WAR AND SPORT."
Andre Maurois

Discipline One
Work Smart

Develop a future-focused, change-oriented mentality for Breakout Success

"Most people see what it is, and never see what it can be."
—*Albert Einstein*

In this chapter:
- ✓ Street Smart essentials for working smart today
- ✓ Manage the complexity of change
- ✓ A timeline of exponential change
- ✓ Analyze your life, career, and business
- ✓ Seek out role models, mentors, and smart people
- ✓ Build a better brain
- ✓ Become a passionate benchmarker
- ✓ Expand your current resources
- ✓ Develop a future-focused and change-oriented mentality
- ✓ Create and execute a dynamic plan for change

Street Smart Essentials for Working Smart Today

Working smart today means having awareness and understanding that today's business environment demands the development of a future-focused, change-oriented mentality and an actionable execution plan to pave the way for Breakout Success.

Incredible advances in technology, communication, information processing, and globalization are occurring at a ferocious pace. As a result, exponential changes in the marketplace, the competitive landscape, and customer behaviors are continually revolutionizing the way we do business. The only safe prediction is that the era of the predictable business environment is over.

Futurist James Canton, in his book *Extreme Future*, has identified a number of factors, such as change, speed, complexity, and ambiguity, as the underlying key drivers in the twenty-first century.

These drivers are fueled by twin mega forces:

Digitization of the world economy: The internet and mobile technology are the most visible factors creating not only millions of new businesses worldwide but, more importantly, drastically changing every element of the way we do business. These factors will continue to threaten the existence of businesses that are not up-to-date, not working smart, and not making the necessary changes to adapt to this endless wave of transformation.

Globalization: This powerful economic force continues to create new markets, new manufacturing and supply sources, and intense competitive pressures from every corner of the globe. In the past decade, India, Brazil, and China, once suboptimal economies at best, have become integral parts of the global economy. China has transformed from a Communist state to become the second largest economy in the world.

FROM THE STREET: IT TAKES A GLOBAL VILLAGE

Companies listed in the S&P 500 generate 46 percent of their profits outside the United States and for many larger corporations this percentage is higher. Coca Cola's vast global empire stretches to 206 countries and nearly 80 percent of its revenue comes from outside the United States.

Manage the Complexity of Change

Today many business models are changing rapidly while others are becoming obsolete as technology and globalization move at terrific speeds; this creates a new business reality fraught with uncertainty. An IBM global CEO study drawn from interviews with over 1,500 CEOs at the world's leading corporations found that "change and complexity in doing business will continue to be on the rise for years to come and only 50 percent of the CEOs are prepared to deal with it."

With change happening faster than at any time since the Industrial Revolution, working smart in the twenty-first century, regardless of the business you're in, begins with a paradigm shift to manage this rapid change and complexity. How are you dealing with it? You don't have the luxury to think, "This is all interesting and would be nice to consider if I had the time." Procrastinating is not an option.

To survive today, you must be prepared for change or suffer the consequences. In an instant, you could find your niche getting squeezed, requiring you to aggressively defend your turf, or worse, you could be blindsided without even the chance to fight off your predators. The unexpected is to be expected. Those who do not prepare for both either will be severely wounded or will die.

History is strewn with examples of companies that have failed to change to meet customer demands, miscalculated a new technology, or simply ignored the warning signs that screamed trouble was coming. The last several years have seen numerous cataclysmic collapses of iconic companies such as Tower Records, Blockbuster Video, Borders, Eastman Kodak, and many others. These companies all failed to work smart.

"The greatest danger in times of turbulence is not the turbulence; it is to act with yesterday's logic." —Peter Drucker

Tower Records set the industry standard for being a music consumer's heaven by providing a massive selection of in-store music titles and also by leading the industry in introducing new artists to the public and promoting concerts. With the concept of building music superstores, it created a huge footprint, selling every genre of music. Then along came digital music, internet-based music-sharing sites, and music download sites like iTunes that devastated its sales revenue. Online retailers put the final nail in the coffin by making vast collections of music available with the click of a mouse, and Tower Records came to a slow and painful death.

Blockbuster's filing for Chapter 11 bankruptcy could probably have been avoided if it had paid better attention to Netflix, founded in 1997 which would eventually crush the mighty icon. Netflix paid attention to changing customer habits and found ways to save them time and money. High-speed internet allowed customers to browse an exhaustive selection of movies online and to receive movies on their doorstep via U.S. mail or by streaming them directly to their computers, which could quickly be hooked up to a flatscreen. This dramatically cheaper distribution model with no brick-and-mortar stores helped Netflix undercut Blockbuster on price.

Netflix also demonized Blockbuster's late fees, which generated enormous revenues but alienated customers. Blockbuster moved too slowly with online programs and got hit by three bullets (price, convenience, selection) all at once and may not recover.

Still, the only certainty is change. Blockbuster's pieces were bought by Dish Network with the plan to reincarnate them into an industry hybrid and Netflix will be challenged by managing its exponential growth. It's not a stretch to predict that emerging companies will eventually knock off all forms of pay/cable TV next with high-bandwidth content streaming, providing convenient, fast feeds for live TV and sports.

Blockbuster and Tower Records experienced what some of us are guilty of: We perceive reality selectively—seeing and hearing only what is comfortable—and often perception is *not* reality. We rush around handling our day-to-day business and personal lives blind to lurking and even out-in-plain-sight dangers until it's too late.

We don't see the cracks until they become chasms of crisis. Ironically, success or perceived success can breed complacency. Don't fall into traps of filtering out the warning signs, getting drunk on your own achievements, or having an irrational sense of imperviousness when you're on a roll. Even the best can get blindsided and collapse in a smoking pile of rubble. Be mindful, completely aware, future-focused, and prepared for change.

"Change is the law of life, and those who look only to the past or present are certain to miss the future." —John F. Kennedy

Often businesspeople figure that if their current methods are working, everything is okay. But often this is not the case. It's easy to get set in our ways. We all get stuck in familiar patterns and routines; we're creatures of habit. This sense of normalcy is misleading in today's business environment, where nothing stays the same for very long. Customers are changing, their needs are changing, and the market and competition are changing. Today you must explore all possible ways to raise the bar. Always be on the lookout for opportunities to ratchet up your business and personal performance.

To stay on top, you must constantly investigate new ways to increase revenues, increase profits, reduce costs, improve efficiency, improve customer/client relationships, increase productivity, and grow your business.

To thrive in a changing environment, the central questions you must ask are:

- What do you need to do to keep on succeeding?
- When was the last time you completed an in-depth analysis of your department, company, competition, marketplace, and even yourself to determine ways to improve, innovate, and safeguard your business?
- How prepared are you and your department, coworkers, and employees to deal with innovation and change?
- Are you truly equipped with the skills and knowledge needed to deal with this highly complex and rapidly changing business world?
- Are you looking for blind spots that could keep you from seeing red flags, fault lines, and your own complacency?
- Are you aware that often the best time for change is when things are going well?
- Do you seek opportunities for change, or are you resisting change?

"The quality of questions we ask ourselves will determine the quality of our lives." —Tony Robbins

It all begins with accepting this endless wave of transformation and more importantly anticipating it by constantly thinking ahead. Become adept at staying abreast of change and, more importantly, staying ahead of it. Attempt to spot trends and seize opportunities wherever possible (more on this later).

FROM THE STREET: EXPONENTIAL CHANGE IS THE ONLY CONSTANT

There has been more technological change in the past twenty years than has occurred in the past two centuries. This has been an overwhelmingly transformative period affecting every fiber of our business and social existence. And this trend will continue with an endless stream of ideas; the number of patent applications submitted in the United States has doubled since the late 1990s to almost a half million a year. "Doubt is the father of invention," said Galileo. "Necessity is its mother," said Plato. We may be getting our jetpacks, and time machines sooner than we think.

A Timeline of Exponential Change

Here's a compilation of consumer-oriented tech inventions and the year they were invented. Many of these products were conceived many years before they were introduced to the marketplace or widely accepted.

1990
World Wide Web
Digital voice recorders

1991
Memory card
Webcam
Lithium rechargeable batteries

1992
Smartphone

1993
Global Positioning System-GPS
HTML programming language

1994
Text messaging (SMS)
Online stock trading
Home satellite TV
Digital cameras
First website for TV
Bluetooth
Amazon.com

1995
Microsoft's Internet Explorer
Debit cards
DVD
craigslist
eBay Inc.

1996
Hotmail
Universal Serial Bus (USB)
High-definition television

1997
Netflix
Priceline

1998
Google
eBook readers
Flat-screen TVs
Video on Demand (VOD)
PayPal

1999
BlackBerry
TiVo
Wi-Fi
Windows Live Messenger

2000
USB flash drive
Video conferencing
Mobile websites and advertising

2001
iPod
iTunes
Tablet personal computer
Wikipedia

2002
MARS Rover
Robot vacuum
Digital camera chip

2003
Apple's iTunes store
Blu-Ray
Skype
LinkedIn

2004
Satellite radio
Slingbox

2005
YouTube

2006
Facebook
MySpace
Twitter

2007
iPhone
iPod Touch
Kindle
Apple TV

2008
The bionic hand
Hulu.com
The Tesla Roadster

2009
3-D camera

2010
LED-backlight LCD television
Third-generation Kindle
iPad

2011
4G smartphones
3-D TV
3-D Camcorder
iPad I

The difficult issue is that business is not a theoretical field but one of practicality: there is no prescription for what will work in dealing with change and complexity. There are no clear-cut answers. The only truly helpful tool is to ask the question "What really works for my specific business and industry?" To get the answer, you have to experiment with various possible adaptations and then test-drive them in the marketplace.

You need every advantage, no matter how small, so you can truly work smart. First get out of your comfort zone. Change the way you think about yourself, your life, your business, and the world. Look at everything in a different light, through new and very different lenses. This is not just a narrative stimulus package; you must become a pathfinder, blaze new trails, thrive on innovation, and constantly be proactive in challenging yourself to relentlessly improve. This demands a fierce willingness to rethink and try anything. Become the architect and executor of your own change plan.

We have compiled the following Guidelines for Working Smart to help you start making necessary changes, become future-focused, and successfully deal with this daunting yet opportunity-filled new reality.

- Analyze your life, career and business
- Identify what you need to know
- Seek out role models, mentors, and smart people
- Build a better brain
- Become a passionate benchmarker
- Expand your current resources
- Develop a future-focused and change-oriented mentality and culture
- Develop and execute a change plan

Analyze Your Life, Career, and Business

You can make sound and qualified decisions only if you know what is going on. Incessant change in today's world necessitates asking hard questions about your business and how it will adapt to the ever-changing realities of the world at large.

Relentless questioning is what leads people to Breakout Success. We questioned and challenged *everything* in our businesses over the years. We made a point to regularly question and challenge the way we were doing things, even when things were going well. We came up with fresh thinking and great ideas and often broke the conventional rules enabling us to gain an edge over our competitors and become even more successful. If it didn't violate church and state, we went for it, and it paid off with many epic breakthroughs.

Begin by doing an in-depth checkup, or Strategic Multi-Dimensional Analysis (SMDA), of your business (more on this later in the Street Smart Workshop). You can't change what you don't acknowledge, know, or understand, and the analysis provides the tools to examine all areas of your business.

You must be able to see the big picture so you can really understand what is going on now and what is likely to come down the road in the next week, year, or decade. Providing the methodology for personal and corporate introspection, the SMDA helps you create the vision to determine where you want to go and how you'll get there.

Starting with a self-analysis of you and your key team members, followed by an extensive analysis of every facet of your company, the marketplace, your competitors and your customers, this vital review process gives you the intellectual ammunition to rethink all assumptions, business concepts, and strategies.

For example, when was the last time you really took stock of your situation and asked,

- What am I/we doing?
- What should I/we be doing?
- What should I/we be doing next?
- What shouldn't I/we be doing?

In this age of innovation mania, forward-thinking strategies are not about creating stability but about successfully creating and managing change. The idea is to build on bright spots—improving on what you have, innovating what you don't have, and protecting what you do have.

Another compelling reason for regularly doing the checkups is that they are an intervention to stay ahead of the game and eliminate lethal myopic thinking and stagnation. Adopt a business, career, and life trajectory where you're constantly channeling your energy and brainpower to be on the lookout for vulnerabilities, red flags, and fault lines, all which of can threaten your business and stall other parts of your life.

Your continued success and competitiveness in the market rests on your ability to change, improve, innovate, and unlock new opportunities. Clayton M. Christensen, a Harvard Business School professor and author of numerous books, including *The Innovator's Dilemma*, boiled it down to three words: "Innovate or die."

"There is nothing more difficult to take in hand, more perilous to conduct, or more uncertain in its success, than to take the lead in the introduction of a new order of things." —Niccolo Machiavelli, *The Prince* (1532)

The analysis will indeed shake up your comfortable world, forcing you to think differently about everything. But with this powerful intelligence, you can recalibrate, reengineer or reinvent your business to increase its viability and profitability and, most importantly, to protect what you have today so you can use it in the future. We have listed a number of critical areas for analysis, including a detailed list of questions and exactly how to complete the SMDA on page 226 in the Street Smart Workshop.

Bottom line: Think bigger than you've been thinking. Develop a fierce willingness to question, rethink, and try anything that could possibly improve your career or business. Greater expectations lead to greater success. This is where the big victories lie in business.

Identify What You Need to Know

One of the most difficult tasks is actually pinpointing what you and your organization don't know. As they say, you don't know what you don't know. And what you don't know can hurt you. Take comfort in knowing that by doing the SMDA, you will not only learn much more than you ever imagined about your business but also uncover potential problems before they have the chance to become business-killing obstacles.

Many businesspeople feel threatened when they're faced with making a decision to change or advance their careers, or to confront new projects they don't know anything about. For many, the intimidation becomes a major roadblock, and they give up before they have a chance to get rolling.

You don't have to be an expert right from the beginning. We launched our first magazine at the American Park Network with very little knowledge of publishing. Having to learn so much was overwhelming at times, but we set our goals and were committed to identifying what we didn't know and to obtaining the necessary knowledge. We immersed ourselves in the information we needed, and the more time we spent learning, the faster our business grew and the more successful it became. Be open to all new ideas, and be eager to learn anything and everything that will help you succeed.

Don't let a lack of knowledge paralyze you. Identify what you need to know, and get the information you need. With it you'll have the confidence to move forward and make change happen.

FROM THE STREET: ASK EVERYONE

Successful people ask questions—lots of questions. Never feel that asking questions is a sign of inadequacy. Get into the habit of asking questions like an unrelenting ten-year-old: "Why are we doing it that way?" "Can we do it a better way?" You can learn from everyone, so solicit ideas from people as often as you can. Not everyone you talk to will have the information you need, but you won't know unless you ask.

"A prudent question is one half of wisdom." —Francis Bacon

Seek Out Role Models, Mentors, and Smart People

It is crucial to learn from the best. Seek outstanding role models, mentors and the smartest people you can find and use their expertise at every stage of your life and your business.

When you don't have the answers and aren't sure of the direction to take, harness the external talent of intelligent, sharp, clever and visionary individuals. If you want to be smart and successful, make it a point to be around smart and successful people.

Develop a Core Group of Trusted Advisors

A core tenet for Breakout Success is to develop and rely on a trusted group of outside advisors. Develop a deep advisory bench from the role models, mentors, and smart people you already know, and in what should be the ever-increasing circle of contacts you make through networking. Consider putting your CPA and attorney on the roster, but also seek others who may not be in your immediate orbit. Form a brain trust with your advisors.

Have a Heart-to-Heart Talk with Your Customers

We learned early on in our business careers that the more we kept in touch with our customers, the more we improved our business, increased revenues, and became more successful. Indeed, customers often proved to be our best sources of information.

After all, who knows better what customers want than customers themselves?

When we decided to expand the American Park Network and develop a national network of magazines, we met with our key advertising clients to discuss our proposed plans. We came prepared with an outline of the expansion plan that included about twenty questions, such as: What factors would be important to them if we were to expand? What areas of the country would be of interest? Would they be willing to participate? How much did they think they would be willing to spend?

The meeting resulted in an endorsement of our expansion plan and the willingness to increase their ad budget significantly. This ultimately gave us the confidence to roll out nationally. As a result of these customer meetings, our company went from two regional magazines to a national network of twenty-two magazines within twenty-four months.

That's when it really hit home: we experienced a defining moment and saw the true value of becoming completely customer-centric and vowed to have high-contact engagement experiences with customers regularly.

Stay in as close contact with all or as many of your customers as you can, especially your best ones, with telephone calls, emails, and even an occasional letter. Show that you care about them personally. Make it a point to show them how much you value their business by making the extra effort to keep it. Take them out for lunch or dinner and ask them how they think you could improve your product or service. Get their opinions on different aspects of your business or new ideas you have. Their feedback is vital.

Your customers are much more than revenue producers. Their insights, needs, and, yes, complaints make you and your company more competitive and better able to adapt to the incessant change that is always looming. Our philosophy has always been this: you need to do more than just provide ordinary customer service—most companies do that already. Your objective, as we will discuss in Discipline Seven—Everybody Sells, must be to provide extraordinary customer service. Why? Because you don't just want satisfied customers; you want customers who are elated with you, your products, your services, and your company. If it wasn't for our customers and the feedback and support we received from them, we would never have been as successful as we are today. Meet, listen to, and learn from your customers regularly.

"If you're not listening, you're not learning." —Lyndon Johnson

Hire Outside Intelligence, Expertise, and Experience

If you can get free advice from your advisors, customers, and others that's great, but if you can't, be willing to pay for it. Hiring consultants can be worthwhile as long as you are well prepared with clear goals and objectives.

Seek high-quality consultation from those who you feel are big thinkers, future-focused, and can bring a unique perspective to your business. We hired these types of consultants regularly for everything we needed to know when we were starting new businesses we didn't know much about, or expanding businesses that were established and ready for growth. We used high-powered sales consultants to help us sell more. We used financial consultants (in addition to our regular accounting firm) to make sure our financial systems and procedures fit our growth plans. We used publishing consultants in our magazine businesses to evaluate our entire operation and offer suggestions on how to improve our design, format, and editorial content. We used general business consultants to help write or update our business plans.

The late Irving Gerson, in *Be Big Somewhere*, wrote about the advantages of using outside consultants, including being able to access additional intelligence, experience, and energy. With consultants you get the skills and expertise not present in your company. You also gain an invaluable outsider's perspective and candid third-party criticism. And finally, you get it all done without distracting your partners, management team, and employees from their important ongoing tasks.

The key to success in working with consultants is to have a clear picture of what you want and need from them. Establish your expectations and the results you expect.

Use these Street Smart Strategies to get the most from a consultant:

1. Know what you're looking for. Do you need a generalist or a specialist?

   - A generalist understands every aspect of a company and how all the departments work together to create a successful company.
   - A specialist knows a specific discipline, like accounting or sales and marketing, but may not have the broader view of the entire workings of the company that the generalist has.

2. Make an outline of exactly what you need from the consultant and what results you expect. Be very specific.

3. Plan how you want that person to work with you.

   - Do you need the consultant to tell you what to do and how to do it or do you need the consultant to do the work and get it done?
   - Do you want the consultant to be imbedded in your organization with full interaction or to work from afar and just contribute direction and completed projects?

4. Conduct face-to-face interviews with potential consultants to help determine the following:

   - Is this person really an authority, and does he have valuable, relevant, and timely information that will help you?
   - Will this person simply confirm what you already know (which isn't necessarily bad), or can he add substantial new ideas to grow the company?
   - Can he separate information that is fact, proven theory, or well-grounded opinion from hearsay, speculation, or unproven theory? (You may have to get several opinions to make this determination.)
   - Make sure he is able to diagnose your current situation and problems quickly and to give you a clear picture of what he sees as potential fixes.

5. Check references. After you have answered these questions, check all of his references and then decide if hiring this consultant is right for you. Sometimes consultants will agree with you just to

please you or because they don't have enough expertise to disagree constructively. Even the best consultants may have only one true area of expertise and one point of view, so be sure to test them with well-prepared questions.

We filtered all the advice our attorneys or accountants gave us (that is, nonfinancial and nonlegal advice), not because we didn't have confidence in their suggestions, but because they had a limited view circumscribed by their professional backgrounds and perspectives. For instance, when we asked our accountant whether we should expand our business from two to twelve magazines (which we ultimately did), he said, "If you're profitable now, why take the risk?" We learned that attorneys and accountants are great for legal and accounting issues, but we had to take their general business advice and weigh it against all our other sources.

Our consulting group specializes in working with startups to medium-size companies to maximize growth, revenue, and value. We work to optimize all operations through the implementation of a disciplined process, providing specific direction for strategic and tactical execution to take the company toward established goals. We've successfully worked with companies across a wide range of industries. If you think we might be able to help you please contact us at www.streetsmartdisciplines.com. Find more information about our company and our services on page xix.

"Many receive advice, few profit by it." —Publilius Syrus

Consider "Unofficial" Consultants

We had great luck hiring people who weren't actually consultants, but who had all the information we needed and were happy to be taken to dinner or to earn some extra money by acting as consultants for an hourly fee. These were usually friends, friends of friends, acquaintances, and anyone we found through our networking efforts whom we felt had the specific knowledge we needed.

We owned and operated a city lifestyle magazine in Buenos Aires, Argentina, called *Buenos Aires Metropolis*. When we started the magazine, we were concerned about our lack of experience operating a business in a foreign market. We thought we had a good business plan, but we were concerned we might have missed something that could sink us. One night we happened to meet a retired Argentine publishing executive while networking at a Chamber of Commerce event. He turned out to be a veteran of twenty years with one of the largest magazine publishers in the country. We offered to pay him for a few hours to review our plan later that week. With his insights, we got an incredible crash course in running a company in Argentina, which gave us the knowledge and confidence we needed to keep going.

"Globalization has changed us into a company that searches the world, not just to sell or to source, but to find intellectual capital—the world's best talents and greatest ideas."
—Jack Welch

FROM THE STREET: EMPLOYEE ADVISORS

Ask your employees for advice. You'll get some valuable suggestions and your employees will feel good about making a contribution. We often checked in with our people and asked: How can we improve? How can we build on our success?

Build a Better Brain—Become a Student Engaged in Active, Lifelong Learning

"Many an object is not seen, though it falls within the range of our visual ray, because it does not come within the range of our intellectual ray." —Henry David Thoreau

As Francis Bacon wrote, "Knowledge is power," and it truly is power: to keep growing, innovating, and achieving your goals.

When we started one of our earlier businesses, the first thing we learned was how much we had to learn. That drove the decision to intensify the learning experience, and we never stopped; we're still driven to learn each and every day. Learning can help you accomplish just about anything you really want, as long as you are 100-percent committed to acquiring the necessary knowledge and also taking smart risks. The more knowledge and information you have, the smarter you become about taking risks.

The quest for knowledge and wisdom must be an ongoing, passionate process. Even when you've reached a reasonable level of success, keep learning to improve and innovate. Learn about what you need to know until you know more than anyone else. Surround yourself with sharp people who know more than you do, and read everything you can get your eyes on. Always be willing to listen and learn from everyone.

We strongly recommend doing the SMDA because it significantly leverages your learning experience by exposing various issues that can lead to improvements, change, and innovations.

One of the most important skills to work smart for the future is to master the art of learning. Learning can keep you from falling into the trap of complacency, eliminates innovation deficits, and paves the way to become future-focused and prepared for change.

Always be looking for new ways to learn and to build a better brain.

Grow Your Mind

An indispensable way to learn about change and to fill in knowledge gaps is to read, read, and read some more. Discipline yourself to set aside a certain number of hours each week to read books, magazines, newsletters, websites, and other publications on the subjects you need to know about. We regularly read the *Harvard Business Review, McKinsey Quarterly, The Economist, Bloomberg Business Week,* and *The Wall Street Journal.*

We always had an insatiable thirst for more knowledge in our different businesses over the years. In the early days we became voracious readers out of sheer necessity to keep the business alive. We read—more like devoured—books on all aspects of business (and continue to do so when we're not writing them). Take a look at our selection of books in "Street Smart Recommended Reading" on page 255 and find ones that suit your interests or needs. Spend time with some of the best brains in business and begin the brain gain.

"The man who does not read good books has no advantage over the man who can't read them." —Mark Twain

Go Back to School

Another way to get a brain gain and sharpen up on various topics is to take classes from local colleges, seminar companies, and adult education programs.

As we were building our earlier businesses, we made the time to attend lots of classes and seminars. We attended financial seminars to get a better understanding of what our accountant was doing, went to sales seminars to help us sell more, and attended numerous advertising and publishing seminars each year to gain a better understanding of our industry. We also encouraged all our employees to attend seminars. Identify the areas where you need a brain gain, and jump into a class or a seminar.

"Thinking will not overcome fear, but action will."
—W. Clement Stone

Create and Foster an Active Learning Culture

Everyone must be responsible for his or her own learning. But if you are in management or an owner of a company, you have to motivate people to learn as well as establish clear goals about what knowledge you want them to acquire. The most effective method to drive successful performance is to make learning a component of job descriptions and performance appraisals. Make ongoing education a company-wide imperative.

To foster a learning culture:
- Encourage employees to use a mentor, coach, or a more experienced colleague to accelerate the learning of skills and competencies either from inside or outside the company.
- Allocate one day a week or month to develop new and creative ideas not related to your specific job description or work in a different department to obtain different perspectives.

- Develop high-contact experiences with customers regularly to find out what they really want and need and how you can improve your products/services and service orientation.
- Subscribe to audio and book summaries, newsletters, and trade journals relevant to your business, and distribute them throughout the company.
- Encourage and pay for courses or seminars for employees.
- Implement formal learning and training sessions that are planned, systematized, and structured.
- Develop professional manuals wherever applicable to facilitate and enhance learning.

Gather ideas and information from every corner of the organization. Have departments get together for periodic focus group-style brainstorming sessions to share ideas and strategies on existing, new, or upcoming projects and important issues. Swapping stories and cooperating on projects deepens the learning process.

"The greatest treasure is a wealth of information."
—Grover Cleveland

Tap into the Intellectual Capital of Information Technologies

There is an intelligence bonanza waiting for you in all the latest technology that continually floods the market. Harvest and glean as much information as possible from these new and exciting information technologies. Technology has changed forever the way we interact, connecting us in new, profitable ways of sharing information and insights. Clay Shirky of New York University aptly calls this tsunami of technology a "massive cognitive surplus" whose wealth potential is mind-boggling.

Futurist Ray Kurzweil states, "Our intuition about the future is linear. But the reality of information technology is exponential and that makes a profound difference. If I take 30 steps linearly, I get to 30. If I take 30 steps exponentially, I get to a billion." Harness the power of information technologies.

Become a Passionate Benchmarker

Benchmarking in its simplest form is learning about successful ideas, strategies, and practices used by companies and adapting them to your business. It is commonly used when trying to determine the most effective way to handle a particular business process. You may already be benchmarking, but become adept at the strategy and use it regularly. It is crucial to learn from the best.

Anything can be benchmarked. Use it for all facets of your company, including operations, finance, sales and marketing, human resources, customer service, products/services, manufacturing, advertising and public relations, and all the other functions in your business.

Keenly observe the successful practices of companies both in and out of your business sector. In our magazine publishing businesses, many of our clients were Fortune 500 companies, so we were in an ideal position to study how the best of the best operated. We identified the standout performers in this group, scrutinized their business practices, and then adapted the ideas and strategies we felt would help us increase revenues, grow, and succeed.

We learned the art of negotiating from one of our customers and applied it to our dealings with suppliers, which saved us thousands of dollars. We learned some innovative telemarketing techniques from companies that regularly called to solicit our business. By incorporating these techniques into our sales efforts, we significantly increased the number of appointments we made with prospective advertisers. At trade shows we picked up all our customers' and competitors' literature to see how they were positioning themselves in the marketplace. This helped us develop a strategy to differentiate and better position our business.

Make it a point also to constantly seek out and study best practices by staying abreast of what is going on in the business world. Regularly read business trade journals, business sections of newspapers, and business magazines and books.

A well thought-out benchmarking effort should include the following:
- Get a clear idea of what you want to benchmark.
- Determine what company or companies you will benchmark.

- Obtain as much business intelligence as possible about best practices and how the leader or high performer achieved the results.
- Determine how you will adopt the best practices.
- Determine how to measure results.

Benchmarking today is more important than ever, not only to keep up with, but also to surpass your competitors. It must become an integral part of your overall, ongoing improvement process and larger change plan strategies. Practice benchmarking regularly.

"One key to successful leadership is continuous personal change. Personal change is a reflection of our inner growth and empowerment." —Robert E. Quinn

Expand Your Current Resources

Increase and optimize your circle of resources by aggressively networking. In today's fast-paced business world, networking has taken on increased importance. Absolutely make schmoozing with a mission part of your game plan. (See Discipline Five—Get More Business, for more on strategic networking.)

Harvey Mackay, motivational speaker and best-selling author of *Swim with the Sharks Without Being Eaten Alive* once said, "I could lose all my money and all my facilities but leave me my contacts and I'll be back as strong as ever. Networking is that important."

Have your antenna up at all times to seek out and connect with those people who could help you achieve what you need. However, successful networking and more importantly the building of solid alliances begin by making the first move to genuinely help others. Find out about the other person by asking questions and listening for ways you could help. Create the bond and strengthen the alliance by doing something for the person. Pay it forward. When the time is right you can introduce your story. It's all about genuine ongoing exchanges. Your tentacles should be everywhere. Establish the connections and build the relationships *before* you need them. Consider it part of your work, and regularly get out of your comfort zone and meet new and different types of people inside and outside of your business and social circles, with these core objectives:

- To broaden your horizons and get you thinking outside of the box.
- To get exposed to new ideas and ways of looking at your business to foster innovative thinking.
- To surround yourself with role models, mentors, and smart people.

It takes a bit more than digging deep into your database or LinkedIn contacts to network effectively. Try these techniques to jump-start your networking efforts. Think creatively to expand the list based on your particular business situation.

- Join business organizations including chambers of commerce, small-business groups, investment groups, industry associations, and business social clubs.
- Attend industry conferences, seminars, trade shows, and conventions.
- Engage in social-media networking including LinkedIn, Facebook, Twitter, and others
- Join networking clubs and associations in your field.
- Join Toastmasters.
- Tap the networking potential of your interests and the things you enjoy doing in your spare time. If you're a sports enthusiast and enjoy working out, running, hiking, skiing, or yoga, join a sports club or organizations involved in these activities.
- Join a book club or an opera club.
- Meet and work with peers in your organization, competitors, or industry-related companies.
- Seek out alliances and partnerships with other people and companies.
- Try something new and different such as taking language, photography, cooking, or dance classes or something else that you've never tried before.
- Do volunteer work.

Seminars and classes are vital learning experiences, but we've also found them to be valuable networking opportunities. When we attend seminars, we're always looking for people who could serve as consultants, prospective employees, and even prospective clients. At one seminar we met a public-relations expert who was a master at creating presentation materials. We hired her to review our materials, and she came up with two breakthrough ideas that actually helped us increase our advertising revenue by 25 percent the following year.

Effective networking requires good people skills. (Refer to Discipline Three—Deal with People) Although it's People Skills 101, we don't see enough people taking the initiative to put their hand out first to introduce themselves, and prepared to have a productive conversation. Have your agenda prepared in advance, knowing specifically what you want to accomplish for all networking encounters. If you're persuading or trying to gain commitment, then you are presenting, so be prepared. (Refer to Discipline Two—Present Everything) To truly master the art of networking, we recommend also reading *Networking Like a Pro: Turning Contacts into Connections* by Ivan Misner, David Alexander, and Brian Hillard.

Don't limit the channels through which new ideas and information flow. Go out and meet new people to increase business intelligence and to continue propelling growth, change, and innovation.

FROM THE STREET: NURTURE IMPORTANT CONTACTS

Networking takes discipline and effort. When you find people who have valuable knowledge and information, make an effort to develop and nurture these relationships

Develop a Future-Focused, Change-Oriented Mentality and Culture

The idea is not only to create a vision of the future but also to attempt to *create the future*. Make a pivotal decision to look far ahead and capitalize on potential shifts in consumer thinking and emerging trends. Become a futurist! What do you see and what would you like to see in one, five, ten, twenty years in your business, the marketplace, the competition, and the customer?

For example, take a close look at your specific business and industry. What is the typical business model? Look at it through a different lens, and dig deep, real deep, to the nth degree. Pull it apart. How is it working? Why is it being done this way? Why has it become the common model? Look at it through the eyes of your customer. Look at interesting models in other business sectors outside your industry and strategically benchmark. Could any facet of those business models work in your industry? You may come up with some unconventional ways to alter your business or to reinvent it, to increase revenues or to develop new revenue streams.

We did exactly this. After we published our first magazine at American Park Network, we met with one of our consultants, who had years of experience in the advertising and publishing business. Our objective was to create a new and different business model that would give us the ultimate competitive advantage in the marketplace and substantially increase our advertising revenue.

After a few intense brainstorming sessions, we hit on something. We realized we could offer our advertisers more than just an ad in our magazines, we could give them the opportunity to leverage their investment by including a merchandising or "value-added" program. (Such packages are now very common in the magazine business, but they were unheard of at the time.) The following year we went into the marketplace and were no longer selling advertising but an Integrated Marketing Merchandising Sponsorship. Our entire marketing strategy changed dramatically, and our revenues more than doubled.

What else can be done to foster a change-oriented mentality? Begin by forcing yourself out of habitual methods of operation and try fresh approaches for *everything*. Stop operating on autopilot in your daily business activities. For every project ask, "Are there different, new, and better ways to tackle the job?" At the end of every week ask, "How can I improve my performance? What can I do to make the business better?" Train your brain to methodically anticipate, look for, and implement change. Develop a sixth sense for it.

Turn off the autopilot when you're seeking out information sources. We all have favorite websites, apps, TV shows, magazines, movies, and books we watch or read regularly. Stretch your mind by trying new and different entertainment and information sources. The idea is to see things in a different dimension. You may end up with a wheelbarrow full of new and exciting information and ideas that will open up new vistas for looking at your life and business.

Become the champion of change and innovation in your organization. Embark on an ambitious effort to develop a mentality to strategically align the corporate culture into one that is future-focused and change-oriented.

This usually requires some reengineering to steer the company in a new strategic direction, but over time this new thinking and change-based culture will automatically foster ongoing innovation.

There is no one success formula for the innovation-change game, but we offer potent, time-tested guidelines that have worked successfully over the years on page 240 in the Street Smart Workshop.

"The only way companies survive is to be miles ahead of the competition. That's what we do."—Sir Richard Branson

Create and Execute a Dynamic Plan for Change

"In the long run, men hit only what they aim at."
—Henry David Thoreau

A change plan is developed to facilitate the implementation of projects that have been isolated for change. It is usually utilized in conjunction with the Strategic Multi-Dimensional Analysis (SMDA), which highlights areas that need attention for possible change or improvement. See page 226 in the Street Smart Workshop.

A growing body of research indicates that a doggedly future-focused, change-oriented mentality that integrates and embraces ongoing plans for change and improvement into a company's DNA produces better decision making, drives growth, and facilitates success.

It's important for companies of all stripes to have a change plan, but it plays an even more significant role in small companies, because the very nature of being small lends itself to greater potential growth and change.

Change requires undeniable courage, a certain degree of risk, some discomfort, and often a lot of hard work, but today an ongoing change plan should be the norm rather than the exception.

The development of a change plan is an integral part of all successful people's playbook, and you, too, should prepare yourself for ongoing change by developing a plan. Developing and executing a change plan involves the following:

- Identify projects for change.
- Develop an effective communication plan.
- Eliminate implementation barriers.
- Develop the change plan.

Identify Projects for Change

Because of its inherently comprehensive nature, a change plan initially can seem so overwhelming that people sometimes don't know where to begin and often hesitate to act. Many that do act often use no methodology for dealing with change.

Begin by doing an in-depth, company-wide assessment utilizing the SMDA. As discussed earlier, it will help determine which areas of the company could be initially identified as proposed projects for change.

There is no right or wrong answer as to exactly where to begin. After doing the SMDA, you should be able to prioritize what needs immediate attention, improvement, or change. Cross-functional collaboration among partners, peers, management team, trusted advisors, consultants, employees, and your customers may facilitate the process.

Talk with as many people as appropriate and possible before adopting and communicating any change plan. Explain the proposed area of change and simultaneously get an understanding of your organization's appetite and aptitude for change, including how people will react to the change and what will have to be done for successful adoption and execution. Obtain 360-degree feedback, in other words, get feedback from everyone whom you deem necessary.

Make it a point to find out what is really going on by asking carefully thought-out and well crafted questions. Determine what is working and what isn't, as well as improvements and changes that could be made. Importantly, while you're checking in with your people, also get their perspectives on many facets of the company, the marketplace, the competition, and your customers.

Consider one-on-one meetings, informal hallway conversations, focus groups, brainstorming/free associating sessions, or any other methods to gain vital insights. Remember to check in with your customers and have that heart-to-heart talk we discussed earlier to explore what they're thinking; they have valuable information to influence your proposed change plan.

"First ponder, then dare." —Helmuth Von Moltk

Develop an Effective Communication Plan

To instigate and manage sustainable change, you must communicate a clear vision of the project. After developing the proposed change plan, you'll be able to frame an effective communication strategy for company-wide adoption, which is the cornerstone for the support, execution, and success of the plan.

You will have already informally introduced the proposed project and received feedback, so now you can finalize and deliver your formal communication plan. Set an upbeat, energized tone from the get-go. Be open and freely share all information about the pending change.

Follow up with your people with these essential steps:
- Share the change plan
- Explain the goals and objectives of the change
- Explain why the change is necessary and is occurring
- Discuss what the change may look like and how it may affect departments and individual employees
- Speak in terms of how the company and everyone will benefit from the change

- Establish roles and responsibilities for how the change will be achieved; that is, who is going to do what, when, why, and how
- Discuss the project timeframe and timelines
- Establish the desired results
- Keep providing progress updates
- Encourage feedback from all employees to continuously improve the plan

Involvement is the operative word for this complicated and emotionally challenging undertaking. Whenever possible, have all the appropriate people involved in any change discussion, and do it in a timely fashion to eliminate information vacuums, rumors, and resentment. Make them part of the entire process. Be honest and direct, and don't spin or withhold facts about pending changes. (People are smarter than you may think; they will figure out quickly that something is going on.)

An open-door policy with ongoing two-way communication for sharing information, ideas, suggestions, and concerns is the best way to diffuse simmering resentments or misunderstandings. Above all, actively reach out to ask questions and, most importantly, carefully observe how the change efforts are being handled and managed.

"The block of granite which was an obstacle in the pathway
of the weak becomes a stepping stone for the strong."
—Thomas Carlyle

Eliminate Implementation Barriers
Everyone perceives change in different ways. Keep in mind that change can be disruptive and upsetting to people. There will be those who are stimulated by the change and welcome it, but you can't expect everyone to be happy—it just isn't going to happen. It's often difficult to get everyone to play in the same sandbox all the time. The truth is, some people will complain and some will view the change as a weapon of mass disruption and resist its implementation. Be prepared to maneuver through some minefields, to deal with a plethora of fear and concern, and to experience violent hiccups when introducing change.

In our consulting practice, we create significant change in many companies we work with. Interestingly, the first barriers we often face are from the very executives who call us in to make the changes. They are tentative about taking on the unknown, disruption, fears, and concerns that accompany the change process. We help them prepare for the tidal wave of potential opposition with an overwhelming, compelling, and persuasive communication plan to ensure successful adoption.

Understand the potential obstacles from all quarters for the change plan you have in mind. Strive to avoid scattershot actions. Focus your energies with laser-like accuracy. You also have to dig in your heels and become more strategic when you're introducing innovation initiatives. To give the project and yourself the highest level of credibility possible in this uncertain situation, anticipate problems and peoples' objections, and prepare viable answers and solutions. Make sure that the feedback you received during the planning stage addresses what problems might happen or what resistance you might encounter.

It's very likely you'll encounter resistance regarding the following issues, so be prepared for objections from fellow managers and employees:

- A belief that the change is unwarranted, not practical, or will not improve the situation
- A dislike of the way the change has been introduced and planned
- A lack of trust and confidence that the change will work and succeed, or even worse, create more problems than it solves
- The likelihood it will result in job losses or a change in job descriptions with diminished autonomy or authority
- High costs that make implementation unfeasible
- A considerable amount of risk
- A fear among employees of not having the skills or competency to deal with the impending change

Factor into your execution plan the time to deal with potential resistance. If the project is thoroughly planned and you've communicated it well to the organization, you'll have less resistance. Regardless how well you plan and present the project, you will still encounter some degree of opposition, so be patient and prepared to deal with it. You can't look at the plan's adoption in black and white. There will be many shades of gray on how the people in the organization will assimilate the changes.

Most certainly you don't want to force acceptance. For some ideas, a long gestation period may be required before people accept them. Make a point to give the straight facts continually; regularly resell everyone on the benefits of the change and offer wholehearted support to everyone, whether they're for or against it.

"Courage and perseverance have a magical talisman, before which difficulties disappear and obstacles vanish into air."
—John Quincy Adams

Develop the Change Plan

In its simplest form, a change plan is an explanation of the proposed changes and the steps needed to achieve them. Length and formality depend on your particular situation.

Here are the essential elements:
- Formulate a crystal-clear vision of the proposed project and its goals
- Understand exactly why you want to tackle the specific area
- Understand what you're looking to change and its scope, and how it will impact other areas
- Isolate potential implementation obstacles
- Determine projected costs
- Determine risk factors and all potential downsides for the proposed change
- Establish evaluative criteria for success and how it will be measured
- Determine best and worse-cases and pros and cons
- Design an Action Plan that includes who is going to do what, when, why, and how
- Set timeframes for implementation and completion

It's essential to put your change plan in writing. As Steven C. Brandt, former professor at Stanford University, shared in his book, *Entrepreneuring—The Ten Commandments for Building a Growth Company*, "Until committed to paper, intentions are seeds without soil, sails without wind, mere wishes which render communication within an organization inefficient, understanding uncertain, feedback inaccurate and execution sporadic."

Create your change plan with a clearly expressed written document that provides the necessary road map to ensure flawless execution.

Working smart is perhaps the most far-reaching discipline. It demands that you take a step back and clearly assess the basic foundation of your career or business and how you run it. It also asks you to examine yourself because your career and business are extensions of your life. As you develop a process to work smart you'll find that your life and business will run better because you now know not only how but also why you want to achieve Breakout Success.

Discipline Two
Present Everything

Set the Stage with Influential Presentations

"All the world's a stage." —*William Shakespeare*

In this chapter:
- ✓ Eliminate conversational chatter and begin presenting
- ✓ Create powerful and compelling presentations
- ✓ The art of presenting: entertain, influence, and be memorable
- ✓ Four key steps to a successful presentation
- ✓ Preparation-The single most important step
- ✓ Practice, practice and practice
- ✓ Present-It's show time
- ✓ Create a presentation question plan
- ✓ Conclusion-Finish strong
- ✓ Establish advancement by staying top of mind

Eliminate Conversational Chatter and Begin Presenting

You're probably already making many more presentations than you realize. But because you're not viewing them as presentations, they may often end up just being "conversations."

But you don't want to have mere conversations in business situations if you're trying to persuade or gain commitment from someone. You want to make compelling and winning presentations.

Successful businesspeople recognize when a presentation, not just a conversation, needs to happen, and they see that they're almost always making presentations. They're making them not only to customers and clients but also in meetings with business partners, coworkers, bosses, subordinates, management teams, employees, suppliers, bankers, and attorneys—and the list goes on. These interactions may be short and informal, depending on the situation, but disciplined people still view them as important and valuable opportunities to present.

We can't stress strongly enough that you are presenting any time you're trying to persuade anyone to execute a course of action, buy into an idea, gain commitment, or sell a product or service.

Create Powerful and Compelling Presentations

In our magazine publishing businesses, we made regular sales presentations to advertisers, but we also made presentations to all our suppliers, including printers, designers, photographers, and freelance writers. Why did we make presentations to these people? Because our goal was to get the best prices, terms, service, and work. We had to convince them about our financial stability, our success, and our potential to deliver more business in the future.

When we were interviewing talented job candidates, we were often competing with larger, more established companies. We used well thought-out presentations with candidates to get them to buy in and join our company by emphasizing the benefits of working at an innovative, entrepreneurial, and rapidly growing firm.

It's irrelevant what business ecosystem you're operating in: if you're engaging, persuading, trying to gain commitment, or selling a product or service, you *are* presenting.

For years we've championed the presentation as the heart and soul, the philosophical underpinning of Street Smart Disciplines because, arguably, everything related to your Breakout Success has its genesis in the presentation. Powerful presentations are a critical component of a success playbook.

Making persuasive presentations is not a mystic art. Rest assured you can learn how to perfect your presentation abilities, but it does require specialized skills. Practice to keep your audience engaged and to achieve your objectives. What you're about to read may be a quantum change from the way you view and make presentations, but our method achieves winning results.

The Art of Presenting: Entertain, Influence, and be Memorable

The presentation is an art form. It must entertain. It must influence. It must be memorable. It must sell.

A presentation must be written like a finely crafted short story and choreographed like a ballet. It must have the structure of a great symphony and the flexibility of a perfectly executed Super Bowl game plan. In short, a powerful professional presentation must be live theater at its best.

Just like a play, a presentation must be scripted, staged, and rehearsed. It starts with careful preparation and has an opening, middle, and conclusion.

If this sounds melodramatic, you're right, at least about the drama part. With your presentation, you must create high stakes and then show how you can deliver on them, just like a hero in a thriller who must overcome great odds to save the day and get the girl, or in your case, gain commitment, make the sale, or satisfy the customer.

As you read the following steps to a successful presentation, take your time and relax. You don't need to get it all right away (there won't be any exams, but read the material as if there was going to be one). For important presentations we review the material to be sure we have all the elements covered.

Once you're familiar with the basic ingredients you can pick and choose the elements required to achieve your specific objective in any business situation.

The Four Key Steps to a Successful Presentation:
- Preparation
- Practice
- Present
- Conclusion

Step One: Preparation
The single most important element of a presentation is preparation. Successful businesspeople often spend about 80 percent of their time preparing and 20 percent actually presenting. This is not unlike professional athletes who spend weeks practicing for a game or match that lasts just a few hours.

Understand the importance of always factoring in some uninterrupted, high-quality planning time for situations that require a presentation. If you don't prepare adequately for these encounters, you'll end up having that conversational chatter we talked about earlier and not making a presentation that will successfully achieve your goals.

We often made one-hour presentations to top executives at Fortune 500 companies. It was tough to get appointments—real tough! We had only one at-bat, so we would spend a couple of hours preparing and practicing to deliver crisp presentations.

We all know luck favors the well prepared, so be mentally, emotionally, and physically ready for every presentation whenever it happens.

"Before anything else, getting ready is the secret to success."
—Henry Ford

Identify Your Objectives

The key driver for the creation of the presentation is your objective. Ask yourself:

- What is the true purpose of the presentation?
- What am I really trying to accomplish?
- How will I achieve my goals?
- What must the people to whom I'm presenting do in order for me to achieve my goals?
- What do I absolutely, positively need to know and do before leaving the presentation to advance commitment?

Do Your Homework

It's important to learn as much as you can about the people to whom you are presenting.

- Get an understanding of the size of the audience. Is the presentation only to one person or to a group? Knowing this in advance is important for tailoring the presentation effectively and determining the delivery format (laptop, flipchart, PowerPoint, or other presentation tools).
- Will the type of meeting be informal or formal? What type of venue: an office, a boardroom, or a coffee shop?
- What expectations does the person or your audience have?
- What do you want the person or audience to get from the presentation?

When in a selling situation, garner as much information as you can about your prospective customers and their company, products and services, target markets, and competitors. See if you can uncover facts in their business or personal lives that create a need for your product or service.

Doing a Google search on the person and the company to which you're preparing to present is a great way to get information. Annual reports provide a wealth of information, so try to get the latest one at the company's website. The message from the CEO, for example, usually outlines the company's philosophy. Do a search on the potential customer's industry and competitors to get a clear picture of its current situation. Are there any strengths or weaknesses on which you can capitalize?

Your knowledge of the potential customer, his industry, and your product or service should be encyclopedic. Study your industry, your marketplace, and your competition. Peruse trade journals, newsletters, and every other source of available relevant information. Gather all the information you may need, and anticipate questions you may be asked during a presentation so you're not caught in a less-than-impressive, "Um, let me get back to you on that" moment. But if you don't have an answer, the smart thing to do is be honest and say, "That's a good question and I'm not exactly sure. Let me find out and get back to you."

"The man who is prepared has his battle half fought."—Cervantes

Create Your Basic Presentation

One of the most important facets of giving winning presentations is learning to see the world from the perspective of the person or people to whom you are presenting.

Spend time thinking about what you're going to be presenting and organize your thoughts and ideas. As we discussed earlier, determine what you want to accomplish. Write down your ideas and goals— and commit them to paper. This will clarify your presentation mindset. Also, define the value statement or key message you're trying to get across, which will be the person's number-one take-away, the crux of your presentation.

If you have to gain commitment from *anyone in any situation*, always prepare a written outline. Sometimes it'll be just a paragraph, sometimes much longer, depending on the situation, but always commit your thoughts to paper.

We stress to our consulting clients that if the presentation is very important or relatively long (thirty minutes or more), they should write out the *entire* presentation. That's right, script the entire thing, word for word. This gives you the opportunity to drill down deep to determine all the content you'll need and most importantly to see what is working, what isn't, and how to fine-tune its effectiveness. Writing it down also helps you practice the delivery so it sounds natural, not wooden.

We often develop and write master sales scripts for our clients. The salespeople tailor key plot points and presentation lengths to specific customers, but we recommend that if they are selling the same product or service, they follow the same script.

Like actors, salespeople must rehearse their scripts before the "performance." By taking this course of action, you develop presentations that are compelling and winning, and that successfully accomplish your objectives. One of the world's most masterful presenters, the late Steve Jobs, visionary cofounder of Apple, was known to rehearse his presentations exhaustively. For keynotes he typically did a week of dry runs before going on stage.

"There are always three speeches for every one you actually gave. The one you practiced, the one you gave, and the one you wish you gave." —Dale Carnegie

We can understand your possible wariness about scripts. They could be construed as disingenuous, but that's not the case if you're genuine. Show people that you really care about their needs and wants, and believe in what you're presenting.

Although we use scripts often for important presentations, we always appear natural because we make it a habit to rehearse, rehearse, and rehearse some more. We view our time in front of the person we were presenting to as "show time" or "prime time," with the objective to give an award-winning performance. We *never* go into a meeting without being totally prepared and rehearsed.

The Opening

It's not difficult to deliver winning presentations; anyone can do it. We work with complete novices and watch them pull off outstanding presentations after they read and incorporate the elements we discuss in this discipline. Their success is directly proportional to the amount of time they spend reviewing this material and adequately preparing. If you put the time in, you too can do it.

When developing your presentation, always start with the big picture and explain the objective of the meeting. People have their own agendas, and as you're speaking, they're silently asking themselves, "What's in this for me?" Your opening statements should answer the following questions, which most people will be thinking about:

- What are you and your company all about?
- Are you reputable, reliable, and financially stable?
- Do you have a genuine interest in me?
- Will you help me solve potential problems?
- What specific benefits will I get from this product or service?

"We rule the world with our words." —Napoleon Bonaparte

Words That Hit Home

When preparing your presentation, choose your words carefully. Use words that convey your strong and positive beliefs, that are precise and that have an emotional appeal. Weave in interesting and entertaining anecdotes wherever applicable. Whether you buy into it or not, you're on stage and you want to make this theater. Use hooks or startling statements that enliven your presentation and keep the audience emotionally engaged. Use whatever words you're comfortable saying that will help you achieve your objectives. Richard Bayan's book, *Words That Sell: More than 6,000 Entries to Help You Promote Your Products, Services, and Ideas* is a good source for finding words that really hit home.

Brainstorm and choose the most persuasive words and phrases for your specific presentation situations. Don't go MIA on us here. Give it ten to fifteen minutes of your concentrated brainpower.

Here are some phrases to get you started:

- We can work with you on this and ensure a productive outcome
- We have had significant success with our product and would like to share it with you
- We can generate results you'll be able to see on your bottom line
- This is truly an outstanding program
- Here's what's important to you
- We can save you time and money
- We can help you optimize your productivity
- We're here to help you with this project
- This will achieve winning, quantifiable results for you
- Try something new; this is a bold and innovative (contemporary, state-of-the art, revolutionary) program that has successfully broken new ground
- It's easy (simple, uncomplicated, easy to understand)
- Our goal is to help you outsmart, not outspend, your competitors
- These unsettling economic times demand a unique or competitive advantage, and we can help give you that

Tailor Your Presentation

Using the information you've gathered about the person you're presenting to, customize the presentation to address their specific needs. Your approach to tailoring should always be the same: through your preparation, figure out what is most important to the person, and then frame that information in the context of what you're presenting.

Be sure to address issues the person understands and can relate to. People don't pay attention to things they don't understand. Importantly, be as concise as you can; always get to the point. Spend high-quality time fine-tuning what you feel the person will respond to.

Be Prepared for Shortcuts

Be ready in case the person you're presenting to suddenly cuts short the time, for example, from a previously agreed forty-five-minute meeting to ten to fifteen minutes. Create a ten- to fifteen-minute plan with a shortened version of your presentation that still delivers the information as effectively as the longer version. Also be ready for an even more truncated version, the five-minute plan, also known as the Elevator Pitch. If doing this is impossible or counterproductive, consider rescheduling the appointment.

Prepare Presentation Materials

As we all know, a picture is worth a thousand words. A raft of research shows that people tend to remember and find what they see more persuasive than what they hear. Almost 80 percent of what they glean from presentations is visual. That's just the way we humanoids work; we're wired that way, so why not turn this physiological reality to your advantage? You want a super-engaged person or audience to gain maximum mindshare. Good visuals maximize attention, understanding, and retention.

Wherever possible, use professionally prepared charts, graphs, and visual elements to illustrate various points in your presentation. In most cases, a PowerPoint presentation is the way to go. Clear, colorful exhibits and visual aids take your presentation to that highly professional, winning level where you always need to be. Money spent on top-quality presentation materials is money well spent. Always strive to produce the best materials possible.

"It's not the will to win that matters—everyone has that. It's the will to prepare to win that matters." —Paul "Bear" Bryant

There is such a thing as PowerPoint overkill. Our rule of thumb with Power Points is to minimize the "Power" aspect and focus more on the "Point." Simplicity rules. Keep your exhibits as simple as possible, get right to the point (no more than ten lines of text per page, and when in doubt, leave it out) with impactful, value-oriented, benefit-laden words and phrases. Have more graphics and pictures than text.

This is about image. In our consultations to companies and lectures to business students, we underscore the importance of creating a professional image by spending the time and money necessary to develop the best possible portfolio of information for prospective clients and customers, including:

- Brochures
- Information on rates and prices
- Written summaries of features and benefits
- Testimonials from satisfied customers
- Newspaper articles about your company
- Product samples
- Information on special offers
- Company newsletters
- Publicity releases

At *Buenos Aires Metropolis Magazine,* we didn't have much of a budget to spend on a media kit (printed promotional materials, editorial overviews, and advertising rates) when we started the company. Nevertheless, we wanted to make a bold statement and create a competitive advantage to set us apart from other publishers and magazines in the city. We also wanted to make the company look bigger, international, and more established than it was at the time. We made a decision to spend nearly every marketing dollar we had to produce the best media kit in the marketplace. We did, and it paid off handsomely, enabling us to attract numerous prestigious advertisers.

Identify Decision Makers

Even the best presentation is ineffective if delivered to the wrong person. Identify the person you really have to persuade or gain a commitment from. You'd be surprised how often people are not presenting to the right person. In sales situations, we found out it always behooved us to start at the top of the target company's staff for whatever we were presenting.

When we were trying to sell a corporate marketing sponsorship for a venue in Los Angeles to a multibillion-dollar petroleum giant, we placed a call directly to the chairman and CEO of the company. We got the chairman's executive secretary and briefly gave her an overview of our program. She said the chairman was out of the country, but she would give him our message and get back to us soon. Sure enough, a day later she called to say that the chairman was interested in our program and had asked the president of the company to call us.

Within a few hours, the president phoned. "I understand that you have something interesting, and I'd like to hear what your program is all about," he said. We made a phone pitch, and he said it sounded good, "but I don't make that decision. I'd like you to call our VP of Marketing and set up a meeting." We called the vice president and mentioned we spoke to the president and he recommended that we see him.

We made the appointment, and a couple weeks later, made our presentation. We ultimately landed the business. The CEO didn't make the decision, but he put us in touch with the person who did. We made this sale and many others by having the moxie to always start at the very top and get high-level introductions to the ultimate decision makers.

"Talent alone won't make you a success. Neither will being in the right place at the right time, unless you are ready. The most important question is: 'Are you ready?'" —Johnny Carson

Step Two: Practice

Practice and fine-tune before *every* presentation. The amount of time required to practice and do the fine-tuning really depends on what you're presenting and to whom. But the bottom line is, practice and fine-tuning make for a peak performance. They sharpen your presentation skills and boost your confidence. And confidence is valuable currency when presenting.

Top NFL players practice religiously, watch videos of their performances, get tips from their coaches—and then they go back on the field and practice some more. When they're playing, every move is so well rehearsed that it comes naturally, and the pressure of the game doesn't affect their performance as much as it would if they weren't so well-prepared. Be on top of your game with dedicated practice and fine-tuning habits.

FROM THE STREET: BRAIN FREEZE REMEDY

Some people experience brain freeze—a complete loss of their train of thought—during presentations, usually to large audiences. Sian Beilock, a professor of psychology at the University of Chicago and an expert in human performance, sees this as a common misfire of the prefrontal cortex of the brain, the area that allows a person to block out distractions and stay focused on the situation at hand. In her book *Choke: What the Secrets of the Brain Reveal About Getting It Right When You Have To,* she states, "Worrying about the situation and its consequences" saps the working memory of the brain. To overcome brain freeze, pause and take a few deep breaths, then continue. She likens this to rebooting a computer when it crashes. Research has shown that practicing and rehearsing, especially for high-pressure presentations, reduces the likelihood of brain freeze and enhances the quality and outcome of the presentation.

"When you are not practicing, remember, someone somewhere is practicing, and when you meet him he will win." —Ed Macauley

Here are a few tips for practicing presentations:
- Practice in front of a mirror. It may feel awkward at first, but doing this really improves your performance, gets you charged up for a presentation, and gets you into your "stage persona."
- Practice with colleagues, employees, and friends. Have someone play the role of the person you're presenting to and, if applicable, have him or her pose questions. Videotape the rehearsal. Observe your body language and listen to your voice. Pay close attention to your vocal speed, pitch, pauses, and energy level.
- Visualize each presentation beforehand. Picture yourself delivering a successful presentation and achieving your desired outcome. This mental walk-through will help you be relaxed when you're making the actual presentation.

FROM THE STREET: GEAR UP FOR EVERY PHONE CALL

Just as you would for a face-to-face presentation, prepare yourself mentally, physically, and emotionally for handling business by telephone. Remember, even though you're on the phone you are still presenting.

Prepare for phone calls as you would an in-person meeting. Don't make the call without having a game plan to achieve your objective. If you don't have a game plan, you'll end up with a conversation, not a presentation, and you'll probably get nowhere. Before every call, ask yourself the following questions:

- Why am I making this call?
- What are my objectives?
- What do I want to accomplish?
- What obstacles or objections might I encounter?
- How will I respond to resistance?

Write a checklist of things you want to accomplish before every call. It's challenging to present on the phone without the benefit of face-to-face contact, so put positive energy in your voice on every call. Fire yourself up!

Charge Your Batteries

Enthusiasm sells more than anything. The word *enthusiasm* comes from the Greek word *entheos*, which means "to be instilled with god-like energy and spirit." No bones about it, unbridled enthusiasm is the number-one attribute of successful businesspeople. Project enthusiasm throughout your presentation—from the opening right until you're wrapping things up.

"Nothing great was achieved without enthusiasm."
—Ralph Waldo Emerson

We always have a strong belief in whatever we're presenting and make it a point to tap deep into the well of *entheos*. And often we're charged up. In the middle of one of our presentations, our customer caught the spirit and got genuinely excited. He was beaming and said, "These are really some great marketing services that can really work for us." He immediately got on the phone and called two people from his department to join the meeting.

Once they arrived, he took over our presentation (we didn't have a chance to get a word in) and began sharing the benefits of the program and selling his coworkers on our services. Within fifteen minutes, he asked if we had the paperwork that he could sign so they could begin. We guess we had our entheos on maximum strength that day. Enthusiasm is contagious. Try it.

Achieve the "Selling Mind"

Before every presentation, give yourself some time to get centered and energized so that you're firing on all cylinders. We usually spend about fifteen to twenty minutes. Find a quiet place and rehearse before the meeting. Work on achieving the Selling Mind, that ultra-positive attitude required for a successful presentation. The process of achieving the selling mind is a conscious psychological preparation, an inner dialogue that gives you a shot of adrenaline to raise you up to your highest performance level.

With the selling mind you're on stage–it's show time and you are presenting in high definition! The selling mind keeps that charged, positive attitude throughout the presentation. Whether you're presenting or selling, sell yourself and or company and its products and services with entheos. Achieve the Selling Mind *before* every presentation.

"There are those who work all day. Those who dream all day. And those who spend an hour dreaming before setting to work to fulfill those dreams. Go into the third category because there's virtually no competition." —*Steven J. Ross*

Step Three: Present

Put Your Best Foot Forward

In the first few minutes of your presentation, you must create a good first impression, and you only get one chance to do it. Greeting people with a warm smile and a firm handshake always works well. People do business with people they like, so do your best to get the person or people attending the presentation to like you right from the start. Supersize your personality to set the tone for a positive meeting and to engage your audience immediately.

Organize all your materials so you're not fumbling around before you begin. Drill down your opening lines to make them sharp and attention grabbing. The first twenty words out of your mouth are more important than the next five thousand words.

Make Small Talk

Before you begin your formal presentation, break the ice with brief, casual conversation. Don't try to make it up on the spot. Prepare some sort of opening dialogue in advance that will help you build rapport. It might be about the weather (the perennial favorite) or geopolitical events (but be careful). If you are in someone's home or office, look for photos and memorabilia or any other things to glean information about the person's family, sports, and entertainment interests and hobbies—anything that can be a topic for small talk.

Use Names

Doesn't it make you feel good when people you just met sprinkle your name throughout a conversation? It does because it immediately establishes rapport with you quickly. If it works on you, it will work on the person to whom you are presenting. Use people's names throughout the presentation.

Watch the Time

Know how much time people have allotted for your presentation, and pace yourself accordingly. Stay on schedule so you won't have to rush through your conclusion or leave out critical material. Ask for a specific amount of time when you set up the appointment, and confirm the time allotment when you begin. Completing your presentation in the agreed-to time (or a little bit earlier) prevents the person from feeling annoyed that you're keeping him or her from getting back to work. Don't overstay your welcome.

FROM THE STREET: RECIPE FOR RAPPORT

- Personalize yourself. Set yourself apart from other people. Be different. Be unique. Be entertaining. Be memorable.
- Use the other person's name often to establish a personal connection.
- Use small talk to break the ice.
- Use noteworthy statements to differentiate yourself, to make your presentation memorable, and to set yourself apart from other people. For example, open with, "This could very possibly be the most important presentation you will see all year long. What we want to do in the next twenty minutes is show you how you can make the needle move in the marketplace and sell more products than you ever dreamed possible."
- Use big-name clients to establish your credibility. Mention some of the important customers that are doing business with your company (but do it in a way that sounds natural and not like overt boasting).

Keep Your Audience Engaged

We're in the camp that feels strongly about using a multitude of methods to keep your audience vitally engaged throughout the presentation. There are a number of techniques you can weave into your engagement repertoire, such as drama, urgency, humor, benefits, testimonials, and precise questioning.

Make it dramatic. To dramatize your points, include periodic pauses throughout the presentation. You may be uncomfortable with moments of silence, but force yourself to get used to the idea. Occasional silences are a key device to add drama and a sense of importance or gravity to the information you're presenting. Stop from time to time, remain silent, and let the points you have just made sink in. Get into a good tempo of raising and lowering your voice appropriately to highlight and emphasize certain points.

Add some humor. You don't have to set the room on fire with laughter, but adding levity is always a good idea in a presentation. Keep it short and sweet. Don't tell random jokes. Draw on humor from your life experiences. People want to know about you, and giving them information about yourself in an entertainingly funny way builds rapport. Perhaps talk about an embarrassing experience that wasn't funny at the time, but that you and others can laugh about now. As the adage says, "Humor is simply tragedy separated by time and space." But run your jokes and anecdotes by a team member to make sure you don't inadvertently offend the person to whom you are presenting, that you've struck the appropriate tone, and above all that they are actually funny and entertaining.

Point out the benefits throughout your presentation. We can't impress on you enough about speaking in terms of benefits with regularity. Weave into your presentation as often as you can benefit-oriented words or phrases. For example, share how your idea, concept, or product will save the person time and money or make work, and thus his life, easier, more efficient, and more fulfilling. Most people are taxed to the max in life between business and family and just living. Importantly, note that really all they want to know is what's in it for them. A great way to keep them engaged is to highlight benefits regularly.

Use testimonials. Testimonials are a core element in every presentation. They are real-world, tangible tools to promote and market yourself, your company, and your products or services. They add creditability. It's not boasting; it's a third- party endorsement of how you have helped past customers. Tell the story using the client's name, and tell it from his or her point of view.

It's easy to get testimonials—if you have satisfied, happy clients or customers. People usually like to help if you've given them a positive experience, so ask them, perhaps by saying, "You've told me that you've been very satisfied with our services over the years, and I was wondering if you'd be kind enough to help me by writing a short letter on your letterhead highlighting that." If they agree, you should add, "I know you're busy so I'd be more than happy to draft it, and then you can edit it. Would you like me to do that?" Usually the only obstacle in getting them to agree is the time it would take to do it, so make it easy for them.

We usually used ten to fifteen testimonials from our clients. We had the testimonials professionally printed and brought them to every presentation. Usually fifteen or twenty minutes into the presentation, we would say, "We've been talking long enough about our services, so now we'd like to let some of our clients tell you what they think." Then we handed out the testimonials and let them read for a few minutes before we continued. Impressive testimonials give tangible creditability, which paves the way to making successful presentations or a sale.

Ask precise questions. A winning presentation engages people by combining precise questioning with skillful listening. People hear what they want to hear so the precise use of questions guides their thinking to make sure they're hearing and understanding exactly what you want them to take away from the presentation.

Be careful not to ramble on in a presentation; pause to ask questions. Every presentation should be crafted to incorporate numerous opportunities to ask questions, especially in the first few minutes and then strategically throughout the remainder of the presentation. The consistent use of questions naturally guides a presentation to your desired result and ensures that the person has truly absorbed your pitch.

Ask questions that do the following:
- Get vital information about the person's needs.
- Encourage participation.
- Pique interest and secure commitment.
- Reveal misunderstandings, concerns, and objections.

"The more you say the less people remember." —Francois Fenelo

Watch your listen-to-talk ratio to maintain a balance between talking and listening. Most people have short attention spans, and in this internet-driven, sound-bite world, those attention spans are getting shorter and shorter, so make sure people are vitally engaged. To achieve an on-the-edge-of-their-seats command of your audience, never talk for more than a few minutes without reinvolving them in the presentation by using reactivation questions, such as "How do you feel about that?" "How would you use something like this?" "What benefits do you feel you would derive?" "How does this look to you?"

Sprinkle these participation pauses throughout your presentation with the development of a Question Plan.

Create a Presentation Question Plan

The use of a Question Plan is a key element of a successful presentation. A lot of information is necessary to prepare an effective one, and, for most people, the material requires a few reads and studying to absorb the techniques. So again, take your time. A good part of our preparation for presentations is devoted to the development of well-thought-out questions. For important presentations, revisit this section to be sure everything is covered.

Every presentation should have a question plan that includes:
- A list of questions tailored to the person or audience
- Optimal phrasing of the questions
- The best time to ask questions

The type and frequency of questions used in a presentation depend on what you're presenting and to whom. Familiarize yourself with the different types of questions, and strategize which ones to ask and when you should ask them.

Opening questions. If you've done your homework, you should already know about the person and the company to whom you're presenting. Get every bit of information that will help you make a successful presentation. Ask yourself before the presentation, "What else do I need to know about the person or business or situation so I can tailor my presentation to meet their needs?"

Use opening questions to confirm your research and to get additional information. Find out what the person really wants and needs. Begin the presentation where applicable by asking questions to get the person talking. If you aren't totally sure what someone wants or needs, find out. Ask questions before you forge ahead.

Ask the person if you can pose some questions with a statement such as "Would it be okay if I asked you a few questions to better understand your situation and how I can help you"? This is always preferable to announcing, "I'm going to start with a few questions." A person is likely to respond more positively to a request than to a declaration. With an opening question instead of a statement, you instantly become a potential partner instead of simply a presenter. Make it a habit not to tell a person something when you can ask a question instead.

Another example of an opening question is "I've done quite a bit of research on your company to make sure our time together is productive. My understanding is that you are planning on implementing a public-relations effort and might need the help of a team of technologists to explore the use of social media. Is this an accurate assessment? What else can you tell us about your company or specific situation that will help us gain a greater understanding of exactly how we can be of service to you?"

Tailor the questions to meet your specific situations. Here are a few examples:

- How do you differentiate your company and products from your competitors in the marketplace?
- How could you save more money when working with your suppliers?
- What do you feel we can do to increase sales at each of your stores?
- What are your most important considerations as you plan your expansion?
- Are there changes in your life or business that are creating new opportunities, challenges, or needs?

Open-ended questions. Include open-ended questions in your presentation. Open-ended questions begin with who, what, when, where, or why; they can't be answered with a simple yes or no. They stimulate informative answers that help you meet the needs of the person or, in sales situations, match your product or service to the customer's needs. Open-ended questions also help you determine what is required to bring your presentation to a fruitful close. The following questions are guidelines for sale situations:

- How can I help you justify your decision to expand your staff?
- What kind of research do you need to support the marketing of this product?
- What are the most important functions this product/service must do for you?
- How do you normally use this type of product/service?
- Why is this type of product/service important to you?
- Who else gets involved in decisions about this type of product/service?

"Asking the right questions takes as much skill as giving the right answers." —Robert Half

Trial questions. Trial questions are those that confirm interest or prompt commitments. Any time you can get some form of confirmation, you're moving in the right direction toward either a positive commitment on what you're presenting or a disapproval or "no." Either way, depending on your presentation scenario, testing the waters by using trial questions is an effective technique to get a reading of where you stand. Use them at various points in a presentation.

- As an opener: "How do you feel this product/service would be of value to your company? If I can show you some additional benefits you could derive, would it make sense for you to take a closer look at getting the product delivered soon?"
- During the presentation: "How do you think you could use our product/service most effectively?"
- At the conclusion: "If we can get the product specifications you mentioned, and it is available in our warehouse, when would you like it delivered?"

Questions as answers. Responding to a question with another question helps you determine what people are really asking. There are usually several possible answers to any given question, especially if it's a general one. Precisely define the real question to give a persuasive answer.

When a person asks a question that you need to think about or needs further clarification, begin with the statement "That's a really good question." This compliment also buys you a moment to think about your response. To further clarify the questioner's thinking and open up more opportunity for constructive dialogue, ask follow-up questions like these:

- "If you don't mind me asking, why specifically are you asking that?"
- "May I ask why you feel that is important to you?"
- "I might be able to answer your question more effectively if you don't mind telling me more about your concern or issue. Would that be all right?"
- "What do you have in mind?"

Listen with skill. Questioning and listening are two essential elements of the presenting process. But asking the right questions is only half the battle. You must also listen—really listen—to what people are saying and read between the lines to get the subtext of their answers. This, in fact, is actually more important than the literal answer.

"Nature has given to men one tongue, but two ears, that we may hear from others twice as much as we speak." —Epictetus

Most people are lousy listeners. The art of communication is 50 percent listening; But, unlike reading, writing, and speaking, good listening habits are seldom taught in school. As a result, most people woefully lack the ability to listen effectively. You can train yourself to listen so that you hear not only the literal answer but also the subtext, which holds the hidden truth of what the person is saying.

The key factor is to concentrate. Focus 100 percent of your attention on what the person is saying and how he or she is saying it. Don't let your mind wander. Don't assume you know what someone will say next. Don't be mentally rehearsing your responses when you should be listening. And by all means, don't interrupt.

Listen actively. Effective listening is not passive. Take actions that will boost your concentration, help you hear the subtext, and convey to the other person that you're fully engaged in the conversation.

- Respond with body language. Sit forward in your chair and maintain direct eye contact.
- Respond to what someone is saying by nodding, smiling, and saying, "I understand," or "I see."
- Take notes. Jot down key words and main points. Note taking keeps you actively involved and forces you to listen. It helps you remember what was said, and it impresses people by demonstrating your keen interest in them.
- Ask questions. Use them to clarify what the person is saying to avoid misunderstandings later on.
- Paraphrase the answers your audience members give, saying, "To be sure that I understand you correctly, let me reiterate what you have said," or "Would you mind if I summarize my understanding of your situation?"

In Dale Carnegie's classic 1932 book, *How to Win Friends and Influence People*, he says that a basic human need is to feel important and significant, to feel appreciated and to feel that we matter. Nothing does this better than active listening.

Step Four: Conclusion

At the end of the presentation, spend a few minutes summarizing key points and check to see how the people feel about what you've just presented. You may want to ask what they perceive are the major benefits of your proposal, product, or service. Most importantly, uncover and address any concerns or problems they may have that prevent you from gaining commitment or making the sale. This process requires skillful questioning, anticipation, and preparation, which we cover in greater detail in Discipline Five—Get More Business.

Create a Sense of Urgency

Many presentations require a call to action which will elicit a commitment or agreement, or a reason for the person to buy now. Most people just don't like to make decisions. You have to give them a reason to overcome their natural inclination to postpone commitment.

For example, in a sales situation, prompt your prospects to act by mentioning there may be a short window of opportunity, such as an impending price increase, and if they don't act now, they will have to pay more. Or there is a dwindling supply of the product, and if inventory runs out, there will be a significant wait before the product could be delivered. You can also create a sense of urgency with exclusive offers, special promotions, or limited-time deals

When we consulted a magazine company, for example, we encouraged them to have their sales force create a sense of urgency through advertising category exclusivity. When they approached telecommunications companies such as AT&T, Verizon, and T-Mobile, we suggested that they take only one company in that sector as an advertiser in the publication. This worked well, and they secured the business within a few weeks. They also got their prospects to act quickly by mentioning that advertising space was limited, that there were only a few pages left.

A well-planned approach to create a viable sense of urgency helps you speed up the decision process. There are many ways you can create urgency; just make sure you use them.

Gaining a Final Commitment, or Closing the Deal

Don't stop now. You have one more critical step to take: you have to ask for the commitment or the sales order. In presentations that require gaining commitment and in selling situations, there must be closure. You've spent many hours of valuable time preparing and presenting. Closing is simply the logical conclusion to a successful presentation. One of the cardinal rules of successful presenting is to achieve closure in situations that warrant it. We will cover this topic further in Discipline Five—Get More Business.

Develop Your Advancement Strategy

If some form of commitment is required and you haven't received it, ask yourself, What is going to happen next? What still needs to be accomplished? Who still needs to be presented to? When and how will I do follow-up activities?

To establish advancement, you could say, "Just to clarify my thinking, what do you feel we have to do to get this program implemented, to begin providing our services, or for us to do business together?" Never leave without knowing exactly where you stand.

Journal It!

Get into the success-oriented habit of journaling. Immediately after all presentations, write a quick summary. Do it right away while the experience is fresh in your mind. Review your notes, and ask yourself what happened during the presentation, including what went well, what could have been done better, what issues or concerns the audience raised, and what your advancement strategy is. Follow-up is vital to ensure that your hard work bears fruit.

Establish Advancement by Staying Top of Mind

If you didn't gain commitment or close the deal, frequent contact with the person must continue until this happens. Stay in the "important zone," that is, in the forefront of your person's mind. There are many strategies for doing this, such as a series of emails, phone calls, and follow-up meetings. For greater impact, consider sending letters and even handwritten notes, a lost art in today's fast-paced, digital world.

Throughout the process, keep an eye out for relevant news articles or other items that might be of interest to the person and forward them to him or her. In executing this type of follow-up, of course be tactful and be sure it is well timed so you don't turn into a nuisance. A well-conceived, well-executed Top of Mind strategy will help you gain commitment or sell your product or service successfully.

We have used these presentation techniques over the course of our journey to achieve Breakout Success. Incorporate them into your success strategy playbook so your every interaction with people, whether in a formal meeting or a chance conversation, is a winning presentation.

Discipline Three
Deal with People

Cultivate People Skills that Pave the Way to Breakout Success

"Success in life, in anything, depends upon the number of persons that one can make himself agreeable to." —*Thomas Carlyle*

In this chapter:
- ✓ Understanding the Great People Truth
- ✓ Conduct a personal audit
- ✓ Street Smart people skills and strategies
- ✓ Have Patience - Everyone is perfect, with all their imperfections
- ✓ First Impressions - Yours and Theirs
- ✓ Be interested in people
- ✓ Don't be a critic
- ✓ Deal with people's moods- Bad mood immunization techniques
- ✓ Let's talk about you
- ✓ Be the best person you can be

No matter what type of business you're in, you are in the "people business." Without people, you have no customers, no clients, and no employees. *Every* job requires some sort of interaction with people, and interacting skillfully is a central discipline to master.

It's simple: people do business with people they like. Finely tuned people skills make you more likable, but most importantly, they help you achieve peak levels of success in your professional and personal life.

It never ceases to amaze us how many people we encounter in the business world who lack good people skills. Over the years, we have dealt with intelligent professionals from all walks of life—doctors, attorneys, accountants, business executives, entrepreneurs, and many others. But it's hard to understand why many of these otherwise talented people fail outright in their dealings with others, often hurting their careers or businesses. Remember, being smart and great at what you do doesn't cut it if you can't work well with people.

We have made our share of social blunders by not employing the best people skills at times. But we think that those of us who have made missteps and learned from them are the most qualified to impart that wisdom to others.

Why are so many people clueless in the way they deal with others? The simple answer is they're humans, and humans are imperfect. What is truly puzzling is why, with so much at stake, interpersonal-skills education is not a required subject in high schools and universities. Most people learn these valuable skills the hard way by making costly social blunders.

Courses about effectively dealing with people are now being taught at Columbia, Stanford, and Berkeley's business schools. This educational remodel was the result of feedback from corporate recruiters who found that business students had plenty of "hard skills" (like finance and accounting) but were falling short where it mattered most—the "soft skills" of dealing with people. This skill set especially becomes paramount as people ascend the corporate ladder and begin to oversee employees or run companies. Actually, corporate leaders are often not the smartest guys in the room, but are masters of the art of the relationship (and leadership). They are able to handle the small talk, deliver a well-told joke or interesting anecdote, and give a pat on the back.

As we were writing this chapter, we reflected back to when we were kids. We realized we learned most of our people skills from our parents, and that was pretty much where the education ended. We can still hear our folks saying, "Smile, be friendly, have a firm-handshake, no staring, be polite, say 'please' and 'thank you.'" Overall, we think our moms and dads did a pretty good job, and we feel lucky that they valued good manners and passed on that mindset to us. Maybe we didn't learn from our parents about which fork to use first at a dinner party or how to play polo like the kids who came from the fancier part of our town, with their moneyed childhood and rarefied parentage. But we wonder in amazement how these smart, successful, and affluent masters of universes were sometimes the most hopelessly rude and socially clumsy people at the party.

Psychologist Daniel Goleman quantified levels of social skills with his emotional intelligence (EI) scale (analogous to the intelligence quotient IQ, which measures cognitive intelligence). According to Goleman, EI is the skill "of managing feelings so that they are expressed appropriately and effectively enabling people to work together smoothly toward common goals." Most of us enhance our people skills and EI as we keep moving through life.

Often the problem doesn't revolve around a lack of people skills or EI, but rather is the result of bad behavioral habits. Sadly, because of the fast-paced and stressful lives most of us lead, we forget, don't have the time, or just don't bother to deal with people as well as we should.

EI and effective interpersonal skills come into play every day in fundamental ways in business and in our personal lives. We need communication skills to speak articulately, listen actively, and write effectively. We need conflict-resolution skills for those heated times of high tension between people. And finally, we need negotiation and motivational skills to influence others to achieve mutually beneficial results in all our interactions.

The challenge lies in utilizing your EI and tweaking your people skills to deal effectively with all the different personality types you encounter, especially those that are polar opposites of yours.

Understanding the Great People Truth

We have to admit that we've damaged a few business relationships in our day by having zero tolerance for various personality types. There were times when we lost all patience with our fellow human tormentors—sorry, beings—and were often on the verge of total meltdowns. It made things very difficult at work, to say the least.

But our salvation, our defining moment, which burst forth in Technicolor and became permanently seared in our minds, was our discovery of what we call the Great People Truth. This epiphany happened many years ago while attending a Zen Buddhist seminar in Marin County, outside of San Francisco. This was the perfect antidote to our toxic thinking.

The Great People Truth is simply embracing the wisdom of openness and acceptance with all people and understanding and accepting the following:

- People are all wired differently.
- People may be difficult and hurtful.
- People may not live up to all your expectations and may disappoint you occasionally.
- People often do not act the way in which you want.
- People will not complete your fulfillment of peace and happiness; it must come from you.

The secret is to downsize your expectations of people. They are the way they are, whether we like it or not, and we must accept that. The wise person fights nothing. Acceptance frees us from having to confront feelings of frustration and disappointment when dealing with others.

Unfortunately and ironically, people don't accept or embrace the Great People Truth as often as they should. (This includes us; we're a work in progress and giving it our best every day to truly accept and practice it). But if you don't completely accept, internalize, and practice it daily, you will lead a life of frustration and unhappiness. Your measure of mental health and overall happiness really depends on completely buying into this truth. It is not easy, and for many people, it requires a paradigm shift.

"Our greatest joys and greatest pains come with our relationships with others." —Steven Covey

Conduct a Personal Audit

Effectively dealing with people must begin with a personal audit or self-assessment. Look closely at yourself and at how you deal with people daily. Sometimes we are self-saboteurs in our dealings with others. Often we don't see ourselves as clearly as we should. How we think and feel about ourselves is only our perception. We really only see the person who we think we are.

Much of what we regard as a problem or issue with another person is often our own issue and our lack of good people skills. We quickly see character flaws and faults with others, but we are often blind to our own predominant behavioral dimension and shortcomings.

If you happen to be trudging through life asking, "What's wrong with this person or that person?" stop for a moment. Have you considered that you may be the problem? Reexamine the filters through which you are seeing yourself and the people you encounter. We all see and hear what we want to see and hear from people, situations, and ourselves. Take the time to connect all the dots to get a true picture of you.

It all boils down to being mindful and consciously getting in touch with how you think other people perceive you. It's also about seeing people exactly as they are and not as you wish them to be.

Furthermore, the world and people are a true reflection of you and your thoughts and of the energy and behavior you emit and exhibit. If you're rude, angry, or impatient with someone, how do you think the person will react? Usually your behavior or something very close to it will be reflected right back to you. If you take a sincere, close look, be ready to see a sharp-edged reflection that you might not like to see.

Carefully examine what is going on inside your head that you're not even aware of unless you stop and listen to it. Be acutely conscious about what is going on. Listen to your inner self-talk when interacting with people, and clean it up when necessary. (More on this in the next section, Street Smart People Skills and Strategies).

You may be thinking this is a bit too Dr. Feel Good or Zen-like, but strip it down to its essential element and it's just common sense. Remember this as you step out of your old social-skills comfort zone, and try these new ways of dealing with people.

Ask yourself if you are truly using good people skills every day. And if you think you are, pay attention to what is going on inside your head and what is likely going on inside theirs when you're dealing with people.

"Working with people is difficult, but not impossible."
—Peter Drucker

There are lots of difficult people in the world, and you may already be dealing with some of them—those impossible coworkers, the difficult boss, unfriendly suppliers, and trying customers. If you haven't dealt with them yet, you will sooner or later. The most trying case is when you have to work with them daily. This is when it's most important to know how to deal with everybody as professionally and effectively as possible so everyone can get his or her job done and achieve the goals that move the company and their careers forward.

We all have personality quirks, idiosyncrasies, and annoying habits. And we know that sometimes we just have to let Harry be Harry and Mary be Mary and do the best we can to deal with them. But what about those people who border on being antisocial?

"It takes less character to discover the faults of others than it does to tolerate them." —J. Petit Senn

Jim Morrison of The Doors summed it up well in their song "People Are Strange." Yes, they sure can be, and Morrison should know. After a combined fifty-plus years in the business world, we believe we've dealt with some of the strangest. Here are a few of the most difficult types with whom we've had to work with:

- Bulldozers: they bury you with a nonstop monologue, preventing you from getting a word in edgewise, droning on with their own soundtrack, sucking up all the oxygen in the room while you try to keep yourself from telling them to just shut their traps.
- Narcissists: the legends in their own minds.
- Hyperactives: those who can't stay focused for very long and are running around the room like fourth-graders while you're trying to carry on a conversation.
- Fragile ego types: these sensitive souls are usually suffering from some sort of inferiority complex.
- Neanderthals: they stand out because of their highly limited social skills and low emotional intellegence.

How do you survive, let alone deal with these … colorful personalities? You'll need specific skills, the willingness to sometimes ride a slippery slope, and the ability to pay some mental transaction costs. We'll show you exactly how.

"Everyone thinks of changing the world, but no one thinks of changing himself." —Leo Tolstoy

Street Smart People Skills and Strategies

For the most part, people skills are truisms that have been around for a gazillion years. But we know for a fact (we see it every day) that despite seeing ourselves as reasonable and intelligent people, we all exhibit unflattering behaviors at times.

No one employs optimum EI and people skills with the consistency that he or she should. To correct this deficit, think of it as a challenge to keep the world happily spinning by doing a better job at how we deal with one another, not only in the business world, but with our family, friends, and strangers as well.

Some people are naturally warm, friendly, and open, effortlessly connecting with everyone they meet. But not everyone has that naturally winning personality gene that creates instant chemistry to make connections with others. And even these social-skill Einsteins are tested when dealing with the "colorful" personality types.

You can learn and improve people skills. Take a personal audit of those covered below. Adopting and practicing them daily can be pivotal in forging effective relationships in your life and business.

"Patience and perseverance have a magical effect before which difficulties and obstacles vanish." —John Quincy Adams

Have Patience

Patience is one of the greatest virtues and unequivocally the single most important strategy to learn and practice in dealing with people. As Benjamin Franklin said, "Genius is nothing but a greater aptitude for patience."

If you're thinking, "Of course it's important—it's one of the greatest virtues. But why are you wasting my time telling me what I already know." Don't have the time to explore whether you have a fully developed knack for patience? I think you see the problem we all have with these big truths in life that are so big and so true, that we take them for granted and roll right by them.

Impatience is one of the major and most obvious causes of interpersonal problems. Maybe you're one of the enlightened few with an abundance of patience. But what about all the people you'll have to deal with who don't have this golden gift? You'll still have to deal with them, calling even more on your patience reserves, which can always use new deposits.

Author M. J. Ryan wrote in her book *The Power of Patience*, "Indeed, the longer I study and practice patience, the more I've come to see that it is a critical factor in whether or not we have satisfying lives." Her comment hits the mark dead on, stressing the importance of developing patience and how it can improve your life.

Patience is a distinct mindset that requires for many a mental reframing and constant practice. Developing a patient personality begins with consciously controlling our minds and our thoughts before and when dealing with people. Expect and understand that all dealings with people will not be smooth sailing, so it's essential to embrace the Great People Truth.

The core elements of achieving higher levels of patience are cultivating self-discipline, self- control, and inner strength. During personal interactions, employing some internal monologue when necessary helps immeasurably. Try these on for size:

- "I will be kind and patient."
- "I will not let this person or situation upset me."
- "I can and will handle this; it's just another test of my patience levels."
- "I am seeing and hearing the good in this person and situation."
- "One, two, three, four, five, six, seven, eight, nine, and ten." Yes, it's the tried and true "count to ten" before saying or doing anything. You've surely heard this one, probably first from your parents, but have you ever tried it? It works!

This internal chatter may sound weird at first—a little New Agey, perhaps. But it's not just happy talk; it *works* at keeping your impatience in check. We'd love to get into your head for a few minutes to find out what you're thinking right now. We hope you're not looking to get off the bus because you think the material is not heading in the direction you expected, but stick with us—have patience.

Here are additional techniques that can help you succeed in developing patience:

- Practice being nonjudgmental. It took us years, but we realized that being nonjudgmental about others (and about ourselves) is a key element for increasing patience levels. It's difficult and takes daily practice, and as we get older, it's tougher to eliminate judgmental thinking.
- Know when to put the brakes on. Relax, take a few deep breaths, and take in what is going on with the person you're dealing with. Maybe he or she is on edge and now is not a good time to deal with a certain issue.
- Sometimes you need a total stop. If a situation gets too heated, disengage from it, and take a cooling-off period if you must. It's in your best interest to postpone the conversation or table the topic.

Employing these techniques combined with the additional people skill strategies we'll discuss further will increase your patience levels to cope with people—and they will enrich *all* aspects of your life.

First Impressions—Yours and Theirs

Don't make snap judgments. Don't label people before you have a chance to find out what they are really all about. Remember the old warning against judging a book by its cover; in many cases people are not what they seem at first glance.

How many times have you met people who appeared to be detached, unapproachable, or impossible to engage in conversation? How many times did you label them as rude, stuck up, or unfriendly, only to find out later they were simply painfully shy? We all have stories about times we misjudged someone; they should serve as a reminder not to allow first impressions to rule your dealings with people. Make it your goal to get to the bottom of each person's personality. Give them the benefit of the doubt, and find the gold in each person you meet. Or at least try!

"Fear makes strangers of people who could be friends."
—Shirley MacLaine

Make Your First Impression a Strong One

Create a strong, favorable, and memorable impression when you first meet people. Is your game face on when necessary? Research has shown that most people form an impression about others in the first ten seconds of their initial meeting, and it's very difficult to reroute that brain wiring for a more favorable take.

Most of us send out conscious or subconscious messages about our thoughts and feelings. Make sure the signals you send are positive, cheerful and enthusiastic. Even if you're not in an upbeat mood at the moment, act the part and surprisingly you'll start to genuinely feel that way when you get good feedback from the person you've just met.

Here are some Street Smart strategies for making a great first impression:
- Greet people with enthusiasm
- Smile
- Maintain direct eye contact
- Remember peoples' names and use them often

Greet People with Enthusiasm

Be outgoing and enthusiastic when interacting with people. Radiate! Some days you may feel that you're not even fit for human companionship, but you must force yourself to step into that crowded elevator car, put on your game face and get in the happy zone. Another way to describe it is to put your charisma in high gear. Don't overdo it, but project the notion that you like to meet people, and they will usually respond in a good way.

Always make the first move. How often are you the first to shake someone's hand and introduce yourself? Try it the next time you're in a social gathering, event, or party. You'll be amazed at how many more people you meet and how much they appreciate your effort to break the ice.

"For every disciplined effort there is a multiple reward."
—Jim Rohn

Smile

A smile is the universal welcome, an always-understood gesture of warmth, friendliness, and kindness. A smile helps establish rapport and makes you more approachable, yet most people don't smile enough. Look around you and see how many people are smiling. Probably not many. Smiling is an underutilized but powerful technique for dealing effectively with people.

FROM THE STREET: THE LAND OF SMILES

Having spent considerable time in Thailand (affectionately known as the Land of Smiles) over our years of traveling, lecturing and consulting, we can say that it's an oversimplification to state that all Thais are always smiling, friendly, and happy, but the day-to-day life is filled with ten times more smiles than in most other countries.

Interestingly, smiling (*yim* in Thai) is the appropriate response to show not only happiness, but also embarrassment, fear, tension, resignation, and so forth. Raised as Buddhists, Thais don't want to burden others with complaints, negativity, and problems, so the smile is perceived as being the appropriate answer to most situations, a fascinating behavioral trait that seems to work well. The smiling, relaxed Thai way attracts millions of tourists every year. Not surprisingly, a good mood is good business. All the smiling in Thailand immediately generates a genuine warmth and friendliness, and quickly forges wonderful relationships that are unmatched anywhere in the world. It's quite obvious; the shortest distance really between two people is the smile. We can learn something from our Thai friends.

We can't make our own cultures start smiling overnight, but try it and see if you get unexpected results when you smile in a situation that would ordinarily bring out the complainer in you. Of course, some events can't be smiled off, even in Thailand. But if the stakes aren't dire, try to smile, and see if you get a better result than with confrontation.

Research suggests that making a conscious effort to smile makes you feel more optimistic. When you're smiling, it's difficult to feel bad. Even if you don't feel like smiling, do it. You'll feel and look better, and you'll make others feel good too.

A smile costs you nothing, but will pay big dividends. The world looks brighter from behind a smile, and nothing beats it for turning strangers into friends. Work on it. Practice smiling more. Smile on the phone. Smile while you're driving. Smile on the train. Get everyone you interact with daily to smile. Tell people about the Thai people, whose cultural imperative starts with a smile.

Maintain Direct Eye Contact

People communicate with their eyes so *always* maintain direct eye contact. Direct eye contact is a common courtesy, a sign that you are interested in what the other person has to say. If you look someone in the eye, you can see important clues to their thoughts and feelings. Don't let your eyes wander when speaking with someone. Gazing around the room or at other people during a conversation is rude and distracting.

Remember People's Names and Use Them Often

It always impresses people you've just met when you remember their names, but 75 percent of us promptly forget them. Sprinkling a person's name throughout a conversation sounds and feels good, puts a nice spin on the conversation, and gets things going in a positive direction.

To help you remember names:
- Go into situations with remembering names as a priority.
- Pay close attention during introductions. Focus on the person's name.
- Associate a new name with someone you know with the same name.
- Say the name to yourself at least five times.
- Use the person's name as often as possible in your conversation with him or her.
- Get the person's business card, or write down his or her name as soon as possible.

If you happen to forget a name, instead of saying, "I'm sorry, I forgot your name," extend your hand and say your name; people usually respond by saying theirs.

"You must look into other people as well as at them."
—Lord Chesterfield

Be Interested in People

Find out what people really want. Put yourself in their heads. See things truly from their perspective; strive to understand their wants, needs, and desires.

Be mindfully aware of people and their situations. Be sympathetic: feel, hear, and see the person you're speaking with. Speak in terms of his or her reality. Find out what's important to those you talk to and weave the issues they care about into your conversations.

The world-renowned people-skills guru Dale Carnegie said, "You can make more friends in two months by becoming interested in other people than you can in two years trying to get other people interested in you."

Here are some guidelines to understanding people and getting them to like you:
- Always put the other person first.
- Focus completely on the person you're speaking to.
- Observe carefully. Remember, people communicate with their bodies and eyes as much as with their words. A UCLA study found that 55 percent of communication is nonverbal, from facial expressions to body language.
- Always listen more than you talk. Encourage others to talk.
- Listen intently. Pay attention to what people are really telling you.
- Make the person feel genuinely important.
- Ask questions.

Be mindful of your actions, the attitude you're projecting, and the tone of your voice when dealing with others. People respond more to these signals than words. Sending negative and conflicting nonverbal signs are the root cause for many petty conflicts and misunderstandings. If necessary, reprogram yourself and make improvements.

FROM THE STREET: MULTICULTURAL MINEFIELDS

Having lived and worked in a number of countries throughout the world, we know that multicultural differences in nonverbal communications can be a minefield. Body language, facial expressions, boundaries of personal space, and gestures are enormously different from culture to culture and can be misinterpreted with disastrous results in business and personal relationships. For example, in Asian and Middle Eastern cultures, the feet are considered the lowest part of the body, and pointing them at people, even unintentionally, is considered rude.

Listen Actively

We discussed active listening in Discipline Two—Present Everything, but we mention it here, too, because it is an absolutely essential people skill.

We've worked and met many top-level executives of companies from all over the world, and every one of them says the same thing loud and clear: "Learn to be a great listener." The problem is, most people are lousy listeners, in part because it's a skill that's never taught in schools or universities. Teach yourself to listen artfully by concentrating, responding, questioning, and paraphrasing.

"Hear the meaning in the word." —William Shakespeare

Observing many people over the years, we've concluded that people don't listen as effectively as they should and miss a lot of what is going on.

Here's what you should *not* be doing when trying to listen actively:
- Don't run a rehearsal in your own mind about what you're going to say next when you should be focusing on what the other person is saying.

- Don't have mental filters on. Eliminate selective listening. Focus on the content of what is being said and not the delivery. Ignore people's irritating personality quirks and speech habits.
- Don't be a derailer. Often we change topics inappropriately when the other person is speaking. This communicates that you're not interested and makes you look rude.
- Don't be quick on the draw to criticize or discount what is being said. Take it in, listen, process it.
- Don't try to be telepathic; that is, don't think too much about what is going on in the other person's mind.
- Don't let your ego get in the way. Nothing blocks or distorts effective listening more than an overbearing ego.
- Don't be "me focused." Don't interrupt someone with an anecdote of your own. Wait until the speaker is finished, and then share your related experience.

FROM THE STREET: THINK BEFORE YOU SPEAK

Before you open your mouth, weigh the importance of what you're about to say. If it doesn't help, encourage, or in some way benefit the other person or the situation, consider not saying anything at all. As the old saying goes, "Better to be silent and thought a fool than to open your mouth and remove all doubt."

"The art of being wise is the art of knowing what to overlook."
—William James

Don't Be a Critic

Avoid being critical or argumentative. Before you speak, ask yourself, "Is it my place to criticize? Did anyone ask for my opinion? Will my input really help the situation?" If your point of view isn't vital, keep it to yourself. If you do offer a critical opinion, don't phrase it negatively. Make your comments as constructive as possible. Try providing some examples of others who have successfully handled a similar situation in a different way.

Never tell people they are wrong, even if you know they are. Ask yourself whether it really matters if they're wrong. If it doesn't, don't worry about it. Let it go. If you must correct someone, always say something like, "I may be mistaken, but ..."

Recognize that people have strengths and weaknesses. Focus on their strengths and potential, not on their weaknesses and flaws; otherwise you'll drive yourself crazy. Mahatma Gandhi summed it up well when he said, "I look only to the good qualities of men. Not being faultless myself, I won't presume to probe into the faults of others."

You'll occasionally be in situations where you must offer criticism. The most important element when giving criticism is where you do it. Praise in public and criticize in private. Don't turn what could be a beneficial private exchange into a public blunder.

Make your criticism constructive. Remember, you are criticizing to help a coworker, partner, vendor, employee, or subordinate do a better job. Be sincere and patient, and show concern when communicating. Take the time to frame your criticism correctly *before* you meet with the person to get the results you want. Don't criticize off the cuff.

When criticizing, speak in terms of benefits, explaining the improvements that the person will experience if he or she applies your suggestions.

Accept criticism from others with the same openness you want from them. Further, let people know you seek constructive criticism. You'll get feedback on how you can improve, and it shows people that you practice what you preach.

FROM THE STREET: DON'T QUIBBLE

Avoid petty disputes; choose your battles wisely. Over the course of your life, there will be too many battles you'll actually need to fight.

Most disputes are just not worth the time, energy, and aftermath. Even if you win the argument, you often lose the war by creating anger and resentment, not only with the immediate combatant, but also with the innocent bystanders, the argument's collateral damage.

"Nobody stands taller than those willing to stand corrected."
—William Safire

Admit Mistakes Immediately

If you make a mistake, admit it immediately and apologize. Everyone makes mistakes. To err is human, after all. The worst thing you can do is to fail to acknowledge mistakes.

In our businesses, we make an all-out effort to promptly investigate and resolve any problems that arise. In many cases, it doesn't take much to solve the problems, and our professional and prompt efforts on the customer's behalf impresses them more than the actual solution. It's our quick and sincere response that makes the difference.

In dealing with a large food and beverage company, we accidentally violated a contractual term for an advertiser to have category exclusivity for their product. We took responsibility and responded quickly. As soon as we discovered the problem, we notified our client and told him about the issue. We apologized sincerely. We said we would look into the circumstances and get back to him with a solution as soon as possible. He was impressed with our response and our willingness to take care of the problem.

We allowed the ad to run in the magazines at no cost—a loss of revenue of twenty thousand dollars. It was a huge financial blow to our small company, but the client was happy and continued to do business with us for several years. Had we not handled the problem as we did, we might have lost a customer who ultimately accounted for more than 400,000 dollars in business in the ensuing years.

"The secret of many of man's successes in the world resides in his insights into the moods of man and his tact in dealing with them."
—J.G. Holland

Deal with People's Moods

Everybody has a bad day now and then (some more than others). You can try to avoid people or keep contact to a minimum when you know they're a bit testy, but often there's no way to avoid them and their bad mood. The key is to understand how to deal with them in friction-free ways while they're in a grouchy frame of mind.

Hit the reset button, and make a constant, conscious effort to completely edit out the disturbing emotional by-products of bad moods. Do not take someone's outlandish behavior personally. Learn to be strong to deflect bad energy and negative comments. Navigate through the situation. Don't get shipwrecked on the rocks of another person's negativity.

Try these bad-mood immunization techniques:
- Realize that the person's behavior probably has nothing to do with you.
- Define what you need to accomplish in an exchange with a bad-mood person so you can get in and out quickly.
- Remain calm and positive. Smile and gently try to turn the situation around.
- Exercise restraint. Before commenting, listen to what people are saying. Pay attention to what they're not saying (the nonverbal cues) as well. Try to understand what has gone wrong. Ask, "Why do you feel that way?"
- Empathize. Say, "I understand the way you feel," or "What can I do to help?" or "I can see that you're a bit upset/unhappy/angry. If you want, we can work together to resolve the situation that's bothering you."

Use your interaction to help the person get over the bad mood; you'll feel better for lightening the situation and, hopefully, accomplish your goal as well.

FROM THE STREET: THE CASE OF THE CRANKY AGENT

One day John was in line at an airport ticket counter in Singapore and the man in front of him gave the ticket agent a nasty dose of verbal abuse. He really ripped her head off, calling her names and questioning her ancestry. By the time John got to the counter, the agent was in a very foul mood, but he handled the situation the same way he would have if he didn't know what had just happened, by remaining positive, smiling, and being empathetic. When it was his turn, he smiled at the agent and said sympathetically, "Would you like to yell at me for a while? I can take it." The agent laughed and said, "Thanks, I needed that." They had a pleasant conversation, and she upgraded John to first class.

Lighten Up

Use appropriate touches of humor to break the ice, ease a difficult situation, or diffuse tension. You don't need a barrage of one-liners, but some sort of comic relief always adds a nice spin. If you're having trouble getting through to someone, humor goes a long way to create bonds. It's a potent, constructive force. (And good for the health, too. As they say, "The one who laughs lasts.")

Never take yourself too seriously. Drop in some self-deprecating humor here and there to make people warm to you quickly.

"Once you get people laughing, they're listening, and you can tell them almost anything." —Herbert Gardner

We were once giving a presentation to a manager who had pulled the senior vice president of marketing into the meeting. Senior vice presidents usually don't have to sit through these types of meetings, and this guy was really uptight about being there. We kept trying to get him to participate, but he just sat there with his arms folded and never cracked a smile. We sold our hearts out with a very enthusiastic, entertaining presentation, but the vice president would not respond.

We kept plugging away, telling him about the great value-added package that came with our program that included a boat ride through alligator country in the Florida Everglades. Mark told Mr. Stone Face that he could send his top customers on this wonderful Everglades trip. "Or you could send your top competitor, and we could arrange to take them to the park's alligator-infested waters for some added excitement. We smiled and paused for a moment of silence while our joke sank in. Finally, the VP smiled, and we all had a good laugh.

A few weeks later, when we followed up, he told us he really liked our program and decided to give it a go. All it took was a little humor to crack his shell and accomplish our goal.

Don't Complain and Don't Be Negative

Complaining and being negative is a waste of time and energy. No one enjoys hearing complaints and negativity. And they don't make you feel any better when you share them with others, so why bother? All you really do is bring others and yourself down. If you're about to drop a complaint or a negative comment, bite your tongue, then say something positive or don't say anything at all. You'll feel better, and the other people around you will appreciate your restraint.

Let's take a breather here and take thirty seconds for some big-picture thinking on the subjects of complaining and negativity. People, places, things, situations—the whole world is imperfect. If you want to remain sane, let alone be happy, the only way to view life is this way: "It is what it is. Everything with all its imperfections is perfect." We often find ourselves repeating this throughout the day. If you progress through life with this attitude as a centerpiece of your philosophy—which, make no mistake, does take habitual repetition to weave into your psyche—you'll always maintain a big happy/healthy quotient.

"You're either part of the solution or you're part of the problem."
—Eldridge Cleaver

In our company, we have a policy for employees: be proactive problems solvers; don't bring us problems without trying to offer solutions; don't complain or be negative unless you can suggest a way to resolve the problem or issue. Our goal is to get everyone thinking about how to solve problems instead of focusing on the problems themselves.

FROM THE STREET: ASK, DON'T TELL

Don't tell people to do something when you could ask or suggest that they do it. Instead of giving orders, try making a request or asking a question:

- "Would you be kind enough to help me with…?"
- "Have you considered resolving the situation by…?"
- "I wonder if we could solve the problem by…?"
- "Do you think this would work?"
- "Why don't we give it a try?

Let's Talk About You - Don't Be Your Own Favorite Subject

Don't talk too much about yourself. Reduce your use of the word *I*. You can't avoid talking about yourself from time to time, and sharing your thoughts and experiences is part of building a relationship. Just don't overdo it, or you'll end up being like one of your "colorful" friends (the ones who suck all the oxygen out of the room).

Try to get the other person involved in the conversation, and pay close attention to your listen-to-talk ratio. Don't dominate the conversation with talk about yourself, your business, or your interests. Bring other people into the conversation with questions about them, their business, or their interests. Whatever the topic, try to solicit the other person's thoughts instead of rambling on about yourself.

- Instead of saying, "I think…," say, "What do you think about…?"
- Instead of saying, "In my opinion…" say, "What's your opinion of…?"
- Instead of saying, "Here's how I handle…," say, "How do you handle that sort of thing?"
- Instead of saying, "I'm working on a great new project," say, "What new projects are you working on?"

"Our ego is our silent partner, too often with the controlling interest."
—Cullen Hightower

Respect People's Need for Power and Authority

People often feel the need to exert their authority, to display their power, to be in control, to be victorious. When you encounter a power play, eliminate any head games and wasted energy. Keep your ego in check. If you let the other person think they have won the battle, you will be able to win the war.

We learned this lesson the hard way. After two very successful presentations to an outdoor equipment company, we persuaded the executives in charge to purchase a sponsorship program. All we needed to close the deal was a final meeting with the product designers. Much to our surprise, the designers mounted a serious challenge to the program. We let our egos take over, and we counterattacked with a defensive barrage that really didn't address the designers' concerns. When they backed off, we figured we had won the battle.

When we got back together with the executives in charge of the entire project, they said the designers didn't think we would get along very well together in our joint efforts. We had lost the war. By letting our egos get in the way, we let the business slip right through our fingers. If we had listened to what the designers really wanted and had acknowledged their need for authority, we could have answered their concerns, dealt with them courteously and effectively, and perhaps landed the business.

"Treat other people as you'd like to be treated by them."
—Jesus, in Matthew 7:12

Be the Best Person You Can Be

Do you think you have a handle on modern manners and proper etiquette? If you really do, you're in the minority. Recent studies show that good manners are a dying art. Many younger people erroneously think it is old-fashioned or boring and uncool to exhibit good etiquette and manners. Politeness and proper etiquette are at the core of interacting well with people, yet basic courtesies and social skills are often overlooked.

Every company has its own corporate culture and complex dynamic, but basic social skills, rules, proper etiquette, and manners should remain valid regardless of the work environment. Companies where people treat one another well are usually more successful.

To wrap up this crash course in the emotional care and feeding of your fellow human beings, here are additional tips for putting others—and as a result, yourself—at ease in social situations. The most salient reason to incorporate these tips into your behavior is that they will pay huge dividends throughout your life.

"Never lose a chance to say a kind word." —William Thackeray

With every person you encounter, marshal all your people skills and positive energy to be the best person you can be.
- Be kind, pleasant, and polite at all times.
- Make positive and genuine contributions to your relationships often, Whether they are thoughtful compliments, kind words of praise, small gifts, advice or knowledge—anything that will be of value or interest to the people you're dealing with.
- Create win-win relationships.
- Offer genuine praise whenever possible.
- Make a conscious effort to smile often.
- Offer a helping hand.

In dealing with people, remember that style can be as important as substance. When it comes to success in business and life, it's not just a matter of what you say, but how you say it; not just what you do, but how you do it.

Discipline Four
Watch Your Money

Developing Financial Fitness and Maximizing Profits

"Some of life's greatest enjoyments and most of life's greatest disappointments stem from your decisions about money. Whether you experience great peace of mind or constant anxiety will depend on getting your finances under control." —*Robert G. Allen*

In this chapter:
- ✓ Develop a specific plan to pursue profits
- ✓ Establish bulletproof financial controls
- ✓ Instill a relentless cost consciousness throughout your organization
- ✓ Adopt cash-is-king strategies
- ✓ Negotiate everything
- ✓ Incentivize your people
- ✓ Use the best financial and legal advisors
- ✓ Reduce labor costs and maximize profits by outsourcing
- ✓ Optimize employee productivity and manage head count
- ✓ Know how and where to get capital before you need it

Budgets, banking, bookkeeping, tax deadlines, contracts, CPAs, regulations, financial statements, audits, raising capital, collecting receivables. These activities do not brighten the hearts and souls of most businesspeople.

It's not unusual for people to find finances difficult to understand, intimidating, or just a numbing bore. But grave dangers lie in wait for those who don't pay close attention to financial matters, or even worse, avoid them altogether. Lack of financial discipline is the primary driver of financial instability, financial chaos, and unraveling—even the death spiral of companies.

But on the positive side of the ledger, you don't have to be a financial genius to keep control over this vital success factor. What you do need is fiscal discipline and enough financial literacy to keep your financial house in good order.

Our objective in this chapter is not to delve into every aspect of financial mastery, but rather to shine a beam of light on essential strategies that you can put into action immediately. From these strategies, you can develop what we call the Financial Checklist Manifesto, our ten essential strategies for developing financial fitness and maximizing profits. Use these strategies to develop an actionable financial plan. Even if you already use some of these tools, it's always a good to periodically reexamine your financial situation.

One: Develop a Specific Plan to Pursue Profits

You can't just hope to make a profit. Profits don't magically appear; they must be pursued. To do this, you need a disciplined plan to stay focused on the bottom line at all times. This is your number-one priority.

"The engine which drives enterprise is not thrift but profit."
—John Maynard Keynes

As management guru extraordinaire Peter Drucker said, "What gets measured gets managed." Start formulating a plan to pursue profits by asking the following questions. These are not rhetorical questions, by the way. They need specific answers. Get focused and look at both the big picture and the smaller details within it to reveal the profit picture that drives your business and inspires you to work to achieve your goals. If you find that you can't answer some of these questions, ask your CPA or trusted financial advisors to help you clear the brush that's obscuring your view of exactly what your business is and how it generates profit.

- What business am I really in?
- How does my company actually generate revenues and profits?
- What is my profit goal?
- What are my short- and long-term goals for the business?
- What is my differential or competitive advantage? What is the true value of this advantage?

- How can I prioritize and further monetize my competitive advantage to increase profits?
- What areas of my business efforts are generating the most profit?
- What areas have the most profit potential?
- Am I focusing on the areas of the business that are most profitable or that provide the most profit potential?
- What areas are marginally profitable or unprofitable? Are any areas a waste of time, and if so, why? Can I make these areas more profitable? If so, how?
- If I can't make unprofitable areas more profitable, have I considered discontinuing, eliminating, or minimizing them?

In our magazine publishing businesses, we answered the first two questions in one short paragraph. It kept us focused on where we were making money: "We are in the publishing business and earn our revenue by selling advertising in our network of magazines. Our profit comes from selling ad pages at a price that is significantly higher than the cost to produce the supporting editorial and design, and the general overhead of the magazines."

You may have numerous products or services. Understand the profit dynamic of each one. Thoroughly analyze their current profitability and projected profitability as well.

At American Park Network, all twenty-two of our magazines were successful and making money. But after taking a hard look, we realized that two of them no longer fit into our long-term plan for creating a national network of magazines. They were local in nature and would never interest the type of national advertising clients we were seeking. They were not as profitable as the other publications and would continue to stress our profits. They took up 40 percent of our time for only 20 percent of our profit. They had to go so we could achieve our long-term profit goal. We shut them down, which enabled us to focus on our more profitable publications.

When you highlight the most profitable areas of your business, it shows you where you should be spending your time. Is there any area of your business that has nothing to do with your key goals and provides only marginal cash flow or profit, or takes up more time than it generates in revenues/profits? Most importantly, does it keep you from focusing on other goals? If so, eliminate it. If you can't eliminate it, at the very least minimize it to the point where it creates little or no impact on your time and energy. Don't become attached to anything that is not generating enough profit. Don't let your ego or sentimentality get in the way.

Every quarter, do a profit audit to analyze areas of your business to determine how and where you can maximize profits.
- List each revenue source in your company.
- Calculate the profit percentage of each revenue source.
- Compare each profit percentage to the time, effort, and resource commitment it takes to generate the profit.

Where should you spend your time and effort? One of our consulting clients had a sales and a service division. Both were growing at a fast pace, and he wanted to understand the specific financial impact that each would have on the company so he could use his people, time, and money for the best return. We ran models on each division to project revenue and profit. While the service division had a higher gross profit than the sales division, the cost of more service techs, administration, travel, and transportation made this division less profitable to the company as a whole. With this new information, the client was able to make an informed and effective decision regarding the amount of investment of people, time, and money he allocated to each division, based on bottom-line profit.

Dramatic outcomes will result when you focus on where the most revenue and profit come from and take action to spend your time and efforts where they count—profits, that is. Develop a profit-oriented mentality, and make profit a priority.

"Formal education will make you a living; self-education will make you a fortune." —Jim Rohn

Two: Establish Bulletproof Financial Controls
Financial reports help you manage your finances, but a surprising number of businesspeople get reports from their banks, accountants, and financial advisors that they don't understand and don't know

how to use effectively in running their day-to-day operations. Don't let this happen to you. These reports are critical to your financial health.

Do you need to be able to prepare a financial statement? Certainly not.

Do you need to know how to analyze and interpret one? Emphatically, yes. If you are weak in accounting, take a course or read a book written for nonfinancial executives. Of the many books we've read on the subject we found *Finance and Accounting for Non-Financial Managers* by Samuel Weaver and J. Weston to be an informative brain-gain, and we recommend it to our clients and students.

If you still feel that your financial IQ is not up to speed, you may want to consult with a CPA or a financial advisor to provide the extra help you need.

One of our clients complained he didn't understand what his CPA was telling him and wasn't getting much value out of the reports and meetings. We asked him what exactly he wanted to learn from his CPA and what questions he was asking to glean this information. His answer was he wasn't sure. He had not outlined exactly what he wanted to know and had not asked specific questions to elicit useful answers.

To prove that it's not always the number cruncher's fault and show our client how to work with his financial advisors, we offered to run the next meeting with the CPA. We put together a list of topics and specific questions and emailed them to the CPA and told him what the management team wanted to accomplish. The CPA came to the meeting with easy-to-understand financial documents, illustrations, and formulas. It was an incredibly productive meeting and a newfound world of financial comprehension for the client and his executive team.

"Money is only a tool. It will take you wherever you wish, but it will not replace you as the driver." —Ayn Rand

Develop your financial foundation with sound financial architecture. Organize all your business finances before you grow. Otherwise, small mistakes and bad habits could morph into much larger and more serious problems as your move forward.

We worked with a former executive from an international equipment manufacturing company who set out on his own and started a brokerage organization in the same industry. He began from a home office and by the end of the first year the business was doing so well that he had rented a warehouse. In the second year, the business went into high gear, and he more than doubled his revenue. The third year was better, and revenue doubled again. Now things started getting complicated. Office overhead was growing too quickly, the volume of transactions was overwhelming the current tracking and inventory system, and the real profit number was getting blurry.

We first conducted an operational audit, bringing in an accounting advisor to develop an appropriately sized accounting process that could grow with the company. Next we built an inventory system that interfaced with accounting and was able to track every piece of equipment throughout an entire transaction and assign all costs to each unit. Within two months, our executive was once again in complete control of the company's revenue, overhead, inventory, and profit. He is on target to double revenue again and is totally prepared with a solid financial process.

Create a Finance Team

There are plenty of alternatives for helping you prepare income, profit and loss, and financial statements. In addition to bookkeepers, accountants, and CPAs, you can buy accounting software to help manage your business and personal finances. The programs come in many formats and varying levels of sophistication to match transaction volume and frequency. Input is easy, and reports can be customized to help you get the information you need to manage your finances at the appropriate level.

Create Budgets

Budgets are a vital management and planning tool for monitoring income and expenses. You need to know when and from whom you'll receive income and when you will incur expenses. This provides a visual working tool to see cash flows in and out of your business. It also helps planning by identifying the sources and timing of your costs and expenses. With a budget, you can quickly see where you need to make adjustments if your revenue or cost estimates are different than expected. Budgets are an integral part of planning your success and provide a clear vision of your financial goals.

Clear, digestible financial reports are also vital for securing a loan, attracting investors, or selling a business. Lenders, bankers, investors, or buyers want reliable and accurate financial information. In light of the recent global financial meltdown, lenders need reassurance that you understand your finances, value financial controls, and run a tightly controlled, sound operation.

Three: Instill a Relentless Cost Consciousness Throughout Your Organization

Ruthless, relentless, and regular expense auditing has been and always will be one of our mantras and should be one of yours too.

One of the easiest ways to increase profits is to reduce expenses. Understand exactly where your money goes. You must control every expense, not quite at the counting-paper-clips level, but close to it.

Every quarter, look at all areas of your business, and determine how costs can be reduced, cut, or at least controlled. Conduct a quarterly company-wide cost control audit, and ask each person to submit an outline of exactly where he or she thinks costs can be trimmed.

Let your people know that saving money and eliminating waste are an important part of their jobs. How do you motivate them? First ask them what they need to do their job better, faster, and easier. Then tell them the money they save will go toward the equipment, tools, or software they want and also toward their bonuses. Set up specific guidelines to assist them, and in certain cases, offer additional monetary incentives to achieve cost-cutting objectives.

"Success produces success, just as money produces money."
—Nicolas Chamfort

There are a number of simple actions you can take to further reduce costs:

Double-Check Bills and Invoices

Read, review, and check all your bills carefully. Don't assume that your vendors are always correct with their invoices and their records. Over the years we have cross-checked every bill and found the error rate to be staggering. Additionally, we double-checked our invoicing to our customers and always caught mistakes too. This is money you're just giving away. Pay attention! This is the easiest money you will ever make.

Know the System

Understand the billing practices of your law firm and CPA. Ask how they will bill you. What are you paying for? Ask if the grunt work will be assigned to a lower-priced associate instead of a high hourly paid partner. Always meet with your financial consultants in advance of an assignment to discuss what you expect and ask what you should expect from them. Whenever possible, and especially when beginning a new relationship with an attorney or CPA, try to control the clock.

If you assign a project, ask them to put in three hours *only* and then check back with you. This way you can see how they're progressing and make decisions as to how to proceed. We work like this often with our CPAs and attorneys to control costs and monitor work quality. They aren't fond of our method, but, hey, we're the client. We're also pleasant to deal with, and we always pay our bills on time. Carefully review their invoices just like you would for any other supplier.

Travel Smart

Don't let travel expenses eat up your profits. Create a detailed company travel policy, and make sure every employee that travels as part of his or her job sticks to it. Get corporate discounts for hotels and rental cars. Demand that travelers plan in advance to find the lowest prices on airfares. Establish a per diem for food and hotels. This may sound overly frugal, but the money you save goes right to the bottom line and can be reinvested to help you reach your goals.

Monitoring establishes the enforcement policies that are integral to the cost-cutting process. Everyone at our company knows that if they go over the limit, they'd better have a good reason, because somebody is going to check their expense reports and ask for an explanation.

Appoint an Office Supply Sheriff

Put one person in charge of ordering and distributing office supplies. Put dollar limits on items, and require advanced approval on higher-priced items. Make employees submit a request form for the items they need. Procurement is a function ripe for abuse, so monitor it closely and regularly. We've had several clients with employees who were getting kickbacks from suppliers. You can only hope that the person chosen for this job is honest, but at least you have to monitor only one person. Keep a watchful eye on close relationships between employees responsible for finances and your suppliers and customers.

Audit Your Agreements

Audit your telephone service plans and contracts every six months for land lines, cell phones, internet services, and any other communications services you use, such as teleconferencing. With the fierce competition in the communications industry, it pays to do frequent reviews of your company's plans and to ask your providers for discounts. These companies are used to it. Get a corporate rate, drop multiple carriers, try to bundle all your services, and see what you can save.

Other areas that merit periodic audits:

Insurance	once a year
Shipping/freight	every six months
Banking	once a year
Magazine subscriptions	at renewal
Automotive	every six months
Utilities	every month

Auction Opportunities

Look for public auctions for used office furniture as a less expensive way of equipping your office, store, or plant. There is always a huge supply of barely used items that work just fine.

"Prosperity is the fruit of labor. It begins with saving money."
—Abraham Lincoln

All businesses today are making changes in the way they manage expenses, manufacture products, and deliver services to save thousands and, in many cases, millions of dollars. A major automotive company decided to use unpainted screws instead of black ones inside the doors of each car. The move cut ten dollars per vehicle and saved close to one million a year. A consulting client bundled its land lines, cell plans, and internet service and saved a thousand dollars a month. Another switched from using new 55-gallon drums at 45 dollars each to reconditioned barrels that cost only 15 dollars each, saving the company 100,000 dollars a year.

Another example, though vexing, is the way airlines nickel and dime us for services that used to be a part of the ticket price: meals, checked bags, calling to make a reservation instead of doing it online, reservation changes, and a host of other fees and charges. It's beyond irksome, but you have to admire their cost consciousness and amazingly aggressive measures in pursuit of profits.

If you are going to set guidelines, make sure you monitor adherence. The cardinal tenet once again is "Inspect what you expect." Make profit a priority, and instill cost consciousness in everything you do. Keep the cost consciousness mantra ringing in your ears.

Four: Adopt Cash-is-King Strategies

Money rules. Cash is king. And it is good to be king. Cash reserves provide significant advantages both physically and emotionally. Having cash in the bank is a sign that you know how to make a profit and you know how to keep it. When you're talking with bankers or investors, it shows you run a good business. It also provides you leverage in negotiations with suppliers to pay quicker for better service or price concessions. And you never have to worry about making the payroll. Look at your cash position daily.

Use the following techniques to make sure you always have enough cash:

Aggressively Manage Your Receivables

There is no excuse for letting your receivables slide. We've seen companies hemorrhage cash yet not pursue their receivables. The sooner you get your money, the sooner you can put it to work by reinvesting it in the company, paying down loans, or earning interest. Create a system that puts you on top of your receivables and in control of your money. You will not lose a customer worth keeping over requests for timely payment.

- Review your receivables weekly.
- Act quickly on overdue accounts.
- Manage your payable/receivable ratio. Always have more owed to you than you owe to suppliers.
- Be aggressive with your collection process. Develop the mindset "If they owe us money, they are the enemy."
- Email, fax, and call to make sure invoices are paid on time.
- A few days before an invoice is due, send a friendly email reminder note and attach a copy of the invoice.
- A week after an invoice is due, fax or mail a copy of it.
- If the invoice is not paid within two weeks of the due date, call the customer.

People who owe you money often need to be prompted to make payment, and they typically first pay the bills of the people who remind them. Most people don't want to get an email, fax, or phone call about late payments, so in the future they avoid the embarrassment or the hassle by paying their bill on time. Use this desire to avoid embarrassment to your advantage as part of your strategy to maximize profits by aggressively managing your receivables.

Get Your Money Faster

Why not try to reduce or even eliminate the receivables issue? Get as much as you can before or at the time of delivery of your product or service. Try to get full payment in advance rather than deposits, retainers, or partial payments.

We're aware that there are certain payment customs in industries, but that doesn't mean you have to slavishly stick to them. There were payment rituals in the advertising industry in which publishers normally would be paid 90 to 120 days after publication. At American Park Network and *Buenos Aires Metropolis*, we developed business models that fueled our growth without the need of outside capital. We had a very concise and persuasive plan to get a hefty two-thirds deposit months in advance of the publication. If the prospective customer balked at the deposit, we told them:

- Our program is not just an advertising buy; it's a comprehensive sponsorship.
- We have a limited number of sponsorships available, and we need the deposit to reserve it.
- You are not just reserving a sponsorship but an exclusive category as well. That means we can't sell it to anyone else, so we need a substantial financial commitment.
- Once we receive the deposit, we start working with you to plan and execute the integrated merchandising package.

By aggressively implementing the strategy of requiring customers to make this two-thirds deposit, we dramatically reduced our receivables and funded our entire national expansion.

Nowadays, many businesses are asking for significant deposits, if not payment in full, before or upon delivery or service. Some customers always grumble about up-front payments, especially if it's a new policy, but if you tactfully explain your reasons in a creative and compelling fashion, you might get at least a partial payment.

When a client signs a contract to work with us, we don't view the deal as closed until their payment is deposited in our bank account. We also wait to pay our salespeople commissions until after we get paid, so they're naturally motivated to keep close tabs on the client until the bill is paid. Additionally, clients seldom cancel an order once they have paid the deposit.

These tactics work well, so give them a test drive. You'll get your money faster. And remember, a deal is not a deal until the cash is in your bank.

Bill Immediately

Tighten your billing practices by creating shorter sales and delivery cycles if possible. Always bill as soon as you can. Absolutely do not let this clerical task get sidelined for other priorities. The sooner customers get the bill, the sooner they will pay.

Here are a few additional cash-is-king strategies:

- Get vendors to give better terms if you pay early or upon delivery.
- If they won't or can't, it's in your best interest to take as long as allowed to pay them.
- Take payment via a customer's credit card instead of offering credit.
- Every situation is different. Brainstorm your own cash-is-king strategies.

Five: Negotiate Everything in All Aspects of Your Business

Negotiation is essential for financial fitness and maximizing profits, a vital part of every successful businessperson's playbook. Become an astute negotiator and plan to negotiate for *everything*.

The art of negotiation is an invaluable skill. There is absolutely nothing wrong with trying to get the best deal in every situation. The only way we were able to realize a profit in our first few years in business was by using tactful negotiation in everything we did. You'll be amazed at the amount of money that drops to your bottom line when you begin negotiating for literally everything.

"You don't get what you deserve, you get what you negotiate."
—Charles Karas

When we consult with companies, we instill a negotiating mentality not only in the owners and top-level management, but also in every employee. Negotiate with suppliers to get the best prices and terms with your customers to close profitable deals and with your employees on their compensation packages. Negotiate with your bankers, attorney, and CPA on their fees. Everything is negotiable. Be tough and demanding, yet fair, honest, and always pleasant to deal with. You want to create outcomes where everyone feels good.

Plan your negotiations well in advance. Understand what's important for your side and what's important for their side. Set your limits by establishing a range of acceptability with minimums and maximums so you will know what points you're willing to adjust and the points that are simply nonnegotiable. That will help determine where and how far you can go in a negotiation and still come away with exactly what you need to make a rational deal. Be bold, because the more you expect out of the negotiation, the more you will usually get.

FROM THE STREET: GET NEGOTIATION INTELLIGENCE

General George Patton once said he would give up an entire frontline battalion for one good piece of intelligence. In business negotiation, as in battle, it is important to have detailed information about all aspects of the deal's specifics and with whom you are dealing. This information greatly improves your chances of creating a profitable deal.

In our businesses, we set up a crash course on negotiating for all frontline people responsible for purchasing goods and services. We work with them on overall strategies and the questions to ask so they can always get the best deals.

We usually ask these questions when making a purchase:
- Is it possible to receive a discount?
- If this really is the best price you can give us, is there a chance you can speak to your supervisor or manager to possibly get us a better deal?

Never lose the negotiating edge, especially when you have reached some level of success.

"Let us never negotiate out of fear, but let us never fear to negotiate." —John F. Kennedy

Six: Incentivize Your People

Hard work and outstanding performance should be generously rewarded. But in many companies, especially where annual raises are nearly automatic, the best workers are not fairly compensated for their outstanding performance. We believe in a good salary with a heavy emphasis on merit bonuses or profit sharing.

Meritocracy has always been important to us to ensure the best people are rewarded and promoted. In our companies, we pay for performance, not for just showing up. Automatic raises each year for our employees? Why? In fact, we rarely give raises. Instead, we pay generous bonuses. We set up specific guidelines and goals for every employee, and if we see that they have hit their marks at the annual performance review, they get bonuses. Likewise we pay our salespeople huge commissions with no cap on what they can earn. Every employee is highly motivated. And because there are no automatic raises, everyone strives to achieve bonuses and commissions.

"He is well paid that is well satisfied." —William Shakespeare

Stock options, profit sharing, and 401(k) plans, daycare, flex-time work schedules, job share, health spending plans, game lounges, and free food and drinks on site are just some of the ways to incentivize your employees. Perhaps the most extreme example is the Google campus, or Googleplex, where employees can go to yoga and exercise classes and get free massages during the workday.

But these perks are no longer the sole province of giant corporations or high-tech companies with venture-capital backing. Businesses of all sizes are offering employees incentives at every level that used to be reserved for top executives. Such incentives are a great way to keep your employees as motivated as you are. Even in a bad economy, companies that are smart put these programs in place and find that their employees are so incredibly grateful for these extras that they are even more productive.

Consult with your CPA, attorney, or compensation specialist to tailor incentive plans for your business.

Seven: Use the best Financial and Legal Advisors

If finance is not your area of expertise, it is absolutely critical to find the best financial people to advise you. The same goes for legal advisors, since legal and financial matters often overlap. Think of financial advice as preventive medicine; use financial advisors not only at tax time, but also periodically throughout the year to plan, budget, and get advice to safeguard your financial fitness. Don't wait until your company's or your personal financial health declines. Take advantage of the expansive range of services offered by financial experts. Develop a team of financial advisors you can call at any time to diagnose potential problems or assist you in meeting your financial goals.

Accountants, CPAs, and Tax Advisors

These individuals not only prepare and place their stamp of approval on tax returns and audited financial statements, they can also provide experienced advice to help maximize your profits.

A CPA can help you find a full- or part-time bookkeeper to do the nuts-and-bolts financial work at a lower cost. A bookkeeper prepares periodic financial statements or cash-flow forecasts, sets up accounting programs and software like QuickBooks or Peachtree, and can fill out important tax forms.

CPAs are not all the same. They vary in experience, quality, service, resources, and price, from simple tax preparers to ultra-sophisticated financial and investment advisors. Over time, as your business prospers, you are likely to need an increasingly broad range of services.

FROM THE STREET: FINANCIAL SERVICE NEEDS ARE A BAROMETER OF YOUR SUCCESS

In our first years in business, we used a one-man CPA firm. His only job was to prepare year-end financial statements and tax returns. He didn't do complex work for us, but he was effective and inexpensive. As the company grew, we needed more comprehensive financial reporting, so we hired a firm that specialized in helping small businesses organize and computerize internal reports and budgets. This is a good thing. Think of your growing need for financial services as a gauge of your success.

Attorneys

Like a CPA, an attorney can be an asset to your team, and a good one is much more than just a legal expert. He or she can often become a trusted advisor on a host of issues and an important element of your growth and success.

When selecting a law firm and an attorney within that firm, look for an organization that not only can help you now but also possesses the capability and resources to grow with you. Get at least four—and more if possible—referrals from trusted colleagues and associates. Set up an introductory meeting, which typically lasts for about an hour. Tell the candidate that you are interviewing several firms and attorneys and will make a final decision within a couple of weeks. For this initial meeting, there should be no charge, but confirm this when making the appointment. Never pay for initial consultation fees. It's a red flag that indicates the firm and attorney may not be at the high level of professionalism you are seeking.

Ask the attorneys specific questions about their and the firm's experience in handling clients similar to you. Tell them about your business, your goals, or the problem at hand, and ask them what they would do to solve it.

The final decision in choosing attorneys comes down to their:
- level of expertise in the business areas you need now and could need in the future
- level of service that you expect
- hourly billing rate
- chemistry between you and the attorney

You should have a grasp of basic business law and the principle regulations governing your type of business. If you don't already know the basics, there are helpful, easy-to-understand books written for the layperson that will bring you up to speed. Don't waste billable hours having your lawyer teach you what you should already know; that would be an expensive education. Your attorney's function is to keep you on the right path and to deal with problems. Any more than that and your legal bills will balloon way out of proportion to their worth and throw your budget way off.

You may spend more time than you would expect with your attorney, especially if you try to raise money, go public, or sell your business, so make sure it's someone with whom you work well.

If you have limited funds and not much of a budget for legal advice you can consider alternatives to get you started. Some of the online legal sites have become very sophisticated with extensive customer service and live support. LegalZoom (legalzoom.com) is a leader in this arena and provides a full array of legal documents and forms that can get you up and running without a large investment. There are plenty of companies that use these services successfully, but be informed, compare pricing and check references. As your company grows and your legal needs become more complicated you should reevaluate the need for a legal advisor.

Here are a few more Street Smart legal and financial tips:

- Periodically review all important legal agreements. You'll be surprised how much you've forgotten and how handy this information will be in negotiating future arrangements.
- Keep your corporate legal records organized and up-to-date. This will save you time and money when you need information quickly, try to raise capital, or sell your business.
- Be adequately insured. Find a well-qualified business insurance agent who can help you determine the coverage you need. Understand exactly what the policies say and consider having your attorney review them. Look into key-man coverage. This is life insurance on employees or partners whose participation is vital to the business. Review all policies once a year to make sure you are adequately covered, and check with other insurance companies to make sure you are getting the best possible prices.
- Have buyout agreements with partners; otherwise you may find yourself in business with your partner's spouse, ex-spouse, or children.
- Make partnership agreements as thorough as possible at the beginning of the relationship, while the parties are still friendly.
- Put arbitration clauses in your contracts.
- Avoid litigation, even when you are right. Never sue anyone over a matter of principle.
- Have employee agreements and employee manuals to outline responsibilities, establish rules, communicate operational procedures, and protect all of your intellectual property.

- To prevent internal fraud, if you have delegated the responsibility of accounts receivables and disbursements, have different people handling each task. You may consider bringing in an outside accountant once a year for a complete financial review. It's worth the extra money to prevent fraudulent accounting practices. List specific goals and objectives you want the outside accounting consultant to analyze.

Be aware! Not all fraudulent activities leave a trail. One example is skimming—stealing cash at the point of sale with no record of the transaction. This crime is tough to monitor, and the problem usually surfaces only when you notice inventory shortages or an unusual reduction in cash flow. Ask your banker for tips on internal organization and services for anti-fraud measures to protect your revenues.

"If a man empties his purse in his head, no man can take it from him. An investment in knowledge always pays the best dividends."
—Benjamin Franklin

Financial Consultants and Investment Bankers

CPAs and attorneys are subject to rigorous educational, testing, accreditation, and experience requirements. Investment bankers who raise equity capital for you and financial advisors who invest your money, on the other hand, may or may not be regulated. Over the past few years, financial debacles from Wall Street to Main Street have put pressure on legislatures to regulate the finance industry.

Nonetheless, regardless of training or experience, anyone can claim to be a financial consultant, investment banker, or private equity firm. As a result, the business landscape is littered with the smoldering remains of deals that have blown up in the hands of inexperienced, unscrupulous, or simply bad advisors. Just ask a former Bernie Madoff client if you want to hear a harrowing financial advisor story.

Be smart. Get solid references when retaining a financial advisor or investment banker. Talk to people who have worked with the candidates and ask specific questions about what they did and if they were successful. Make careful and thoughtful decisions when you need help with money so you don't wind up making matters worse.

Find Your Financial Guru

The year before we sold the American Park Network, we interviewed a number of financial consultants and investment bankers to help us plan and consummate the sale. We talked to individuals and institutions. Some impressed us with their abilities and enthusiasm. Others gave us delusional predictions about a company they didn't even know yet.

We ultimately chose an individual investment banker who had a strong background and experience working with small companies and who agreed to come on board as acting chief financial officer to guide us through the process of selling the business. Know what you need, and hire the person who will achieve your goals.

In evaluating financial consultants, especially those whom you want to raise capital or sell your business, look for experience, integrity, a keen desire to understand your business, and a determination to complete the transaction. Also find someone with whom you have good chemistry. Most states have regulations related to brokering the sale of a business, but the onus is on you to choose a reputable and talented advisor.

An additional caveat about accountants, attorneys, and financial advisors: many people think these professionals and others in positions of authority are the voice of absolute knowledge, wisdom, and truth. It doesn't matter how many diplomas and certificates they have framed on their walls. Forget credentialism. Don't regard credentials as a guarantee of superior knowledge or high-quality work. "Inspect what you expect" in your dealings with them. Discuss their findings with your team members and other advisors, and if the situation warrants, get another professional opinion.

Eight: Reduce Labor Costs and Maximize Profits by Outsourcing

As your department or business grows, you may need additional people, but resist the urge to hire. Every person you bring on full-time creates an enormous expense. When you factor in salaries, payroll taxes, benefits, and health insurance (which alone has been increasing about 15 percent a year)—now we're talking *expensive*. Before you hire, carefully analyze the situation and make sure you really do need another full-time person. Chances are you can out-source the work.

Outsourcing is a proven method to reduce costs and maximize profits. It offers a means to pay outside people or another company to provide the functions or services you need instead of hiring full-time employees.

Finding talented people is hard, but the high cost of compensation packages often becomes a financial burden, and companies almost always under-budget for this added expense. Outsourcing taps the skills of talented people for *only* the time you need them. It also allows you to focus on your company's core competencies. Outsource to reduce labor costs, improve quality, and spend more time where you know you can increase revenues and profits.

You can outsource design and production of all your marketing or product information brochures to an outside design firm. Hire a top website design firm to create your online presence and manage the site. Hire a packaging and shipping company to handle all your deliveries. This enables you to hire the most talented people to do specialized tasks and to pay them only for specific projects, saving a considerable amount of time and money. And if you find you're not getting the quality or quantity of work you need, it's far easier and dramatically less traumatic to replace an outsourced resource than to fire an employee who failed to get the job done.

Also consider outsourcing as a way to build your sales and marketing team. At *Buenos Aires Metropolis Magazine*, we set up a national sales force in the United States by using independent reps. With independent reps, you immediately get the sales horsepower you need in major cities without incurring the high costs of setting up offices and hiring in-house salespeople. Thanks to outsourcing, we didn't have to lay out any capital, and the reps worked on a very lucrative commission-only basis.

When we were overloaded with work and needed more help or felt it was time to hire an additional employee, we used a practice known as temp-to-perm, meaning that a temporary assignment could turn into a permanent position. We recommend this to all our clients. The temp-to-perm strategy gives you an opportunity to evaluate fully both your needs and the employee. It gives you time to identify specifically what you're looking for in an employee and also allows you to refine the job description when necessary. We often found, for example, that we didn't need a full-timer, but rather someone who worked two days a week. Equally important, it gives you and the prospective employee a chance to try one another out and make sure the fit is right. Many of our full-time employees started with us as temps.

Nine: Optimize Employee Productivity and Manage Head Count

To keep your number of people to a minimum or even to reduce head count and to increase efficiency and productivity of every person on your existing staff, conduct a productivity audit.

Here are some Street Smart essentials for increasing productivity:

Provide Personal Management Mastery Training for Your Staff

Help your people learn how to manage themselves more effectively. The mastery of personal management skills makes people incredibly productive. (Refer to Discipline Six—Manage Yourself.)

Manage by Walking Around (MBWA)

To truly maximize productivity, you have to know what's going on with your team. Be people-centric. Don't insulate yourself; get out of your office and have more interaction with your people. They may be telegraphing frustrations that you're missing. Only through face-to-face engagement will you know what is really going on.

Always have your finger on the pulse of the people that you're working with, including subordinates, employees, partners, and the management team. Check in with as many people as you can at least once a month. We call these Dynamic Immersion Sessions. After a bit of small talk ask, "How are you feeling about everything? What do you think about...? Do you have any issues or concerns? What are the biggest hurdles you're facing right now, and how can we help? Is there anything management can do to help you do a better job?"

Create what we call *luminosity*. Through your questions, illuminate people's core concerns. People want to know that you have their interests at heart. Keeping their happy quotients at a high level is a vital component for maximizing productivity.

Periodically, ask people to report on certain issues, projects, and so forth that you deem appropriate. Get their opinions with their personal spin. We always stress the importance of participatory management, and we want, expect, and welcome the good, bad, and ugly news from everyone.

When you ask people for feedback, let them know you don't want a fluffy report. You need real feedback, and it should include what you do well, what you do badly, and where you should focus on improving. We are so serious about this feedback that we make it part of the employee's job description and are never deaf to constructive criticism. You'll be surprised how much you'll learn with direct, honest, and open engagement.

Achieving Breakout Success in business has everything to do with how you treat your people. This recurring theme was covered well and in-depth in two best-selling and impactful books, one in the early eighties, *In Search of Excellence* by Tom Peters and Bob Waterman, and almost twenty years later, *Good to Great* by Jim Collins.

Develop Goal-Oriented, Actionable Plans for All Employees

You're not the only one who should be developing goals and actionable plans and expecting to achieve them. Everyone should have the same to ensure maximum productivity.

After you define your company's goals for the year, share them with *every* person, making it clear you want them to make the company goals their goals and to develop their own action plans to achieve them. An excellent way to keep the momentum going is to have them submit a monthly and quarterly report with goals and a list of actions steps necessary to achieve them.

In our businesses, we always have our managers meet with their direct reports once a week to give and get feedback. In addition, they discuss their weekly goals and to-do lists. You don't have to be a strict taskmaster. Allow people to do their jobs, and don't hinder their performance with useless managerial interference. But definitely check in to get an update and to determine if anyone needs help, direction, or inspiration. (These meetings should last no longer than fifteen to thirty minutes.) This system keeps people focused on accomplishing their weekly and long-term goals and shows that you are in the trenches with them.

FROM THE STREET: BE A LEADER WORTH FOLLOWING

Leaders lead by example. They set high standards and hold themselves to those standards. They walk the talk. They expect the people who work with them to also set and meet high standards.

Leaders get the most out of people by understanding what makes them tick, how they work, how they interact with their coworkers. Then they bring everyone together around company goals. They have team smarts. Leaders challenge and inspire people to do their absolute best work. Ask yourself, "If I were an employee, would I be inspired to work for me?"

You might be thinking that this is control-freak micromanaging. Call it what you will, but somebody needs to keep the trains running on time, and that somebody is you. This continual feedback system has worked well for us and many of our clients over the years. It makes everyone—especially you—more efficient and truly maximizes company-wide productivity. This nose-to-the-grindstone style is what it takes to fast track your Breakout Success path.

To manage your organization's head count, begin by evaluating the staff structure and your number of employees. Do you really need every full-time person? Exactly what does he or she do? Can some responsibilities be outsourced or divided among other employees? Consider paring down your core staff and using outside contractors, outsourcing firms, temp agencies, or consultants.

It makes good business sense to have a small staff of talented people rather than a large one with mediocre workers who may not fulfill their roles, may have duplicate roles, or may be the source of problems that cancel out their productivity. Despite the occasional complaint, morale is higher when people are busy. We always make it a point to keep everyone very busy and wearing many hats.

FROM THE STREET: TIE STAFF SIZE TO THE REVENUE IT PRODUCES

A CEO we worked with in New York used a revenue-per-employee system as a guideline to manage head count. When his target number got out of whack, he would immediately put a hiring freeze in place until staff size got back in line with revenues. It was a simple, effective way to control what can be a runaway cost train. It is better to be understaffed part of the time than to be overstaffed any of the time. Controlling staffing costs is your job, so pay attention.

It may be difficult to let someone go, especially if the person has been doing a good job, but it is a business decision you should consider to reduce costs and maximize profitability. The bottom line is doing what you have to do to get the most productivity possible from each person on your staff. It may very well eliminate the need to hire additional people and save you thousands of dollars. Make productivity optimization an ongoing goal.

Ten: Know How and Where to Get Capital Before You Need It

Finding capital—that is, raising money—is a difficult hurdle. There are hundreds of books on this topic, so consider our brief overview not a tutorial on raising money, but an introduction to acquaint you with this vital element of running a successful business.

"Business? It's quite simple; it's other people's money."
—Alexandre Dumas the Younger

When raising money, you want more than financial capital. You want intellectual and reputational capital as well. It's vital to have investors involved that understand your business and can add value with their knowledge and open the right doors for you within their circle of influential contacts. Financial, intellectual, and reputational capital will expedite the path to Breakout Success.

Raising capital requires masterful salesmanship. No sales effort calls for more professionalism and preparation than raising money. It can be complicated, so create an overwhelming and compelling presentation that provides an airtight case for your business proposition. It's not about the spreadsheet. Most people don't rely on the numbers and projections anyway. It's about you and/or the team. Put yourself in the investor's shoes, and figure out everything that you feel is important to them.

Demonstrate that you thoroughly understand your business and have a concise and detailed plan for successful execution. Show them that your management team has the expertise and experience to get it done.

Whether you seek capital from a bank, a venture capitalist, or friends and family, you have to convince them that you are reliable, trustworthy, and competent. They need to know that you will communicate all the good and bad news and will work extraordinarily hard to succeed. When money is involved, trust and ethics become paramount. Gaining your lender or investor's confidence is paramount in the ongoing process of raising funds for growth.

Inexpensive Sources of Capital

Customers. The very best source of capital is your customers. Advance deposits and upfront payments are capital for running your business. As we mentioned earlier, we required our customers to pay two-thirds of their total bill for advertising at the time of commitment. The deposits were sufficient to fund our operation. We had a credit line and we had willing investors, but we never had to use them because the cash flowing in from deposits and upfront payments was enough to keep us going.

Determine how your customers can help fund your company's growth. For example, always get a credit line before you need it, and use your customer list and payment history to prove to the bank that you're an excellent risk for a loan.

"Always rub up against money, for if you rub up against money, some of it may rub off on you." —Damon Runyon

Vendors. Another source of capital is your vendors. A favorable payment term is analogous to an interest-free loan, and vendors are motivated to offer flexible payment schedules because they want your continuing business. We don't suggest that you string along your suppliers, but you shouldn't pay a bill before it's due unless you're getting a significant discount for the early payment. Do some calculations and see which options make the most sense for the current situation. And be aggressive in negotiating terms. If a new vendor wants your business, ask for a 120-day payment period. Ask for similar terms from existing suppliers who may fear losing your business. Remember, negotiate everything. Don't be timid about transforming your suppliers into vendors of interest-free capital.

Friends and family. Borrowing from friends and family is one of the trickiest situations in business or life. You will almost always get a better deal than you would from a bank, but the nature of your personal relationship may change forever—and for the worse. In the best-case scenarios, everyone comes out a hero. But don't jump off this cliff without some serious thinking about the relationship's chances for survival if your parachute doesn't open. Absolutely do not enter into such a transaction unless your friend or family member is fully informed and prepared financially and mentally for a complete financial loss. And if that does happen, you must be prepared for the drama that will follow. Ask yourself if it is worth the damage it could do to your personal life.

"Before borrowing money from a friend, it's best to decide which you need most." —Joe Moore

We realize that the risks to relationships rarely stop people who are determined to borrow from or loan to family and friends. If you don't qualify for a bank loan and hit up your family or friends, structure their investment as a loan. There is no point in sharing equity ownership if they don't demand it or if they are not going to be playing a vital role in running the company. Keep the arrangement simple and keep them informed, just like you would a banker. Above all, look them in the eye and tell them not to invest more than they can afford to lose.

Expensive Sources of Capital

Banks or lending institutions. Banks are often frustrating to anyone who needs money. They seem to want your business, but they also seem reluctant to lend you money. The bank's problem is that the cost of a bad loan is enormous. Banks can't charge enough interest to off-set losses on bad loans. Although interest rates are at all-time lows, banks are incredibly gun shy about lending money. They're scared, and if you were in their shoes, you'd probably behave the same way.

Banks almost never lend seed capital, so if your business is a startup, you'll have to look elsewhere for financing. But if you have a track record you may be able to get a bank loan to finance expansion or capital investments.

How does a small-business owner tap a bank for anywhere from fifty thousand to five million dollars? It starts with relationships and trust. Examine your existing banking relationship. What type of deposits do you make? When a bank is able to track your revenue volume, you stand a stronger chance of being able to negotiate more favorable loan terms, especially if the revenue is growing.

What services do you pay the bank to provide? Can you consolidate your banking business from two or more banks into one to give you negotiating clout?

Never walk into a bank and simply apply for a loan. After choosing the bank, get someone—you're CPA, attorney, or another business executive—to introduce you to its highest-level lending officer. In most cases you are better off establishing a relationship with the bank's business-lending department than with your local branch. Invite the banker to lunch, but not for a conversation. You will be presenting, and it may be your most important presentation ever, so make it an award-winning performance. Demonstrate that you're a first-rate, professional executive. Show your enthusiasm and belief in your business. Explain what services you need and what type of business the bank can expect from you.

Unless you have collateral or terrific audited financial results spanning the last several years, don't ask for a loan right away. Cultivate the relationship *before* you need the money. If you are going to need a loan in six months, get to know the banker *now.* Then apply for the loan when you're ready, but before you actually need the money.

Does this advance work sound like a waste of time to you? If it does, you need to take a closer look at the process. Raising capital is one of the most time-consuming aspects of any business effort. So unless you can avoid it altogether, build this vital activity into your plans and schedule.

Once you have bankers salivating to do business with an executive of your caliber, you've got to knock their socks off with a great presentation and loan application package. Demonstrate your grasp of your business and its intricacies. Provide professionally prepared financial statements and cash-flow forecasts. Make it clear that you have thought through how you will pay off the loan and have developed contingency plans.

Never let the lenders stump you with an objection. Think through every concern they might have and be prepared with an answer. Don't give them the slightest excuse to say no. When you get the loan, live up to the letter and spirit of the agreement. It will help you get the next big loan under even tougher circumstances and help you negotiate even better deals with the same lender in the future.

You may not have the financial history or collateral required to secure a bank loan. If that's the case, you may be able to qualify for a personal loan based on your income or assets. You can then invest the proceeds in your business.

If you are up against the wall—and utterly fearless—use your credit cards to obtain capital. We have all heard the stories about entrepreneurs who maxed out their credit cards with cash advances to purchase the company they were working for. We know two small-business owners who combined their credit cards to get 45,000 dollars in cash to buy a piece of equipment they needed to complete a lucrative contract. They negotiated the purchase with a thirty-day trial provision that gave them the option when they finished the job within thirty days, to return the equipment for a full refund. But they got so many additional orders, they were able to keep it and pay off the credit card debt from their profits. That was innovative financing.

"Those with the gold make the rules." —Old venture capital adage

Venture Capital and Angel Investors

Despite the difficulty of securing a bank loan, it is often a better option than trying to raise money from sophisticated private angel investors or venture capital (VC) firms. Ironically, startups and small businesses seem to get along better with investors than with bankers, probably because many bankers don't have the time, experience, or inclination to understand an entrepreneurial venture. But venture capital can be more costly than a bank loan. Banks simply take payment via interest on the money borrowed. Investors typically want a percentage of ownership of your company via equity.

Angel investors provide capital, looking for a higher return than they would see from more traditional investments. They are typically successful entrepreneurs or businesspeople who have enough resources to be able to participate in the high-risk business of investing in small-business startups. Usually these investors provide a bridge from the self-funded stage (friends and family) of the business to the point that the business requires the next level of funding provided by venture capital. Funding estimates vary, but usually range from 25,000 to one million dollars.

The term *angel* was coined when wealthy businessmen in the early 1900s invested in Broadway productions. Modern-day angel investors help early-stage companies with funding, expertise, experience, and contacts.

There are extensive networks of angel investors in almost every major city throughout the world. Look up "angel investors" online, and you will find thousands. There are a number of angel directories as well. Newer angel groups offer online screenings and introductions to allow a broad reach for matching investors with ideas and companies that need funding.

To the vast majority of up-and-running small-business owners, we say venture capital is probably not a good idea. They tend to focus on the hottest-trend companies or businesses that have the potential to do twenty-five million, fifty million, even one hundred million plus in revenue within five years. They also like to see a complete management team of proven managers and executives with demonstrable track records in the industry and/or in building successful companies. They also may require a seat on the board and some management oversight. You may not need these headaches and restrictions that, ironically, could wind up strangling your entrepreneurial spirit.

On the other hand, if you have explosive growth potential and could possibly go public or anticipate you could sell the company and you need lots of money to get started, you may want to consider how this style of funding could fuel your effort. In many situations, venture capital can be the jump-start to greatness. Very importantly they have the deep pockets to keep you rolling and relationships with lots of other VC firms in case another round of cash is needed. They also tend to be experienced business executives or former entrepreneurs who can offer sound advice.

Unless you have raised venture capital before, prepare yourself for one of the most challenging sales of your life. As in any sales presentation, you must close by asking for what you want—in this case, the money! In the best of circumstances, be ready to spend six months of full-time effort on acquiring your initial funding.

Remember, you don't have to be a financial genius to make the right financial decisions. Being financially literate and having good fiscal discipline will suffice. Practice the key strategies and rules for this street-smart discipline, and you'll be on your way to creating long-term financial fitness and maximizing profits.

Discipline Five
Get More Business

Find New Customers and Keep Growing Revenue

"There are risks and costs to a program of action. But they are far less than the long-range risks and costs of comfortable inaction." —*John F. Kennedy*

In this chapter:
- ✓ Establish a systematic plan
- ✓ Develop an aggressive prospecting mentality
- ✓ Street Smart sources to get more business
- ✓ Stay close to current and past customers
- ✓ Revisit the lost art of turning cold calls into customers
- ✓ Optimize internet and social media marketing
- ✓ Learn from competitors, market developments and future business trends
- ✓ Overcome obstacles to get more business
- ✓ Street Smart strategies for handling questions and concerns
- ✓ Secure the business

Establish a Systematic Plan

This essential discipline is the art of keeping a constant supply of new business opportunities, new customers, and new revenue flowing into your organization. A well-planned, consistent campaign to find new business and new revenue sources must be a staple in every business plan to pave the way for Breakout Success.

Most businesspeople simply don't spend enough time planning and executing an ongoing effort to find more customers and get more business. They get bogged down with the distractions of their daily routines, running the business or tending to existing customers. Many otherwise capable people simply don't enjoy the task of developing new business or don't know how to find new customers because they have never tried. They get so comfortable with their current customers that they aren't prepared when customers leave and there are no new prospects to replace them.

Every company loses customers from time to time, so don't think it won't happen to you. When you lose customers, you need to find new ones just to stay even, much less move ahead. No matter what type of business you're in, you must develop and execute a system that continually funnels new business to your company.

One of our clients in Honolulu operated a small business that generated 30 percent of its sales from one customer. The client had a close business relationship with the top executive, and the company had been a customer for ten years. The account seemed secure, so our client didn't try to get additional customers. When the unthinkable happened—the top executive got fired—our client lost that business along with nearly a third of his sales revenue. That's when he called us. We quickly were able to help him replace his lost revenue stream using the processes we outline in this discipline. Just because you don't want to think about losing business doesn't mean it's not going to happen.

When we consult with businesses, we analyze what they are currently doing to get more business and then focus on improving their current processes and tailor new methods to improve their sales and marketing efforts to increase revenues.

Getting more business and increasing revenue is straightforward and boils down to four methods. Determine the ones that you can best use for your particular business:

- Increase the number of customers you currently have.
- Increase the size of accounts, orders, or business deals.
- Increase the frequency of customer business transactions.
- Raise prices.

Getting more business is hard work, but it's critical. You may feel overwhelmed just keeping things going in your business, but all those details you're spending time on may not matter if you lose business and are not actively seeking new sources to replace it.

Successful people don't wait for new customers to walk in the door; they are always aggressively pursuing new opportunities. Make finding new customers an ongoing part of your success plan. Prospective customers are everywhere, so be on the lookout in whatever you're doing and wherever you go.

Develop an Aggressive Prospecting Mentality

Prospecting is the search for new and qualified customers and involves compiling leads or target lists of potential customers who may be willing and able to buy your product or service. Always have a ready-made list of leads available to get more customers. When you prospect often and effectively, you will also:

- Learn more about what and how you need to improve your product or service by talking to people who aren't customers
- Learn more about your competitors by talking to their customers
- Sell faster, because more-qualified potential customers make decisions more quickly

Developing a prospecting mentality is the first step in keeping the supply of new customers at full capacity. A prospecting mentality is an ongoing focus and effort devoted to building, qualifying, and maintaining a pipeline of potential customers now and for the future. Building the pipeline is the easy part. Qualifying and maintaining your pipeline of target customers is more difficult and truly requires a long-term commitment to ensure sustainable success.

"Business has just two functions and only two. Marketing and innovation. Marketing and innovation make money. Everything else is a cost." —Peter Drucker

Street Smart Sources to Get More Business

There are many ways to find new customers, and we'll cover the tried and true methods that successful businesspeople regularly use. With incredible advances in information technologies, you also have a range of powerful methods to choose from. Instantaneous resources like search engines, websites, online directories, email, and social networks have provided instant communication and in-depth, real-time research that can dramatically increase efficiency and zero in on targets that are highly likely to want what you're selling.

Not all the methods we discuss will work for your particular business. Experiment with the ones that seem most appropriate, but don't discount any just because they are out of your comfort zone. Explore boldly. Finding new customer and clients requires action and discipline. The important thing is to get started.

- Stay close to current and past customers
- Get referrals
- Revisit the lost art of turning cold calls into customers
- Optimize internet and social media marketing
- Networking
- Learn from competitors, market developments, and future business trends
- Industry outlets
- Advertising, publicity, and sales promotions

"Above all, try something." —Franklin Roosevelt"

Stay Close to Current and Past Customers

Since they are already familiar with your company, current customers are your very best sources of additional business.

Existing customers are usually much easier to sell than new customers, and it's also less expensive to sell more to them than it is to find new customers. Employ ongoing strategies to get more business from them, such as making periodic telephone calls or sending emails that give information about new products or services, advanced notice of sales, reminders for servicing, or customer satisfaction questionnaires.

Think about it for a moment. When was the last time you called a current business associate or customer to ask them how you are doing as a supplier, vendor, or partner? Have you recently asked them about changes in their business that might prompt a new need for your product or service? When did you last call to thank them for their patronage? If you don't keep in touch with your customers, you can't be sure they are completely satisfied. And you can bet that a competitor is keeping in touch to get their business.

There are many reasons to communicate with your customers regularly. They are your extended sales force. Ask them for referrals. Ask them for testimonials you can use in presentations and on your website. And ask them to spread the word about you and your business.

When we were consulting with a real estate client in San Francisco about increasing the company's sales volume and were specifically covering the topic of staying in close touch with clients, one of the realtors was delighted and shocked (and so were we) to hear her results. After reconnecting with her top clients after a three year period, this is what she found out: One client had recently sold his house (a loss of 35,000 dollars in sales commissions); two clients had recently listed their homes with a competing realtor (a potential loss of about 75,000 dollars); two others were thrilled to hear from her and provided updates on their families and had two potential referrals for her (which eventually led to 100,000 dollars in commissions). The invaluable lesson is to stay in close contact with your customers.

FROM THE STREET: DEVELOP "GET MORE BUSINESS" GOALS

As you begin your efforts to get more business, establish goals for exactly what you want to achieve and determine the prospecting methods you'll use. Your goals and the specific prospecting methods you choose depend on your business, but here are a few sample goals and game plans:

- Goal: Get more business from current customers.

Game plan: Call ten customers (each day, week, or month) and tell them about a new product, service, upcoming promotion, or new information.

- Goal: Increase sales with referrals.

Game plan: Get one referral from every existing customer and supplier.

- Goal: Find new customers.

Game plan: Get at least twenty leads for prospective customers (each day, week, or month) from cold calling on the phone, in-person meetings, or trade shows, conferences, and networking functions.

Past customers who are no longer doing business with you may be valuable sources of additional business. Don't let former customers drop off your contact list. Periodically check in with them and find out if there is any new need for your product or service or to find out why they aren't buying from you anymore. If you did something wrong, apologize and tell them you'll handle the situation. Find out what it will take to regain their business.

Even if you can't get the customer back onboard, you can gain valuable insights and goodwill by discussing why an inactive customer is no longer doing business with you.

Remember, situations change, people change, and strategies change. A former customer's need for your product may have changed too. Just because someone didn't need your help or your product or service last year doesn't mean they don't need it today.

Get Referrals

Referrals can save you a great deal of time. With good referrals, you don't have to work so hard in developing new business. You avoid dead-end leads and prospects that never call back. With a referral or recommendation from an existing customer, you automatically get a measure of trust and respect from a prospective customer and significantly increase your chances of getting new business.

It's easy to get referrals. It's harder to get good referrals. And it's very hard to get referrals that actually turn into business. The key is to ask for referrals in a way that will get you sound, qualified leads.

Be very specific about the type of referrals you're seeking. Are you looking for customers of a certain age? A particular income bracket or a specific profession? Do you want leads with children of a certain age? Homeowners? Companies involved in a specific business? Companies of a certain size? Whatever you're looking for, explain your criteria thoroughly when asking for referrals so you get high-caliber candidates that are more likely to become customers.

Get as much information as you can from the person making the referral. Find out about the prospective customer's circumstances and potential need for your product or service. If someone is willing to give you a name, he is usually willing to fill you in on the prospect's background. (He may even be willing to provide a personal introduction or help you set up your first appointment.)

Don't forget to ask the person supplying the referral if you can use his name when you call.

When you ask for referrals, follow up diligently and provide a token of appreciation to the people who gave you referrals; you'll be paving the way to getting more business from them and the people they recommend.

FROM THE STREET: USE INCENTIVES

Offer your customers a reward for referrals. Develop a specific referral-reward program, such as a pool service that provides one free month of service to an existing customer for every new customer referred or a clothing store that lets a customer pick out a free tie for every referral who buys a suit. One blogger we work with advertises on his website that he will pay a thousand-dollar referral fee to anyone who recommends a person whom he hires to join his company. Think of referral incentives as a way to hire an army of salespeople to get what you need. Existing customers know your product or service; why not put them to work for you?

"No one knows what he can do till he tries." —Publilius Syrus

A note of caution regarding referrals: We've recently had a client who, as a result of implementing an effective sales and marketing effort, received a huge number of referrals. Great, you say. Yes, normally that would be great, but the very blessing of having lots of potential business coming your way has hidden dangers that can sneak up on you with potentially dire consequences. Regrettably, our client did not have a systematic, disciplined process for assessing and developing these referrals, so most of them couldn't be converted into customers.

We see many companies, executives, and managers being lulled into a false sense of security with future planned sales and cash flow based on what they think are solid referrals, only to find out that the majority of the referrals were not qualified, resulting in many fewer customers than expected and wasted time, money, and energy.

On the other hand, it's easy to let the all-important job of asking for referrals slip through the cracks. We see sales managers and CEOs from small businesses and multimillion-dollar operations neglect to ask for referrals.

Develop a referral program including specific goals as to where, how, and the number of referrals you would like to obtain and, most importantly, a system to qualify them.

FROM THE STREET: NO SALE? NO PROBLEM!

If you're working with a prospective customer who for some reason can't do business with you at present but seems impressed with you, your company, products, or services, at least ask for a referral. On many occasions, we spent considerable time in meetings with prospective customers but, for reasons beyond our control, the timing wasn't right or we just couldn't meet each other's goals. In these cases, we shifted from selling to asking for a referral. It usually went like this: "Since you now know about our company and the benefits that you would derive, would you happen to know anyone who could benefit from our services?" Often we got the referrals, and in many cases we ended up landing some new business.

"Develop the winning edge; small differences in your performance can lead to large differences in your results." —Brian Tracy

Revisit the Lost Art of Turning Cold Calls into Customers

Cold calling means approaching a potential new customer "cold" with no introduction, referral, or advance appointment. You just walk in unannounced or call someone who doesn't know you from Adam. Few people enjoy making cold calls, and it may or may not work for your particular business, but if you think it might bear

- Do I need to have an online presence to keep up with the competition?
- How quickly will my company see a return on its investment?
- How will the time and effort devoted to the internet business affect my current business?

Be honest with yourself. Don't let the excitement of new technologies get in the way of current business goals. The Web's powerful and ever-improving innovations are very compelling, but still may not be right for your particular business. If they are, utilize them intelligently to maximize effectiveness. Use common business sense, stay informed, do your research, and get all the advice you need before you decide to forge ahead.

Social media has grown dramatically over the last five years with Facebook, Twitter, and LinkedIn leading the pack. The University of Maryland's Robert H. Smith School of Business, which sponsors the Small Business Success Index (SBSI), reports that nearly one out of five small-business owners are using some type of social media in their business. However, faced with all the hype regarding social media and social networking, practitioners believe it is wise to keep a safe observational distance as the world—and most importantly your market—adapts at its own pace so you can then make decisions accordingly.

As we did with the internet years ago, we advise our clients with a standard caution: If you're going to use social media marketing, your audience and customers will demand your extensive participation, which translates to providing them valuable information that is timely, important, and relevant. Trying to cut corners using social media as another form of marketing or advertising, and measuring your success by your Facebook fans or Twitter followers are not productive approaches.

The incontrovertible contribution of social networking is that it has introduced an entirely new high-tech ability to build an interconnected network of contacts and knowledge partners. Access across industries and interests has become increasingly easier, and barriers caused by time, distance, borders, and language have virtually vanished. Moreover, skillful social networking has a compounding effect; it multiplies your impact exponentially. When you network correctly, you tap into all contacts—friends, neighbors, relatives, clients, and business associates—every person you meet. With just one contact, you open up vast new networks of people who may provide you with new customers, new information, new processes, and new suppliers to help you get more business.

The SBSI report also found that there are still formidable obstacles for the business application of social media. Many people currently don't weigh or budget the people, time, and monetary investment required to be effective in a social media environment. Resources are essential to make an impact and provide important, timely, and relevant information to contribute to the social group. Also, many don't understand that while exposing a business or service on a social network provides a live line of contact and feedback to new customers, it also allows customers from anywhere or with any agenda (maybe those of your competitors) to throttle you openly with criticism, innuendo, and trolling.

Most of the social media gurus and advisors that we talked to warn that not making a total commitment to social media is probably worse than not being there at all. Some of the more vocal pundits are even hinting that a state of social fatigue or burnout is approaching, and it may arrive sooner than we think.

There are valuable attributes to social network marketing. These include the ability to contact customers with notifications of interest (sales, promotions, or events) that are fast, in real time, effective, and inexpensive. We suggest you try techniques that make sense for your business and see which ones work while guarding against over investing in a non-proven process.

Networking

Although we touched on networking in Discipline One—Work Smart, we'd like to circle back briefly because it's an over-used term that is woefully underutilized for getting more business.

Networking is a sound prospecting method, and you can do it almost anywhere: at social gatherings, chamber of commerce meetings, industry meetings, conventions, and trade shows; at your church or synagogue; in airports or on planes; while you're waiting in the reception area of a supplier or client. But don't offend people by turning every encounter into a heavy-handed sales pitch. Do, however, consider everyone you meet as a potential source of leads or new business. Just use some finesse when you're developing them.

"Once you have a clear picture of your priorities—that is values, goals, and high leverage activities—organize around them."
—Steven Covey

FROM THE STREET: NETWORKING GAME PLAN

Networking might seem like the random meeting of people, but you should approach it strategically as you would any other element in your business plan. The key is to set measurable goals for your networking activity. You will see that you can increase the odds of meeting more customers.

Have a plan with specific objectives going into each networking situation. At the next business trade show or conference you attend, collect business cards from five people and tell them about your product or service. At your next chamber of commerce meeting, come prepared with a brief, five-minute pitch of your business and its products or services. Tell people about your company's success. Ask them about potential interest in your product or service, ask for a referral, and be sure to follow up with an email or telephone call. This strategy keeps you focused and can help you avoid squandering time just socializing.

Learn from Competitors, Market Developments, and Future Business Trends

These three sources are fertile areas of valuable information that can help you increase business. We also cover this topic in greater detail in the Strategic Multi-Dimensional Analysis in the Street Smart Workshop on page 226.

"Learning faster than your competitors is the only sustainable competitive advantage in an environment of rapid change and innovation." —Arie de Geus

Competitors

Your competitors' customers are your prospects, and their prospecting methods may give you ideas for getting more business. Look at your competitors and explore the following:

- Who are your competitors' customers?
- How can you attract the same customers?
- What are your competitors doing to get more business?
- What are they doing that you're not?
- What are you doing that your competitors aren't doing?
- Review their websites and other pertinent information on the internet.
- Get on their mailing lists.
- Get brochures and other literature by visiting their stores, offices, trade show booths, or by sending in business-reply cards requesting information.
- Talk to your competitors at social functions, seminars, or trade shows.
- Talk to customers who also buy from your competitors.

Market and Industry Developments

Market or industry trends, directions, and forecasts can help you target business opportunities. Ask yourself,

- Are you staying abreast of developments in your market or industry?
- Are there developments that might affect your business?
- Are there new products or services your company could offer?
- Are there new technologies for use in your business?
- Are there new products or services you should be using to improve your business?
- Are there opportunities to sell your products or services in new geographic markets?

- Is the growth into a new market important or profitable enough for you to consider?
- If so, what are you doing to implement the necessary changes in your company?

"There is one thing stronger than all the armies in the world and that is an idea whose time has come." —Victor Hugo

Future Business Trends

Think about future developments—new business ideas, changing customer habits and advances in production or communication—that might have an impact on your business and affect the methods you use for getting more business.

- How will technology continue to change your business?
- How will advancements in communications and wireless technologies change your methods for getting more business?
- Is it possible that new technologies could radically change your business model or make it obsolete? (think Blockbuster, Tower Records, and Borders). If so, which type of technology could pose significant changes or threats?
- How could social networks impact your business?
- Could changing trends affect customers' buying habits enough to affect your business?
- Could customers be paying for products and services in new and different ways?
- How do you stay informed about business trends?

Trade Associations

Trade associations—industry trade groups founded and usually funded by businesses that operate within a specific industry—are good resources for getting more business. They can provide timely news, pertinent industry information, and leads for prospective customers. They usually offer conferences, events, workshops and seminars enabling networking and the exchange of ideas.

Business Publications and Online Information Services

A staggering amount of information in publications and online is available for you to use to find potential new customers and increase your business. American Cities Business Journals, which publish business newspapers in forty cities across the United States, has a page devoted specifically to business leads. Its introductory copy reads, "Business Leads are designed to keep you informed and help you grow your business." That's the whole concept boiled down to its essence. The page includes listings of new businesses, new locations, new corporations, commercial real estate sales and lease deals, and proposed construction projects. Subscribers to the newspaper receive fresh leads every week. How easy is that?

Online information services, directories, blogs, reference sites, and search engines also offer thousands of databases that list prospects by business activity, size, or geographic location. Most of them include useful contact information as well.

FROM THE STREET: ONLINE, EMAIL, AND DIRECT MAIL

Get more business by using online sales and marketing solicitations via email or direct mail. If the email or direct mail approach works for your product or service, you can save a lot of wasted time and energy trying to reach heavily gate-kept prospects or playing phone tag. Make your email or direct mail piece powerful, convincing, and benefit-oriented to grab a prospective customer's attention instead of it winding up in the trash.

Advertising Information

You can get a lot of information about prospective customers—especially companies—from their advertising. An ad usually tells you what a company does, what products or services it offers, how it tries to differentiate itself from the competition, and its location and phone number. Sometimes an ad even talks about the goals a company is trying to accomplish. This is all valuable information ripe for the picking. It may help you determine whether the company is a good prospect and provide you with critical information you need to approach a prospective customer.

When we were selling advertising in our various magazines in the United States and Argentina, we set a goal of finding ten new prospective customers each week using advertising information. We scanned newspapers, magazines, trade journals, billboards, and any other places a business might advertise that could provide us with prospective leads.

Trade Shows and Conferences

There are several ways to prospect at trade shows and conferences. You can mingle and network. You can set up a booth and turn visitors that happen to walk by into leads. Or you can take a more focused, aggressive approach and use these events to make appointments, presentations, and to close business deals, as we do.

We're extremely effective at working trade shows and conferences because we have a game plan. We don't sit back and wait for prospective customers to come to us. Thanks to crisp intelligence work, we arrive knowing the companies we want to do business with and the names of the decision makers who will be attending the event. We make it a top priority to introduce ourselves and make a presentation or at least set up a future appointment with each of them.

Often we're able to get access to CEOs, presidents, and vice presidents by providing a compelling story. How? We craft a concise marketing message about our business, products, and services and how they will benefit. Then we practice it so we can present it with confidence and clarity. We make sure we have a great story or pitch, which helps give us the courage to walk up to these executives on the trade show floor and start presenting. Our competitors at the show set up booths and wait for customers to come to them. We go to the prospective customer and state our case. Can you guess which method generates more new business?

A trade show is the perfect venue to get more business. Potential new customers are there, and you're there to present a product or service that will help them. It's a perfect match. Plus, there are no secretaries or voice mail to screen your calls. You have direct access.

Advertising, Publicity, and Sales Promotions

"If the circus is coming to town and you paint a sign saying 'Circus Coming to the Fairground Saturday,' that's advertising. If you put the sign on the back of an elephant and walk it into town, that's promotion. If the elephant walks through the mayor's flower bed, that's publicity. And if you get the mayor to laugh about it, that's public relations. If the town's citizens go to the circus, you show them the many entertainment booths, explain how much fun they'll have spending money at the booths, answer their questions and ultimately, they spend a lot at the circus, that's sales. And if you planned the whole thing, that's Marketing!" —P. T. Barnum

Advertising

Advertising is expensive. To avoid overspending, you must have clear goals. What is your target audience? What do you want your advertising to achieve? Is current advertising actually reaching your target audience? Is there a more effective advertising medium or a less expensive one available? Are you getting results? Can you measure and track the return on your investment in advertising?

Experiment by advertising in different types of media until you find the formats that work best for your business. Estimate your cost and your return on investment, that is, the number of sales or new customers the advertising generates. Make a habit of tracking the source of your business. Is it from advertising, referrals, word of mouth? When you advertise, include as many ways as possible for customers to reach you: address of your store or office, email address, phone number, 800 number, fax number, Facebook, Twitter, and website address.

Earlier in the book, we mentioned using testimonials in presentations. They are also very effective on your website and in any advertising that you use. Testimonials from current customers are potent advertising tools that work in almost any medium and can dramatically increase your credibility and appeal.

"Efficiency is doing things right. Effectiveness is doing the right things." —Peter Drucker

Publicity

Public relations is the long-term strategic planning businesses and organizations undertake to build awareness and relationships with the public. Publicity is a component of public relations and is the short-term tactic that organizations use to gain awareness.

The key is to find something newsworthy about your business, such as a new product or service, an executive change or promotion, an award, a project that helps your community, volunteer activities, fundraisers, or upcoming events. Write up a press release. Keep it short (two pages maximum), and start with a captivating first paragraph that summarizes your message and sparks interest.

At American Park Network, we hired a San Francisco public relations firm and worked with them closely to develop an effective PR campaign. In a couple of months, we landed on the front page of the business section in the *San Francisco Examiner* and also had write-ups in the *Wall Street Journal,* the *New York Times*, the *Chicago Tribune,* and at least a half-dozen trade magazines. The publicity put us on the map as a successful, innovative publishing company, and our business increased significantly in the next six months.

Good publicity strengthens your credibility in the eyes of your existing customers and helps secure new business from those who have just recently heard about you.

Sales Promotions

Sales promotions support the selling process and attract customers to your product or service by offering incentives directed to produce immediate sales volume impact within a defined period of time. There are an infinite number of sales promotions you can choose, limited only by your imagination and the needs of your particular business. Here are some to get you thinking:

- Price incentives with coupons for a given period
- Packaging offers that include extra product (33 percent more, for example) or include sample-size products in the same package

- Buy two and get one free promotions
- Special coupon incentives to encourage consumers to make a brand switch or to try a new product
- Contests, games, and sweepstakes to create interest in a brand or product
- Sampling or live demonstrations at fairs and trade shows

The techniques we just covered will help you get more business. Focus on the ones that provide the most value for your investment of people, time, and money. Understand exactly what you want to accomplish with any marketing tool you use, and devise a comprehensive plan to execute it diligently. To gauge results, "inspect what you expect."

Overcome Obstacles to Get More Business

We've covered a variety of methods you can use to find new customers and get new business. But keep in mind that you must still land the new customers (getting them to pay for your goods or services). This may require closing, which requires selling. We won't cover the huge topic of sales in detail in this book, but will touch on a number of proven methods to deal with roadblocks to securing new business successfully.

We were lucky to have learned a lot of this material early in our careers in formal sales training classes when we worked at the 3M Company, when both of us were living and working in the Hawaiian islands for several years. Although our early on-the-job education was a great foundation, we have continued to study sales and marketing techniques throughout our careers. This ongoing self-education keeps our sales personas fresh and focused, which allowed us to successfully overcome roadblocks to closing business deals.

We believe that there is absolutely no substitute for personal sales presentations for securing new business. They are by far the most effective way to get new customers, so whenever possible, opt to give in-person presentations. That's why we devoted an entire chapter, Discipline Two—Present Everything, to covering the strategies, skills, and art of presenting. Read it, study it, and learn the key elements for presenting.

"A path without obstacles probably leads nowhere." —Defalque

Obstacles are part of the process of getting more business, so just accept this hard reality and be well prepared to deal with them. The biggest obstacles people usually face are objections. A dictionary defines objection as "an expression of disapproval or opposition; an adverse reason or statement." But you should regard objections as unanswered questions or concerns that people have, not as a potential rejection of your proposal or pitch.

Thus, change your focus: view an objection as an unanswered question or concern. Questions and concerns are good because within them lie the information you need to overcome the obstacles.

Four Truths of Questions and Concerns

- Questions and concerns are part of everyday business life. Expect them and be ready for them.
- Questions and concerns are signs that someone is thinking about buying or is seriously considering your product, service, or proposal.
- Questions and concerns may reveal what the other person wants and needs.
- By planning in advance for questions and concerns, you will be able to handle them more effectively.

Why People Have Questions and Concerns

A look at human psychology explains why questions and concerns are common. They are often the symptoms of hidden fears. Everyone wants to make the "right" decision so they will look good in the eyes of their superiors, coworkers, family, or friends. They manifest their fears as questions and concerns. In many cases they don't verbalize their fears, but these are some of the questions that may be running through their minds:

- Am I making a good decision?
- How will my supervisor or business partners view my decision?
- Am I making a mistake?
- How risky is the decision?
- Is this good value for my money?
- Is this a good deal?
- Could I get a better deal somewhere else?

- Is there a better product or service out there?
- Will everything be delivered as promised?
- Is this person really trying to help me, or is his effort motivated by personal gain?
- Am I being misled?
- Am I being pressured?

These fears often stand between you and getting the business. You can't pretend they don't exist, and you can't ignore them just because they aren't verbalized.

When people are afraid, they often get defensive and even rude. If someone is rude to you, don't escalate the situation with a rude response. Remain calm; don't let your ego get in the way. Address the person's questions and concerns appropriately. With well thought-out answers and explanations, you can help people eliminate their fears and reach a comfort zone that allows you to move ahead.

FROM THE STREET: NO CONCERN IS TOO SMALL

There are times when someone's concern may seem insignificant, even ridiculous to you. Don't dismiss it. Handle every concern with patience and empathy. The person wouldn't be raising the issue if it wasn't important.

People often have an aversion to making decisions; they find the process and the finality of their choice unsettling. By asking questions and raising concerns, they set up a protective smoke screen. They stall. They punt. They buy time. They postpone decision making. Help them along by determining their real questions and concerns. Then address those concerns and resell the benefits to move them beyond their fears.

Why You May Have Difficulty with Questions and Concerns

- You subconsciously fear questions and concerns and view them as rejection. You think that if someone raises a question or concern, he or she is rejecting your product, service, or proposal, and you take it personally.

The solution: Don't be afraid of questions and concerns. Take them in stride by reminding yourself that people aren't rejecting you, your business, or your objectives. They are simply expressing a concern. Never take it personally.

- You have had no training in handling questions and concerns. You are not prepared for them, and they make you uncomfortable.

The solution: Some people make a big deal out of handling objections, but it's not a big deal. If you practice the common-sense techniques in the following section ("Street Smart Strategies for Handling Questions and Concerns"), you'll deal with them successfully.

- You interpret questions and concerns as final no's, as roadblocks you can't overcome.

The solution: Put yourself in the other person's shoes. Don't you ask questions and weigh concerns before making a decision? Most intelligent people do. It's a natural part of the decision-making process. The word *no* is not final, not the end of the line. Many businesspeople quit after the first or second no. Be persistent, handle each question or concern, and get past the roadblocks.

"Never give in; never give in, never, never, never, never...never give in." —Winston Churchill

Street Smart Strategies for Handling Questions and Concerns

- Prepare
- Welcome and acknowledge the question and concern
- Be empathic
- Ask questions to gain further clarification
- Answer the questions and concerns

Prepare

Preparation to handle questions and concerns is one of the most important practices of successful businesspeople. Follow these steps to prepare for dealing with them:

- Always write down questions and concerns you encounter. Then write out your best plausible and persuasive responses. Have your team or employees do this exercise as well. Ask them to submit their questions and responses, then meet to fine-tune the responses.
- Rehearse your responses using a tape recorder or a video camera so you appear natural and at ease, especially when you are using emphatic statements.
- Role play with your coworkers, partners, employees, or salespeople. Take turns playing the customer and firing off questions and concerns.
- Before each encounter with a prospective customer, make a list of the specific questions and concerns you think he or she will bring up. Write them down and develop persuasive responses for each one.

Remember, more than anything, preparation is the key to successfully handling questions and concerns.

Welcome and Acknowledge the Questions and Concerns

One of the biggest mistakes businesspeople make is reacting defensively to questions and concerns. They respond negatively. Avoid confrontation, contention, or debate. Be receptive, and welcome the issues. People sense immediately whether you are negative or receptive. Always take a receptive stance.

Relax and really listen to what is being said. Listening is an active process: focus all your attention on what the person is saying. Don't let your mind wander, pretending that you're listening as you're preparing what to say next. And don't interrupt or try to answer the question or concern, and don't give your opinion at this point. Your goal right now is simply to get the other person to fully explain what he or she is thinking.

Hear people out and try to absorb the core meaning of what they are saying. Create a pleasant environment so they feel comfortable expressing their genuine thoughts. Keep smiling throughout. Smiling and listening are powerful nonverbal signs of acceptance. Smiling is also a way to mask your negative emotions; especially in difficult situations when someone is firing off what you feel are insignificant questions and concerns.

"The person who never objects to anything is a tough person to close." —Tom Hopkins

Be Empathetic

Respond to questions and concerns by acknowledging what the person is saying, and be empathetic. Ask yourself, *How is this person really feeling right now?* Empathy disarms people and makes them feel like you're on their side and are genuinely working to solve their problems.

Demonstrate empathy by verbally aligning yourself with the other person by using phrases that acknowledge their question or concern. These phrases will get you started, but we suggest you brainstorm to develop an empathetic mindset and use words that fit your own personality and style.

- I hear what you're saying.
- I understand the way you feel.
- That's a valid concern.
- I'm glad you asked that question.
- I appreciate your concern.
- You raise an important question.

After stating your phrase, pause, and don't say anything for ten to fifteen seconds. The pause gives the other person a chance to talk further about his or her concerns, which is good. Remember, you want to learn everything you can so you can formulate solutions. The pause also gives you time to mentally prepare your response and next step.

Try a technique known as "Feel, Felt, Found" to effectively demonstrate empathy. Here's an example: "I certainly understand how you *feel*. As a matter of fact, Jim Telson at the Milford Corporation (try to use a concrete example the customer can relate to) *felt* exactly the same way you do. (At this point, add details about the specific concern.) But once he began using our product, he was extremely happy and *found* that the state-of-the-art features of our product and our 24/7 service orientation far outweighed the additional minimal cost."

FROM THE STREET: SUCCESS STORIES

Stories about customers who had questions or concerns but are now extremely happy with your product or service help to allay the fears of prospective customers. Have some written testimonials or references to reinforce your point. Suggest that the person call one of your satisfied customers.

Ask Questions to Gain Further Clarification

You must get people talking to achieve an important twofold objective: to test the person's questions and concerns, and to uncover the true reasons for the resistance. Try questions like these:

- So I can help you, can you tell me more about your concern?
- I think I understand, but do you mind if we talk about that further?
- Do you mind if I ask why you feel that way?
- Do you mind if I ask why that is a specific concern at this point?
- Can you tell me a little more about why you are thinking along those lines?
- Can you help me gain a better understanding of what you mean?
- What exactly don't you like about…?

Also, try turning around what the person has said and rephrasing it as a question. For example, if someone says, "It costs too much," respond with what is known as a reflective question: "It costs too much?" (A reflective question reflects back the original question.) Then pause and wait for the person to say something. Often the person will elaborate, but if he or she simply says, "Yes, I said it costs too much," you can respond, "I understand what you're saying, but do you mind if I ask why you feel it costs too much?"

Pause after every question you ask. Don't be afraid of silence; train yourself to get comfortable with it. Let people think through their concerns. If you keep talking or interrupt, they won't get to fully express themselves, and the issue will never get resolved.

"One of the best ways to persuade others is with your ears."
—Dean Rusk

FROM THE STREET: PARAPHRASE

Paraphrasing demonstrates empathy and helps you clarify situations. Simply restate what the other person has said. For example, say, "If I understand you correctly, you're saying that you're afraid changing suppliers will disrupt your production schedule. Is that your concern?"

Answer the Questions and Concerns

Uncovering real questions and concerns is the difficult part; answering them is relatively easy because most of them are the same question about a particular issue, just phrased in different ways.

Before you answer a concern, put yourself in the other person's shoes. Ask yourself what response would make you feel good about this issue? Make sure you have completely handled the issue and gained agreement before you continue with the conversation or your presentation. Ask, "Have I completely answered your concern?" Also, ask if there are any other questions or concerns that the person feels could stand in the way of doing business together.

"Obstacles are things a person sees when he takes his eyes off the goal" —E. Joseph Cossman

Businesspeople encounter many different questions and concerns; many are unique to their businesses but many are common. The average company typically has about ten to fifteen that come up over and over. We selected five of the most common ones to illustrate how you can answer them effectively.

This is an exercise we use religiously in our businesses. We identify recurring questions and concerns and then write ironclad responses. We memorize and rehearse them, knowing from experience that this method is the best way to eliminate roadblocks to getting more business.

Have you heard these before?

"I want to think it over." This is the classic comment of the procrastinator, someone who has difficulty making decisions. This person is usually very cordial and at the end of your presentation, he or she says, "I'm very impressed (with you, your company, your product, your presentation). I'm very interested, but I want to think it over."

How do you handle this type of person? You have to help him or her along. Be patient. Try to uncover specific issues you can address. Say something like, "I understand you want to think it over, and I agree that you should. (Pause) But while I'm here, maybe I can help you. Exactly what is it that you feel you must think over?"

To uncover specific questions or concerns and move the procrastinator along, try this technique by asking, "Let's discuss for a moment all the reasons you are concerned about this idea and all the reasons you should go ahead now." Help the person list one concern and then stop talking; let him or her come up with any additional concerns. Next, take an active role in helping the person list all the reasons he or she should go ahead and start doing business with you today. This exercise will flush out specific questions and concerns. It will also illustrate that the reasons for going ahead outweigh the concerns.

"The price is too high." Or *"It's too expensive."* Price-related questions and concerns are the most common. You will encounter them, so be prepared. It's inevitable you'll lose some business because of price. Accept it. But don't give up at the first sign of price resistance. In fact, be encouraged when a customer expresses concern

about price. It means he is interested in your product, service, or proposal.

Sometimes, a customer will suggest that your competitor has offered a lower price. It could be a bluff. To find out ask, "Would you mind if I took a look at that price quotation? There may be differences in the features and services that will account for the variation."

FROM THE STREET: A PREEMPTIVE STRIKE— TAKE THE OFFENSE

This might sound counterintuitive, but after you have identified recurring issues in your business, be the one to bring them up to the prospective customer. Weave persuasive preemptive responses to common concerns into your presentation. For example, if your product or service is always more expensive than your competitors', raise the price issue yourself and address the concern right up front. "Our price may be higher than what you had in mind, but our product is the best and our 24/7 service is unrivalled in the market. We are not the cheapest, but no one can offer you more value for your dollar." Sell value over price.

When a customer says, "The price is too high," use a reflective question to get him to be more specific about his concern. "The price is too high?" Another way to respond is by saying, "I agree that many things today cost too much." (Pause and wait for the customer to say something.) "Just out of curiosity, how much is 'too high'? What dollar amount are you talking about, and what are you using for comparison?"

Depending on how the dialogue goes, you may want to ask additional questions, such as, "Is it possible you feel you're not getting enough value for your dollar?" or "Does the product/service lack some features you're looking for?"

You can address a price concern in several ways:

- Discuss the service orientation and reputation of your company. You might say, "You may be paying a bit more, but that's because you are dealing with the best company in the industry. No one will come close to providing the level of excellent service and personal attention we provide. If anything goes wrong with the product, we will replace it with no questions asked. You will be glad you paid a little more to get our superior service."
- Minimize the price difference. Say, "Let's look at it over the long term. It will cost you only two dollars more a week." Then mention again all the benefits of your product or service and say, "Really, for two dollars extra a week, isn't it well worth it?"
- Resell the features and benefits of your product or service, especially those your competitor doesn't offer and the ones the customer has mentioned are of value. Stress benefits over price, and emphasize the price-quality equation. Say, "Someone can always manufacture an inferior product and charge less for it. Our price represents quality materials, quality workmanship, and quality service."

"Our greatest weakness lies in giving up. The most certain way to succeed is to always try just one more time." —Thomas A. Edison

"I want a discount." Some customers can't resist bargaining for a better price. They consider pressing for a discount to be part of buying. The good news: a request for a discount, like a concern about price, indicates that the customer is interested. If your company does not cut prices, be prepared with a list of convincing reasons for your no-discount policy:

- "Unfortunately, the discounts competitors offer sometimes drive them out of business, so you never know they may not be around next year."
- "Our firm price assures you of quality. You won't end up paying more down the road for repairs and service or for the hidden costs of lost time and wasted productivity."
- "We invest a tremendous amount of money in making our product/service the very best, and we keep our profit margins as low as possible."

- "Demand for our product is very high. We don't have excess inventory, so it doesn't make sense for us to cut prices."

"I want to shop around." Respond with, "I certainly understand. It's probably a good idea to shop around. But maybe I can save you time and money, and spare you the frustration of continuing to shop. Just to clarify my thinking, why is it that you feel you need to shop around? Are you looking for a better product? Better price? Faster delivery?" Then pause and let the customer respond.

If he or she comes back with, "We just want to see what's out there," try to uncover specific concerns by saying, "Do you have a concern with our price?" (Pause) Is it the quality? The color? The size? Is it the reputation of our company? Exactly what is it that concerns you? The reason I'm asking is that I'm confident that you can do all the shopping you want, but you won't find a better product for the price from such a quality manufacturer backed by one of the finest service organizations in the industry."

"We're satisfied with our present supplier." People resist change. This is normal. Customers will always ask themselves, "Why should we change if things are going well with our present supplier?"

Your response should be, "I can understand that you are satisfied with your present supplier. You're dealing with a very well-respected firm. Just out of curiosity, what exactly is it about your present supplier that makes you so happy?"

Make a mental note of what customers say they like about their current supplier, but also be thinking about what they don't mention, especially if it's a feature, service, or benefit you can offer.

Next, ask, "Is there anything about your present supplier's product or service you would like to improve? Is there anything you are unhappy with?" Their response is your opening to focus on how your product or service will provide the improvements the customer wants. In this exchange, try to close for at least a portion of their business.

Secure the Business

The ability to make business deals, get more business, and build more revenues is what differentiates truly successful businesspeople from mediocre ones.

Some people are blessed with a product or service they can market without directly asking for the business or closing. But most people must use effective closing strategies and techniques to get more business. To survive in today's competitive marketplace, you have to ask for the business and you have to know how to effectively close a deal. All the great work you put into your business and its products or services—and your selling and marketing—won't matter if you don't get the deal.

Despite the business mythology and mysticism that surrounds it, closing is not really mysterious or difficult. It is the logical conclusion to an effective sales and marketing effort or a strong presentation. Most people find that if they have carefully followed all the required steps in the selling process, closing is no big deal. That doesn't mean the close is automatic. Countless new business opportunities are lost, and countless transactions fall through every day because people fail to ask the single most important question: "How can we do business together?"

What Is Closing?

Closing is the process that prompts people to make commitments. One of the most effective ways to ensure a successful close is to understand someone's true wants and needs. Armed with this information, you can tailor your sales and marketing efforts and be in a stronger position to close comfortably, naturally, and successfully.

Fear of Closing

Many businesspeople dislike closing for the same reasons they dislike handling questions and concerns. They are frightened by the psychological implications of the word *no*. Subconsciously they fear rejection. They fear failure. To eliminate your fear of rejection and failure, understand this simple truth: when it comes to sales and marketing, everyone is working more or less in an environment of potential rejection. It's the nature of business, and it's nothing personal. Accept that you will get a lot more noes than yeses. Change your frame of mind to separate your ego from the situation. Remember, when someone says no, he or she is not rejecting you personally.

Getting Beyond No

A no stops many businesspeople cold. That's a natural reaction that you must overcome. People give up because they feel that to pursue the cause after a no is confrontational. But don't surrender the first time you hear this two-letter word, to which people give way too much power. Successful businesspeople certainly don't let the initial no stop them. When top sales professionals across the country were asked about how many times they attempted to close a sale, the average number of attempts in a typical presentation was five. That means five noes before they got the sale.

The word *no* is not the ultimate rejection. It's essential to acknowledge that you are going to hear no, but understand that each no may bring you one step closer to yes, if you play it right and follow the Disciplines chapters "Present Everything" and "Get More Business."

Confidence and courage are the two vital ingredients to successful closing. In every situation, you must have the confidence to assume that someone will buy and the courage to ask for the business.

"Self confidence is the first requisite to great undertakings."
—Samuel Johnson

Confidence comes from the overwhelming belief that your product, service, or proposal will truly benefit someone. Build your confidence by knowing your product, service, or proposal and the person or company with whom you're dealing. Demonstrate your courage by the enthusiasm you generate throughout the entire selling process, especially at the close.

Watch for Buying Signals

To determine when you should start the closing phase in a selling situation, listen to your prospective customers. Listen for questions that indicate that in their minds they have already made the decision to buy and are now trying to work out details or logistics For example, a prospect might ask, "Is it available in blue?" or "Does it come with a warranty?" Such questions are cues to launch the close of your presentation.

Don't let the opportunity slip away. Too often businesspeople miss out on the prime moment to close by responding with a simple answer instead of a closing question. For instance, if a prospective customer asks, "Is it possible to get it delivered next week?" people usually say yes or no instead of coming back with a closing question such as "If I can get it delivered next week, may I go ahead and order it for you today?" Always respond with a question that requires the prospect to make a commitment.

Watch for these buying signals:

- The customer exhibits body language that shows interest: he or she leans forward and listens attentively.
- The customer brings someone else—spouse, business partner, or other decision maker—to the meeting.
- The customer makes comments that indicate he or she is already thinking about owning the product, such as talking about how it will be used.
- The customer asks for details on pricing or payment plans.
- The customer expresses questions or concerns that reveal an interest in your product or service.

FROM THE STREET: DON'T WAIT

Any time can be the right time to close. Spread closing questions or invitations to buy throughout your presentation; you don't have to wait until you're finished. Ask early and often.

Summarize and Move the Sale Forward

If you are making a personal presentation, you can accelerate your closing efforts with a summary of your entire presentation. The objective is to recap all the benefits of your product or service and to uncover objections that haven't surfaced. The summary is also a subtle, logical, and effective way to ask for the business. Start by saying, "If it's okay with you, I'd like to take a couple of minutes to summarize the highlights of what we've discussed. Before we begin, do you have any questions?"

If the prospective customer has questions at this time, use them to determine where you stand in the sales process and whether you need to handle additional concerns before you proceed to closing. Otherwise, summarize your presentation, and ask questions that will move the sale forward.

"Good fortune is what happens when opportunity meets with preparation." —Thomas A. Edison

Questions that successful businesspeople weave into closing summarizations:

- What do you like about our product/service?" If customers have trouble coming up with a list of things they like, suggest attributes of your product or service they are sure to find beneficial.
- "What aspects of the product/service will benefit you in your work/personal life?" With this question, you get the customer talking about how he or she will actually use your product or service.
- "Is there anything you would change about the product/service?" With this question you uncover any remaining questions or concerns. It is one more chance to confront and resolve potential problems.
- "Is there anything that might get in the way of doing business?" If the customer says no, you have an invitation to close the sale. If something stands in the way, you can find out exactly what it is and what you need to do to move ahead.
- "Is there anyone else involved in making the decision? If so, can we have them join us now?" This should not be the first time you ask this question. You should pose it when you make the appointment and once again at the beginning of the presentation. It's also a good idea to ask again during your summary, because the customer may have seen or heard something during your presentation that suggests the need to involve an additional decision maker. If someone else has to be in on the decision, try to see that person right away.

Ask your prospective customer to introduce you or to set up a meeting as soon as possible. If it will be a joint decision, ask your prospect whether he or she will recommend your product or service. If the answer is "No," or "I don't know," or "I'll have to think about it," you need to get some clarification; move immediately into your techniques for handling questions and concerns.

- "What are the next steps we have to take in order to do business?

FROM THE STREET: CLOSING IS JOB ONE

Even a great product will not sell itself, and good advertising usually isn't enough to make a product fly off the shelf. Most products and services must be sold and when it comes to selling, nothing requires more training and practice than closing. The most successful businesspeople are masters of recognizing the invitation to buy—in other words, the close. Your success in getting more business rests on learning and implementing proven closing strategies and techniques.

Negotiation

We cover negotiation in Discipline Four—Watch Your Money and recommend that you reread it since many closing scenarios often require some negotiation and savvy negotiating skills to successfully close the deal. The give and take of any negotiating situation should always result in each party achieving what it wants and needs. Successful businesspeople combine customer satisfaction with transactions that yield profits for themselves or their companies.

Don't let pressures to get the new business drive you to make concessions that result in unprofitable business. Most customers are looking for a deal, so be prepared with negotiating strategies.

"You miss 100 percent of the shots you never take."
—Wayne Gretzky

When You Can't Close Right Away

If your prospective customer says no, your work isn't done. You have to find out why. The information may help you keep the current sale alive and enable you to be more effective in future selling situations.

Find out if the no means "never" or "not right now." If it's "not right now," you may be able to uncover an objection that hasn't surfaced yet. If you deal with the objection effectively, you might close the sale. At the very least, you can lay the groundwork for doing business in the future.

FROM THE STREET: GO FOR IT

Never forget to ask for the business. If you have a good product or service, have made a good presentation, and have asked all the right questions along the way, then go for it. Ask, "Is there any reason we can't have your business today?" Don't let fear stop you. Ask for the business!

When successful businesspeople have a prospective customer say no, and they feel it is a final no, they usually say, "I really appreciate your time, and I understand that you don't want to buy right now, but could you help me out by telling me exactly what is keeping you from doing business or from buying?"

By asking for help, you get a chance to find a hidden objection, which you might be able to handle then and there. For example, if the prospect says, "We don't have the money until our new budget starts the first of the year," you could arrange a payment plan that starts January 1 and close by saying, "If we could set it up to have your first payment in January, would you go ahead with it?"

Even if you can't close the sale, by asking why, you will get critical information to help you sell future customers. You may discover that your product or service needs changes or that your presentation needs improvements. Whatever the outcome, you will come away with new information to help you sell more.

After the Close

Even a resounding yes is no guarantee that a sale is a done deal and you have secured a new customer. Depending on the nature of your business, you may need to get a signed contract or handle other details required to complete the transaction. In our businesses, we don't view a sale as complete until we get paid. Make sure that a deal doesn't fall through the cracks.

By following these Street Smart strategies and techniques with unrelenting dedication and strategic focus, you'll ensure that you never run out of new customers and always have a strong revenue stream. Integrate them into your daily routine, and you'll experience significant results. And above all, remember that getting more business takes planning, preparation, and hard work.

Discipline Six
Manage Yourself

Organize Your Life to Make Time for Breakout Success

"Work is hard. Distractions are plentiful. And time is short."
—Adam Hochschild

In this chapter:
- ✓ Set goals to create a blueprint for breakout success
- ✓ Understand and execute the golden rules of time management
- ✓ Plan, plan, and plan some more
- ✓ Discipline yourself
- ✓ Be decisive
- ✓ Know your hours of peak performance
- ✓ Get organized and eliminate time wasters
- ✓ Eat smart for top level performance
- ✓ Exercise your way to super productivity
- ✓ Manage your mind

If you are like most businesspeople, you struggle and often fail to find enough hours in the day to juggle life's numerous demands and still accomplish all the things you need to, let alone to make time for family, friends, and to just enjoy life. But you should always find a way to carve out enough time to do whatever it takes to continue on your personal path to Breakout Success.

You are probably wearing many hats in your business and personal life. It's easy to get bogged down with dozens of disparate tasks, some valid but some meaningless minutiae that drain away precious time. Be honest with yourself: even the more important activities can sometimes be excuses to avoid the underlying challenge of working toward accomplishing your life-changing goals. You're only cheating yourself if you avoid the essential tasks that will lead you to success.

We've been masters of deft personal time management through-out our careers. What's the key driver? Personal management helps to control how you spend your time, reduces stress, and raises your energy level. Controlling our time personally enabled us to move at seemingly sci-fi speeds, be amazingly productive, make great money, and have plenty of free time to enjoy life.

How can you make better use of the precious commodity of time and truly maximize yourself? Over the years, we've perfected a personal management system that keeps our business and personal lives in order and ensures we always have enough time to focus on what really matters.

You've probably developed some sort of system already, but do you get *everything* done that you want and need to in your business and personal life? If not, take a hard look at your approach. Is it a true system or just a series of things you feel you must do to get through the day?

We all have blind spots and can stand to improve our ways of working. If you're really going to gain control over your life, you'll have to eliminate your allegiance to old habits and techniques, and adopt new methods to use your time more productively.

Here are the time management disciplines that have worked remarkably well for us and our clients over the years. Make no mis-take—it's a rigid regimen, and not all facets may work for you. We suggest that you take an inventory of the time management tech-niques you currently use and then combine them with some or all of the methods we cover in this chapter to build your own prescrip-tion for self-mastery.

Set Goals to Create a Blueprint for Breakout Success

Most of us know about goal setting, but few people take the time necessary to do it. Why? There are many reasons, but it's usually because it takes effort and time, and it isn't easy.

Goals give you those targets to aim for and provide the catalyst of desire, motivation, and persistence to reach them. As the late Earl Nightingale, author, radio personality, and personal development guru said, "People with goals succeed because they know where they are going. It's as simple as that."

Over the years we've developed and perfected a goal-setting system that is effective, doesn't take too much time, and is relatively easy. It will help you understand and establish what is really important in your life, why you want it, and how to achieve it.

In the Street Smart Workshop on page 202 we cover goals in more detail and will help get you started with the system.

"Nothing happens, unless first a dream." —Carl Sandburg

Most of us are so busy trying to get things done that we don't take a breather every so often to determine what we really want or where we should invest our time and energy. Take a moment to reflect: what really are your dreams for your life, career, and business? Goals are simply dreams with a specific game plan. They provide the mind a road map to take you from where you are to where you want to be, to make your dreams a reality. The power of goals can be awe-inspiring. You can actually have most of the things you want out of life—really.

Larry Page, cofounder and CEO of Google, was the commencement speaker at Mark's daughter, Haley's graduation from University of Michigan. Larry, a U of M alumnus, spoke of the time between graduating from college and founding Google. He shared many fascinating stories about the challenges he faced during those years. Then he closed with some insightful advice: "At some point you have to wake up from the dream and start *creating* the dream."

Clearly defining goals is very empowering, and once you write them down, they take on a life of their own because you've established a benchmark that you must either reach or change. A goal is a commitment. A commitment creates pressure. Pressure, properly managed, generates activity. Activity, properly directed, leads to accomplishment. And accomplishment leads to the achievement of goals.

Goals become a major asset that you must manage just like you would other personal and business assets.

"Man is what he believes." —Anton Chekhov

Understand and Execute the Golden Rules of Time Management

Before you can learn to manage your time, you must analyze how you currently spend it. *Keep a log of everything you do each day for one week*, making notes about what you did and how much time it took. The log will help you identify where your time can be better spent, as well as the time-wasting activities you can eliminate. We recommend that you do this exercise at least twice a year.

Use these rules of time management to reengineer the way you use your time and to literally find more hours in each day.

Get an Early Start

Try getting up thirty minutes earlier than usual each day. You're probably saying, "Hey, I'm already getting up at six!" Noted, but give it try. Use this extra time to hyper-focus and fine-tune your goals for the day. Reevaluate them. Prioritize them. Think through your plans and visualize your activities for the next twelve hours.

Focus on Your Peak Times

Try to get top-priority tasks done during your peak performance hours, which for most people are the first several hours of the day. Stick with the important tasks until they are completed; don't jump around trying to accomplish a bunch of things at once (more on this later).

Identify Important Tasks

Learn to separate important tasks from nonessential ones. Be ruthless in decisions on how you use your time and the tasks you choose to tackle. Most people spend far too much time on unimportant tasks because they are often easier to handle than important ones. Don't get bogged down with nonessential time wasters, which we call "junk." Get rid of it all. (If it makes you feel better, move it to a "Do Not Do List.") Ask yourself regularly, "Is this task essential or nonessential?" Don't get sidetracked by trivial events or requests that come up that divert your attention from the important job at hand.

One of the greatest causes of stress is doing too many things at the same time, so eliminate the octo-tasking or the feeling that you should be doing many things "now." Focus on the most important tasks, and let the nonessential ones go. Pursue priorities; discard distractions.

Be Realistic

You will always have much more to do than time and circumstances allow. It's impossible to get everything done. Be realistic and flexible when you're setting up a schedule. Build in some time to accommodate surprises, and accept that some things may not get done.

Set Deadlines

If no one is creating deadlines for you, it is essential that you set your own. Deadlines provide the incentive and sense of urgency you need to make things happen. Reward yourself when you accomplish tasks by your deadline.

"I'm a great believer in luck, and I find the harder I work, the more I have of it." —Thomas Jefferson

Delegate

If you are in a position to delegate, by all means do so. Delegating is crucial to time management. Always ask yourself, "With all that I have going on right now, what can I have someone else do?" Or "Could someone else be doing this particular task, which would allow me to tackle something more important or something I'm better suited to address?" Carefully evaluate your workload and consider if you should hire a part-time or full-time person or an outside service. Delegate as much as you can.

But that's not the end of the matter. You must make sure that you delegate effectively. Just because you pass tasks to someone else, you can't assume they're going to get done properly. You don't want to over supervise, yet you want to keep tabs on the tasks you delegate. Live by the mantra "You must inspect what you expect."

At *Buenos Aires Metropolis Magazine* we had a publisher working for us who, like many businesspeople, wasn't comfortable delegating. He tried to do almost everything himself, figuring he could get things done quicker and better than handing off work to our employees. Unfortunately he ended up spending too little time on the vital job of bringing in advertising revenue to grow the business. We worked with him a great deal on how to delegate effectively. Our sessions forced him to confront his non-delegation habit, and he realized that if he didn't let go of some of the work, the company would never reach the size we wanted it to reach.

He finally delegated administration duties to our general manager and production to our production manager, which enabled him to focus much more time on bringing in advertising revenue and other areas to grow the business. The results were remarkable: the company doubled its revenues in just one year.

Here are the core tenets of effective delegation:
- Establish the goals and objectives of the project or task.
- Set a deadline.
- Be clear and direct about the task you expect the person to complete, and establish your expectations about the end result.
- Keep in mind that people may not do things exactly as well as you would, but that doesn't necessarily mean they're incorrect. Let them put their own spin on things. They may end up being better than what you would have done.
- Establish an open-door policy so people feel comfortable asking you for additional instructions or clarifications.

"Never tell people how to do things. Tell them what to do and they will surprise you with their ingenuity."
—General George Patton

Don't Overbook Yourself
When setting up your schedule, don't fill every minute of your day.

Leave some free time each day for:
- Thinking, planning, and organizing yourself
- Dealing with unexpected situations that arise
- Relaxing your mind for fifteen to twenty minutes. Some quiet time each day is crucial for maximizing productivity (more about this later in the chapter).

Be Flexible
Realize that everything you're trying to accomplish will take about 25 percent more time than you have planned. Things always take

more time; don't get frustrated. If you start to run out of time, re-prioritize your tasks.

"Genius is one percent inspiration and 99 percent perspiration."
—Thomas Edison

Give That Extra 1 Percent

Sometimes you'll have to work a bit more when you're feeling ill, tired, or even exhausted. Push yourself with a tough-it-out attitude. Tell yourself, *I can do it! I can give a little more to* make that extra telephone call, complete a project, see that last customer or client. Giving that extra one percent each day really adds up over the long haul.

Set Aside Time for "Think Time"

This is uninterrupted high-quality time to do just that, to *think strategically and to hyper-focus*. Because of the fast-paced business and personal lives we lead, we often find too many people multi-tasking. They are buried by a multitude of distractions that prevent them from devoting the thinking time necessary to deal appropriately with their most important projects.

Think Time requires eliminating all distractions and mental clutter so you can hyper-focus on your chosen project or task that demand deep thinking. We find this time especially vital for planning and brainstorming to create clarity of focus (or to re-frame and see things differently), which is usually difficult to accomplish in the typical harried business office environment.

Regularly set up appointments with yourself, become "unavailable," and go to your Think Time "place" wherever that may be.

"Nothing is more terrible than activity without insight."
—Thomas Carlyle

Plan, Plan, and Plan Some More

Efficient planning is vital to allocating more time to spend on doing what really matters. A good plan cuts down on wasted time and makes you much more productive. Make carving out uninterrupted, high-quality time to develop plans a top priority.

Long-Range Planning (Annually and Quarterly)

To manage your time, you must develop solid, well thought-out plans for the future. Do some brainstorming and be sure to take everything out of your head and get it on paper. Become a meticulous chronicler of your business life. Set realistic goals and then develop actionable plans to achieve them.

Refer to your plans often; they'll keep you on track. You'll be revising them regularly because your circumstances and priorities will change, but you must maintain a working set of plans that will lead you closer to accomplishing your goals.

Short-Term Planning (Monthly, Weekly, and Daily Planning)

After completing your long-range planning, you can manage your monthly, weekly, and daily activities by working from to-do lists. There's nothing new about to-do lists, but some people don't use them effectively or with much regularity. We never found a planner notebook that met our specific needs, so we created our own monthly, weekly, and daily to-do lists. (See the daily sample template on page 239 in the Street Smart Workshop, and customize it to your specific needs.)

"I get up every morning determined to both change the world and to have one hell of a good time. Sometimes, this makes planning the day difficult." —E. B. White

Each day, work from one list that is divided into Business Tasks/Activities and Personal Tasks/Activities. At the end of the day, write tomorrow's to-do list. Take a close look at your schedule and anticipate the problems that could arise. Be prepared for unexpected interruptions. The next morning, start your day by reviewing your list, and make adjustments if necessary.

Transform yourself into a habitual list maker. Religiously creating and implementing goals via to-do lists will enable you get more done than you ever dreamed possible. If you make these goal-setting and goal-achieving disciplines part of your daily routine, getting things done will become who you are, your persona, your DNA.

"Obsession is the price you pay for perfection." —Warren Buffet

Discipline Yourself

Once you have made a commitment to achieving concrete goals and a plan of action, you have to muster the discipline to get the job done. Discipline keeps you from wasting time and avoiding tasks that you consider unpleasant. Let's be frank: to achieve all your goals, you must have enormous self-discipline. Get out of your comfort zone and force yourself to do things you find difficult. At all costs, avoid leading an undisciplined life.

After we sold the American Park Network to the Meredith Corporation, we had plenty of new responsibilities and things to do, as part of a large, diversified media company. Many times we just didn't feel like focusing on advertising sales. We allowed ourselves to get sidetracked by other "important" business matters. But we knew that if we wanted to increase revenues and meet our new revenue goals, we had to devote time strictly to ad sales.

That's what we did, and it was critical to our success. We made it a point to set aside Monday, Wednesday, and Friday to do sales—and only sales—activities. Our hours of peak performance were in the morning, so we forced ourselves to make sales calls to set appointments when we arrived at the office. It took all our powers of self-discipline to stay focused, because there were always distractions and fires to put out. When things came up that we couldn't put off, we handled them quickly and returned immediately to our top priority of growing the business.

Banish procrastination! It often results from a lack of clear goals and objectives, fear of failure, perfectionism, or being overwhelmed by the size of the task at hand. Clear your head and embrace self-discipline to take action *now*. Develop a do-it-now mentality. Don't put off an unpleasant job; just jump in and do it. The more you take action, the less discomfort you will feel tackling jobs you don't like.

"Procrastination is the thief of time." —Edward Young

Stick with us on this material, even though we're advising you to break out of your comfort zone and add what seem like more tasks to your already busy schedule. It won't be fun at the outset as you reshape your habits and mindset. But after a few of weeks spent actively applying these disciplines, you'll be getting more things done and achieving many of your goals. You'll have more time to enjoy high-intensity fun in your life. And there are few things better than the feeling that you've earned some time off as a reward for your focus and hard work.

Be Decisive

Smart businesspeople make quick decisions. Granted, you should make decisions carefully, but you never know for sure if you're making precisely the right decisions, so don't agonize over them. Often, going with your gut reaction eliminates brain cramps by overthinking and in most cases achieves better results than a self- induced "paralysis through analysis."

Here are a few ways to be decisive about making decisions:
- Determine the purpose of your decision.
- Determine the criteria you should use to evaluate the decision.
- List possible solutions with their pros and cons and best-case/worst-case scenarios.
- Forget about making perfect decisions every time. If 90 percent of your decisions are correct, you're doing fine. One hundred percent is virtually impossible, will drive you crazy, and isn't worth the extra time.

"To think too long about doing a thing often becomes its undoing."—Eva Young

Know Your Hours of Peak Performance

Everyone has an internal clock that influences peaks and valleys of performance. It's natural for your energy to fluctuate during the day. Don't fight it. Use it to your advantage. Make a mental note of your peak performance times—the times when you have the most mental and physical energy—and use these "power hours" to accomplish your most important tasks. Leave less important jobs for your lower-energy periods.

Get Organized and Eliminate Time Wasters

Most people spend far too much time and energy just looking for things they need at a particular moment (most often car keys) and engaging in other preventable unproductive activities.

The Top Time Wasters of Mass Disruption:
- Telephones: unimportant interruptions and personal calls
- Lack of goals and strategic planning
- Drop-in visitors
- Frequent meetings
- Ineffective delegation
- Being unorganized
- Improper or overuse of digital technologies

"Time is what we want most but what we use worst."
—William Penn

The telephone can be a huge waste of time. To manage your telephone time more effectively, try the following:
- Text or email any time you can, instead of making calls. If the communication at hand pertains to setting up times and places for meetings, always text or email unless you absolutely need to clarify directions or times.
- Learn the best times to make business calls. Determine when you are most likely to get through to the people you want to reach.
- Eliminate phone tag. Find out exactly when you'll be able to speak to someone, and let him or her know when he or she can reach you. Leave a message noting several specific days or times when you'll be available to take the call. Where applicable, let the person know exactly what you need to discuss so he or she can be prepared when you finally connect.
- Cut back or eliminate personal phone calls at work. If you have to, set aside time each day during unproductive downtimes, breaks, or lunch and, importantly, keep them short.
- Minimize telephone interruptions. Shut off your cell phone during important or busy times during the day or have your

calls screened by a receptionist, secretary, answering machine, or voice mail. That way you can complete what you're working on and take or return calls when they will not interrupt important tasks.

- Above all, know what to expect before you connect.

Street Smart Essentials to Make Better Use of Your Time

- Make "waiting time" productive. Bring along material you need to work on when waiting for a plane, standing in line at the post office, cooling your heels in a doctor's office, or waiting before an appointment with a customer. If you commute by train, use the time to read some best-sellers. If you commute by car, listen to audio books.
- Reduce TV watching to an absolute minimum. Program your DVR to record whatever you feel you must see, and watch it when you have free time.
- Cut back on office chitchat. Instead of shooting the breeze at work, set times to get together periodically for coffee or drinks.
- Use the "circular file." Deal with all office memos immediately and quickly. Get comfortable tossing unimportant paper. Whenever you pick up a file or a piece of paper, don't put it down until you have made a decision to take action, delegate, file, or dispose of it.
- Work while you exercise. Finish reading your mail, memos, articles, or business journals while you work out on a stationary bike, treadmill, or elliptical trainer. However, if the objective is to clear you head, let it go and enjoy your workout. Deal with the tasks after you're energized and refreshed.

"We are drowning in information, but starved for knowledge."
—John Naisbitt

Read to Lead

The time you spend reading can be much more productive if you get organized and learn to read efficiently. In this age of information overload with unlimited choices in the battlefield for the mind, be highly selective in what you choose to read. Don't feel you have to read everything.

While reading, ask yourself what you're getting from it and how much benefit you can gain. Periodically review the list of everything you habitually read, including websites, newspapers, magazines, and books. Are they all necessary? They may have little to do with your specific goals, so why fill your head with unnecessary information? Unless something is vital to your life or business, don't bother to read it. If you truly feel you might be missing something, just skim.

You can probably double your reading speed with these few simple exercises:

- Don't read every word; read for general content, basic ideas—the heart of the material.
- Skim. First skim the table of contents, chapter titles, paragraph headings, and any bulleted or highlighted points. Then do an overall skim and, finally, focus on the topics of importance to you.
- Practice moving your eyes from left to right and down the page more quickly than you normally do.
- If you're inundated with things you must read, consider taking a speed-reading course.

We're confident you don't need a detailed primer on all of the digital communication and time-management devices that can help you get organized. Most of us have smartphones, organizers, laptops, e-readers, and tablets—and new ones come on the market every week, it seems. By the time you're finished reading this book, there will probably be a new wave of digital technologies in the marketplace.

One of the most important functions of these various gizmos is the ability to record or write down your ideas. Unfortunately, we regularly see people fail to capture great ideas. Ideas are very elusive, so get into the habit of recording them on either your smartphone or digital recorder, or at the very least jot them down in a notepad.

Wherever you are and whatever the time of day or night—at your desk, after company or client meetings, and even in bed having one of those middle-of-the-night epiphanies—record or write down your flashes of brilliance. If you think you can remember them later, you'll wind up kicking yourself because they are likely to pass into the ether, lost forever.

FROM THE STREET: DON'T DRIVE YOURSELF MAD. WRITE IT DOWN!

In an episode of *Mad Men,* an ad copywriter has a brilliant idea as he's about to fall asleep that he knows will make the perfect advertisement and perhaps lead to a career-making achievement. The next morning he wakes up and remembers he had this fantastic idea. He looks at his notepad, confident that it will be as great this morning as it was the night before. But it's not in his notepad. He didn't write it down. He spends the rest of the episode driving himself crazy trying to remember it, but he never does. Meanwhile, a competing copywriter comes up with the winning ad campaign.

Wired to Distraction

Our taste for digital technologies is becoming truly insatiable. As useful as these digital devices are for increasing productivity, they can actually reduce efficiency when not used properly or are overused.

With always-on technology and constant connectivity, you may think you're entertaining and refreshing yourself. But according to the latest studies by neuroscientists and socio-digital researchers, endless connectivity creates distractions and mental fatigue. Digital technologies have also been found to reduce peoples' attention spans. Addiction to technology is creeping up without our even realizing it.

We don't mean to be spoilsports when it comes to technology, since we personally use all the latest tech products, but many people may be losing up to a couple of hours a day of productivity because of improper digital device usage. To minimize these losses, set up ground rules and police yourself and others. For the oblivious gadget obsessed (or for those with "iPolar disorders"), you may have to do an intervention and follow up with a tech-detox.

Ground Rules for Surviving Tech-Related Disruptions and Time Wasters

- Eliminate personal web surfing during work hours.
- Make sure what you're doing online is productive and is related to your number one priority task at hand. If not, get offline.
- Stop checking your in-box more than absolutely necessary. Responding to email is often an easy way out, a distraction from staying focused on more pressing and difficult tasks you may be working on. You have many options for adjusting your email, text, and voice-mail notification modes on your computer and cell phone. Unless your job depends on instant response, you might want to turn the notification off when you do not want to be distracted.
- Don't deal with any personal emails during the workday, period. If you must, handle them during breaks or at lunch.
- Allot a specific time each day to check and respond to all business emails.
- Eliminate checking and sending personal texts during the workday unless absolutely necessary.
- During important meetings and especially during planning sessions, disconnect from all digital devices whenever possible.
- Don't even consider wasting a nanosecond on Facebook unless it is directly related to your business. Do you really care that your friend just bought some whitewall tires (unless you sell tires)?
- Shut off Twitter during work hours (again, unless it is related to your business).
- If you're not in the business of gaming, don't play games at work. Use your time more productively.
- With respect to your personal time, eliminate potential mental fatigue and give yourself a break from stress by listening to your iPod or watching TV while you tap out a few emails or texts.
- Create an email-free day every couple of weeks.
- Occasionally get out of your digital bubble; power down and unplug from gizmoland and the seductive cocktail of digital

stimuli. Don't confuse constant connectivity with making real connections. Connect to the real world and human surroundings.

"We must learn to balance the material wonders of technology with the spiritual demands of our human race."—John Naisbitt

In her book *Alone Together: Why We Expect More from Technology and Less from Each Other*, Sherry Turkle, a Massachusetts Institute of Technology professor and clinical psychologist, illustrates the digital bubble many of us live in today. She comments, "Our networked life allows us to hide from each other, even as we are tethered to each other. The new technologies allow us to dial down human contact."

Today, being "social" has taken on a new meaning, where the majority of human connections are in the form of emails, texts, and tweets. Turkle's real concern is how the digital world has turned public spaces into private places, highlighted when she sees couples out to dinner, conversing with their smartphones instead of each other. She doesn't discourage technology, but feels it has to be put in its proper place. We hope her book will be the needed intervention for the tech-addicted.

"The wise man should consider that health is the greatest of human blessings. Let food be your medicine." —Hippocrates

Eat Smart for Top Level Performance

You don't need a degree in nutrition to recognize the connection between eating well and increased energy, mood level, and productivity. It is a simple fact that a healthy diet keeps energy at peak levels throughout the day. In other words, the right foods and the right eating habits make you feel good.

Forget about dieting and especially about the hundreds of fad diets du jour. It's obvious they don't work when you learn that around 550 million people around the world are considered obese and 1.5 billion are overweight. In the United States one-third of Americans are overweight and another one-third are obese. For those who exercise but are still overweight, the sad truth is, physical exercise is only part of the solution. It all really comes down to what and how much you put in your mouth.

If you're not already on a healthy diet, you may have to change the chip in your brain and adopt some new healthful strategies. It's not as bad or difficult as you might think. On the bright side, you'll see the benefits right away through weight loss, looking better, and increased energy. What could be more encouraging?

For those that are eating healthy already, we congratulate you. But if you aren't, refer to Eat Smart in the Street Smart Workshop on page 242.

Exercise Your Way to Super Productivity

Exercise is definitely good for heart health, disease prevention, and cognitive enhancement. It's unquestionably a great mental and physical energizer too. It not only boosts your energy, but also reduces stress, uplifts your mood, and contributes to overall performance.

But how do busy businesspeople fit exercise into their schedule? Think of it as part of your job, and make time for it as you would other business activities. Business—and life in general—are stressful as well as mentally and physically draining. Exercise helps you reduce stress and mental fatigue and allows you to operate at peak levels of performance.

And now you may be saying, "I'm working fourteen hours a day, barely making ends meet, got errands to run, got a spouse who wants me to spend more time doing jobs around the house, three kids that I'm schlepping all over town to baseball games, swim meets and piano lessons, not to mention all the other stuff raining down on me right now...and you're saying go to the gym for a workout? Come on!

People get wrapped up in all their own excuses for not exercising. We've heard them all numerous times from our clients, employees, co-workers and friends over the years. But the bottom line is that the benefits of a regular exercise program are downright extraordinary. Do you want to feel and look much better, have more energy, be in better spirits, increase your mojo, think with greater clarity, be more productive, make more money, be more successful, have more fun, and sleep better? We thought so. And for those people who don't exercise, all we can say is, Just give it a try!

"It is exercise alone that supports the spirits, and keeps the mind in vigor." —Cicero

If you're not already on an exercise regimen, where do you begin? Refer to "Exercise Your Way to Super Productivity" on page 246 in the Street Smart Workshop.

Manage Your Mind

To succeed in business, it is imperative to maintain a powerful, positive frame of mind. To rigorously execute all seven disciplines in this book, you must master the mental game.

When you're positive, you're more productive and you get better results in everything you do. For some people, having a positive mindset all the time comes naturally, but for most of us it requires a seismic shift in thinking. Being positive must be learned, developed, and practiced every day.

We all have days when we feel a bit down, when the pressures and struggles of working and trying to get ahead in life really get to us. As Norman Vincent Peale, the guru of positive thinking and author of the best-selling classic *The Power of Positive Thinking*, once said, "Not a day goes by that I don't have to struggle to overcome negative thinking."

But there's no place for a negative frame of mind, especially when you're on the path to Breakout Success. You have to be upbeat, positive, and on top of your game. This type of mindset is one of the most vital characteristics of successful businesspeople; it makes the difference between success and failure.

"Man's greatness lies in the power of his thoughts." —Blaise Pascal

We thought we were positive people. But in our businesses over the years, we realized we had to be even more positive. We not only had to keep ourselves positive, we also had to be responsible for keeping our partners and employees positive as well. We tried a number of techniques over the years and finally came up with a program that helped us maintain a positive mindset in our business and personal lives.

Guidelines for Developing a Powerful and Positive Mindset

Control Your Thoughts

Understand that your mind is your own and that you can train your brain to control your thoughts to optimize your success. It is crucial to develop mental toughness by conditioning your mind. It's just like working out in a gym to condition your body; it takes practice, but you can do it.

Make a conscious effort to control your thoughts by listening to your inner dialogue, the self-talk or chatter that goes on in your head. Eliminate negative chatter such as "I can't do this," "This is too difficult," or "This will never work." Make it a habit to listen to your inner dialogue; you may be surprised how negative your mind can be. Replace nay-thinking with uplifting self-talk.

There are no benefits to negative thoughts, so eliminate them as soon as they enter your mind by turning them into positive statements. You can change your attitude and the way you deal with any situation by adjusting the way you think or repicturing the situation. It just requires practice.

"Sooner or later, those that win are those that think they can."
—Richard Bach

Act Positive

Talk and act as if you have the traits and attributes of a positive person. Develop confidence in yourself and your abilities. Going through the motions, even if you don't feel like it, will help you appear and feel positive, and not surprisingly, will put you in a better mood.

Have a Vivid Mental Picture of Being Successful in All Situations

Picture yourself succeeding in all aspects of your business and personal life. Stay focused, and visualize the successful end result in whatever you may be pursuing. See it in your mind's eye. By visualizing certain events or business situations—even material objects such as a new car, office, or house—we attract them into our lives.

Successful people use visualization regularly, whether it's consciously or subconsciously, to attract and achieve everything they want. These powerful visions and thoughts create a mental reframing, changing our behavioral habits and actions to help us achieve what we want. Visualization is a powerful tool that we don't use enough.

Never Underestimate Your Full Potential

We all tend to place limits on our performance or the success we can achieve. Placing limits on your potential is truly the biggest roadblock to achieving stellar performance. Remember, you have the power to change the way you think, to change for the better, and to achieve success. Success in life is really only limited by your imagination.

"Change your thoughts and you change your world."
—Norman Vincent Peale

Develop a List of Mind Power Affirmations

Mind-power statements or affirmations should be an integral component of any self-improvement program. Used correctly, they can aid in your mental conditioning, providing the support necessary to make the changes you want.

Create mind-power statements that resonate with you. Write them down, and keep them with you so you can easily refer to them. Focus on what you want—focus is power! It can be as easy as spending a few minutes each morning and evening reading and repeating the statements. It's important to show emotion and passion and to believe in what you're saying so that they become embedded in your subconscious. It's really not about what you're affirming, but how you're affirming. If done regularly, it focuses you to achieve what you want in life. If you want some ideas on affirmations, refer to "Mind Power Affirmations" on page 254 in the Street Smart Workshop.

"A man is literally what he thinks, his character being the complete sum of all his thoughts." —James Allen

Reduce Stress and Mental Fatigue

Overworking saps brainpower and creates mental and physical fatigue and stress. Research has shown that taking some downtime, at least fifteen to twenty minutes a day (usually the afternoon is the best, when it's normal for energy levels to drop), can rejuvenate the mind and body, leading to optimal functionality and a more positive mindset.

Unfortunately at many companies the unspoken rule is to arrive early and leave late and take as few breaks as possible. Smart businesspeople today are evaluating performance not by the number of hours worked but by the value created. They recognize that renewal, achieved by taking downtime, is a means to increased performance and value.

Be willing to try and support energy management rituals such as shutting down with a power nap, self-hypnosis, meditation, prayer, or deep-breathing relaxation exercises. These rejuvenation sessions typically start with finding a quiet place where you won't be disturbed. Think of it as your decompression chamber, and visit it at least once a day. It's important to set aside this quiet time to calm yourself, reduce stress, and alleviate mental fatigue.

Some of these exercises or methods may sound a little far out, but find one that works for you and practice it every day. You may be surprised how you'll be able to increase your productivity significantly and you'll feel amazingly refreshed.

Make a sincere and concerted effort to implement the essentials of personal management mastery regularly. You have nothing to lose but roadblocks to your success.

Discipline Seven
Everybody Sells

Develop a Sales and Customer Service-Driven Organization

"People acting together as a group can accomplish things which no individual acting alone could ever hope to bring about." —Franklin D. Roosevelt

In this chapter:
- ✓ Share the Everybody Sells philosophy
- ✓ Integrate the principles of Everybody Sells
- ✓ Explain each person's sales and customer service roles
- ✓ Build a sales and customer service-driven organization
- ✓ Develop basic sales and customer service training programs for everyone
- ✓ Powerful guidelines for providing extraordinary customer service
- ✓ Be proactive in customer engagement
- ✓ Create a customer service mission statement and set standards
- ✓ Manage, motivate, and monitor selling and customer-service performance
- ✓ Reward excellence

It may not be their job titles or in their job descriptions, but everyone in an organization should be selling. It's simple: if your business requires you to deal with people, functionally speaking, you're selling.

Take, for example, the people who answer the phone or greet customers at your office or place of business. Are they "selling"? Unquestionably a resounding yes! They are influencing directly or indirectly the customer-service experience and potential purchasing decisions. The testy manager at the doctor's office who sets the appointments can discourage patients from working with the doctor. These types of people "un-sell" the idea of the patient coming back, regardless of how good the doctor may be. This happens much more often than it should, and the reason is a lack of proper sales and customer-service training.

The very first moment that a customer has contact with anyone in your company, an image, an impression, and a reputation is created. That image, that impression, and that reputation must be conveyed as one of being smart, knowledgeable, positive, enthusiastic, competent, reliable, well organized, detail oriented, creative, courteous, service oriented, financially stable, and more.

The customer's perception is everything. This image is as important—or maybe even more important—than the products or services you provide, and it must be conveyed throughout the customer relationship. You can't do this alone; everyone must be involved.

Most businesspeople are aware that if they have customers (whether they are patients, clients, or even passengers—they're *all* customers) they should be providing good customer service and also basic customer-service training to their frontline people who have regular contact with customers. That's obvious. Yet unfortunately we see far too many companies barely even confronting this vital issue, so stick with us.

If you're providing merely good customer service today, you're not cutting it. Customers are becoming more knowledgeable and more demanding than ever and do not want merely to be satisfied. If your people provide competent customer service, but nothing more, you're likely invisible to your customers. In today's marketplace, only extraordinary service gets noticed and remembered and, more importantly, helps drive your continued growth and success.

The larger issue and the huge differentiating factor between what most people do and what successful businesspeople do is that they have a different model in mind when they develop their organizations. Smart people see the business world through a distinctive lens; they see it through the eyes of their customer. They have the essential customer perspective and, thus, a vital competitive advantage in the marketplace. They recognize and understand the paramount importance of these factors:

- Basic sales training for *everyone* in the organization to increase sales and enhance customer service to drive the continued growth and success of the organization
- Employees providing *extraordinary customer service*, not just good service. And they do whatever they have to do to provide it
- Professional customer-service training not only for customer-service employees and frontline people, but for *everyone* in the organization
- Developing a passionate and proactive sales and customer service-centric corporate culture

These four factors constitute the core of Discipline Seven—Everybody Sells, which is the development of a highly competent sales and customer service-driven organization with an ongoing outstanding sales effort while providing extraordinary customer service. This must be a core value, a fundamental part of the company vision, not just an afterthought.

We've long championed the Everybody Sells philosophy. Everyone should be playing a critical role in the sales and customer-service process, whether it's a four-person dental practice, a twenty-five-agent real estate firm, an eighty-person car dealership, or a ten-thousand-employee multinational, billion-dollar-a-year food marketer. And everyone should be adequately trained, motivated, and incentivized to do it. In today's challenging and competitive business environment, it has become increasingly critical to have everyone contribute to achieving revenue goals, of which exceptional service plays a vital role.

Everyone in your organization is consciously or unconsciously representing your company to customers or potential customers in many ways, some good and some bad. Your accountant, for example, is contacting customers about their overdue accounts. Workers at your warehouse help customers carry items to their cars. And service techs and delivery people are spending more time with your customers than you think. So everyone should be actively and professionally "selling" and "servicing" at all times.

For some people, integrating the Everybody Sells philosophy may require a paradigm shift, a resetting of strategies and in many cases a new skill set. Here are the essential principles of Everybody Sells to help you develop a sales and customer service-driven organization and pave the way to Breakout Success.

Share the Everybody Sells Philosophy

It's important to present the Everybody Sells concept tactfully and to clearly explain to your people the following:

- Selling and customer service are everyone's job.
- Selling/servicing requires continual effort to identify and fulfill the needs and wants of customers, which in turn create optimal value.
- Everyone will benefit by embracing the Everybody Sells philosophy.
- The operative roles that everyone will play in sales and customer service are critical to the success of the company.

As we mentioned in Discipline One—Work Smart, everyone perceives change in different ways, so be well prepared to broker the acceptance of the Everybody Sells philosophy. Change for most people can be upsetting and disruptive, and you can bet on it, when it comes to sales. Especially when you're asking non-selling people to play a greater role in sales, you'll find yourself maneuvering through some minefields (Revisit the sections entitled "Develop an Effective Communication Plan" and "Eliminate Implementation Barriers" in Discipline One—Work Smart). You may indeed be dealing with a range of fears and concerns, from mild resistance to passionate refusal, when introducing this topic.

Non-selling types often attach an unwarranted stigma to salespeople, usually lumping them together with the fast-talking, aggressive spin-meisters selling used cars or the slick time-share salespeople. This negative, cynical view of sales can (and must) be changed for the Everybody Sells philosophy to be embraced and become a company-wide proposition.

Understand that non-selling people are coming from different operational and behavioral backgrounds and business cultures, and are usually hard-wired differently than salespeople. We're talking different languages from different worlds. They might feel it's not their responsibility or the job they chose to sell in any way, shape, or form, or they may find it difficult to integrate the selling practices component of Everybody Sells into their repertoire. This divide is normal and should be expected so, again, be patient and deal effectively with a potential disconnect.

"Individual commitment to a group effort—this is what makes a team work, a company work, a society work, a civilization work."
—Vince Lombardi

So, how do you get the job done? We have had success in our own businesses and with our consulting clients by redefining the concept of sales. We explain that sales and service are two sides of the same coin. We help people understand and change their perception of sales by stating that selling, like service, is about identifying and fulfilling the needs and wants of customers and creating value for them. We encourage them to view it more as "service-selling."

Explain to your team how selling and customer service-related efforts will benefit them. When the company grows, they enjoy greater opportunities and rewards. The company may be able to pay higher salaries and bonuses, provide incentives, offer more benefits, and provide more opportunities to move up in the organization.

Additionally, emphasize how this new role of sales and customer service is vital in order to compete in these fiercely competitive, ever-changing times. Make crystal clear that sales revenue is the lifeblood of the organization. Without sales and customer service, there will be no success and growth, no health plan, no commissions, no bonuses, no paychecks, no money, and even possibly no business and no jobs.

Effective leadership is what builds the Everybody Sells sales and customer-centric corporate culture. So, masterful selling and providing extraordinary customer service begin with you. It's your job to make everybody see the light and become a master at selling and customer service.

Your enthusiasm for the products or services that you sell and your dedication to providing extraordinary service need to be so evident and unwavering that anyone you come into contact with will see, feel, and understand your enthusiasm and devotion. Your uncompromising commitment must be meticulously communicated and executed.

For the successful transformation and adoption of the Everybody Sells philosophy, you must engage the heart and minds of *everyone* involved *in* the organization. The idea is to align the entire company around this priority for at least the first sixty to ninety days from when you implement this new paradigm until it is completely entrenched, embraced, and working.

FROM THE STREET: THE POWER TOOLS FOR SUCCESS

Passion and enthusiasm are your power tools for success. Share your vision and passion for the future and the successes to come.

We started one of our first companies on a shoestring with the two of us and a part-time secretary. We had no fancy office (it barely could be called an office), no salaries, no insurance, no health plans, but we had a solid dream of success and a viable plan of execution. As we slowly grew, we shared our dream with each employee who came on board. We explained to each one that working toward the goal together meant helping the company grow, and if the company grew, everyone would benefit.

As everyone did their part to sell, provide outstanding customer service, and control expenses, the business did grow and became more profitable. Salaries increased. Bonuses were paid. There was additional vacation time given. There were health plans and bigger offices. Employees gained more responsibility and authority through promotion. Several people who joined the firm as temporary help became department heads. The tangible benefits of the Everybody Sells philosophy, although in its infancy at this point, made us firm believers to continue weaving it into all our businesses over the years, and in our consulting sessions and university lectures as well.

Explain Each Person's Selling and Customer Service Roles

Many of your people have a great deal of customer contact and opportunities to sell. You may be asking, "What could possibly everyone be selling, especially non-selling people?" In every customer encounter, everyone should at the very least be selling themselves, the company, its products and services, and your service orientation in the best light by being knowledgeable, positive and enthusiastic, competent and courteous.

Start by asking yourself specifically what each person is or should be selling and how they should be providing or enhancing customer service efforts to reach an extraordinary level. Think about bookkeepers, service techs, office managers, administrative staff, secretaries, receptionists—anyone and everyone who has any contact with customers. They all have an opportunity to sell and provide extraordinary customer service. But you must make it clear what is expected.

For example, what customer sales and service role can office managers, secretaries, and receptionists play? Usually they are a customer's first contact with the business. Are they making a good first impression? The next time you walk into your office or place of business, think of yourself as a customer. Are you satisfied with what you see and hear? Are your people providing extraordinary customer service and selling? When you call the office, pay attention to how people answer the phone. Listen to phone calls coming into the office. You may be surprised what you hear. How would you have handled those encounters? As a manager, what would you have said?

Make notes on how everything could be improved and offer guidelines for what to say and do in every conceivable situation. Make the ideal responses part of a script for frontline employees and those that have regular customer contact.

Develop scripts for recurring situations, questions, and common problems so everyone can respond with confidence and enthusiasm (more on scripts later). Define specifically each person's customer-service and sales roles to make sure they aren't shooting from the hip when taking calls or personally dealing with customers. And the final step that people so often leave out is to practice, role play, and critique. These will guarantee excellence and make the customer's experience as positive and pleasant as possible.

"Setting an example is not the main means of influencing others; it is the only means." —Albert Einstein

Mercedes-Benz, Ritz Carlton Hotels, Amazon.com, and Disneyland are a few standouts that exemplify the Everybody Sells philosophy. They strictly define each person's sales and service roles, and their people are always right there at any moment to cater to customers. These businesses gained their reputations by training their people to see the world through the eyes of their customers and to always put them first.

It is your job to help your team realize that selling and customer service are vital parts of their jobs. Help define their roles, train, manage, motivate, and reward them to ensure the successful adoption of the Everybody Sells philosophy.

"I had to convince my staff that they were in the business of making a difference in the lives of people. I wanted them on board with the idea that everything we did in our company had the potential to change someone's life for the better. There was no task so small that it could be discounted. There were no conversations with a customer that were not of monumental importance. Until everyone could see the bigger picture, they couldn't truly understand how vitally important their role in the company really was."
—Zig Ziglar

Build a Sales and Customer Service Driven Organization

All too often we assume that people know how to handle sales and customer service-oriented situations when, in reality, they may have no idea what to do. (Is it possible you have alienated or lost customers because of this?) We have all experienced it. In most companies, people are utterly undertrained. Everyone must have adequate training before they deal with customers, because today's customers expect to deal with well-trained and knowledgeable people.

Don't leave the all-important job of selling and customer service to chance. Train your team well. *Everyone* is a critical success factor to the Everybody Sells customer-centric philosophy, so it must be integrated into the mainstream of the organization by educating, training, retraining, and coaching. This can be accomplished in a multitude of ways, such as classroom-based training, workshops, seminars, conferences, and web-based training.

Below we provide guidelines to help set up your own in-house sales training program for non-selling people as well as guidelines that can serve as the foundation of your customer-service training, both developed to sell more products or services and provide extraordinary customer service.

There's a huge amount of information out there on this topic, and we encourage you to explore it in more depth. If your situation warrants it, take a look at the many good books on the topic of sales and customer service. Two books we like in particular are Harry Beckwith's *Selling the Invisible* and Tom Hopkins' *How to Master the Art of Selling.* Beckwith's book further explores the importance of customer service and offers a different approach about what a business is actually offering its customers and the importance of packaging and selling long-term customer relationships. Hopkins' is a classic sales text and a must-have for your library if you want to master this art. For seasoned pros and beginners, this book is an outstanding resource for tactical sales information, including the five essential steps to successful selling.

Additionally, there are a number of companies that offer top-quality one- to two-day sales training and customer-service seminars. Check the internet for the training services that apply specifically to your company and are designed for what you want to accomplish.

"Treat people as if they were what they ought to be and you help them become what they are capable of being."
—Johann W. von Goethe

Develop Basic Sales and Customer Service Training Programs for Everyone
To set up an in-house sales training program, begin with the basics. Selling, at least when it comes to adequately training non-selling people to execute the Everybody Sells philosophy, is not difficult and has four basic tenants:
- Presentation
- Dealing with people effectively
- Dealing with issues and concerns
- Closing or gaining agreement

We cover all four tenants in greater detail in Discipline Two—Present Everything, and Discipline Five—Get More Business and suggest you revisit those chapters. However, to save you time, here's a synopsis with the most salient points that can serve as the foundation of your training and the necessary tools to take good customer sales and service to the extraordinary level.

Presentation. Everyone must have a rudimentary knowledge of how to effectively make a presentation, whether it's a ten-minute phone conversation with a customer, a formal customer-service training, or a sales pitch to one of your clients. Keep in mind that you are presenting anytime you're persuading a customer to execute a course of action, buy into an idea, gain commitment, or buy any sort of product or service.

Begin by identifying the objectives of what you'll be presenting. Ask yourself, What am I really trying to accomplish? How will I achieve my goals? What action is required of the customer with whom I'm speaking?

Do your homework. It's important to learn as much as you can about the customer. The more you know, the more successful you will be in delivering extraordinary customer service.

Always prepare for the customer engagement in advance by jotting down notes or creating a written outline for the meeting. Sometimes it may be only one paragraph, and sometimes it may be longer, depending on the particular scenario, but always commit your thoughts to paper (and after the meeting, always recap your notes).

Begin a customer engagement by sharing the objective of the meeting at the outset. Remember, people have their own agendas, and as you're speaking they're silently asking themselves, "What's this all about? What's in it for me? How does it benefit me? How is my problem or issue going to be solved?" So, your opening statements should answer these and similar questions about which most people will be thinking.

Create a good first impression; you only get one chance to do it. First impressions are lasting ones, and you could lose vital business if they're negative. People do business with people they like, so do your best to get the customer to like you right from the start. Super-size your personality, and set the tone for a positive meeting.

Make some small talk and use the customers' name often in your conversation.

Speak of benefits regularly. As often as you can, weave into conversations with your customer the benefits they'll receive. Most people are busy. They may be listening, but all they really want to know is what's in it for them.

In dealing with customers effectively use precise questioning. Questions aid in:

- Getting vital information about the person's needs
- Encouraging participation
- Peaking interest and securing commitment
- Making sure the person understands specifically what is transpiring
- Uncovering concern, issues, and objections

Jack Litzelfelner, a friend and training consultant, has conducted sales and customer service trainings for thirty years. He has trained thousands of non-selling people in the basics of selling. We were auditing one of his training classes for a bank that was changing their retail compensation plan to require employees to sell new services to existing and new customers. These were bank tellers, customer representatives, and loan officers who had little or no experience in sales. The training began as a challenging and unsettling experience for everyone, knowing that their new compensation plan was going to be based on the selling of these services.

Jack, of course, with years of experience and as a masterful trainer, put everyone at ease and thoroughly engaged them with his uncanny ability to soft peddle the topic of sales. He completely repositioned "selling" as "helping" customers by simply stating, "Part of your new job is to share the bank's new services and explain how they can truly benefit the customer. And with our unrivalled customer service orientation, we're here to help them make the most of these of services." By the end of the two-day seminar, Jack had won the hearts and minds of the employees, and the program was adopted successfully.

"Before you can sell yourself successfully to others and thus sell your ideas, your wishes, your needs, your skills, your experience, your products and services, you must be absolutely sold on yourself 100 percent." —Joe Girard

Deal with people effectively. No matter what type of business you are in, you are in the "people business." Without customers, you would have no business. Every job requires some sort of interaction with people, and interacting skillfully is a dominant discipline to be mastered. We cover this in greater detail in Discipline Three—Deal with People.

Here are essential Street Smart customer-service skills:
- See the world through the eyes of your customers and always put them first.
- Greet and deal with customers enthusiastically and have a warm and welcoming smile. (We've all met people who smile but their eyes show no warmth, so their smile comes off as an empty gesture.) Be kind, pleasant, and polite at all times.
- When you're dealing with customers, stop whatever else you're doing and give them your undivided attention; that is, 100 percent of your attention. Focus on them. Make appropriate eye contact, listen, nod, and take notes. Ask questions to be sure you heard and understood everything correctly.
- Take a genuine and keen interest in customers by finding out what they really need and want.
- Admit mistakes and apologize immediately. The worst thing you can do is fail to acknowledge a mistake. Own up to it and take prompt action to rectify the error.
- Always maintain a balance between talking and listening, and when you're listening, actively listen. Listening is not a passive endeavor. You must concentrate and focus on what the customer is saying. Don't let your mind wander.
- Don't prejudge what your customers are saying, and keep an open mind so you really hear everything. Don't assume you know what your customer will say next.

- Don't be mentally rehearsing your responses when you should be listening. And by all means, don't interrupt.

FROM THE STREET: COACHING CONSCIOUSNESS

The management task of coaching is not an event, it's a process. It is something you do with people, not to them, and it's your job to coach your entire team. Regularly coach people in their newly defined customer service and sales roles. Help them prepare for their initial or new sales and customer-service situations. Make suggestions for improvement and encourage them to practice.

Without regular coaching, training, and practice, selling and customer service skills atrophy. Don't let that happen. Periodically monitor everyone to ensure that you're achieving the necessary progress and the desired results. Help people reach their full potential and yours will follow.

Dealing with issues and concerns. When dealing with customers, you typically have to deal with a range of issues, problems, concerns and objections. Getting past these obstacles is just a part of doing business. Accept it and deal with it. This is easier said than done, but it's essential to deal with these roadblocks professionally and effectively.

The key is preparation. It should be no surprise that successful people are well prepared for these situations and likewise have their people well trained and prepared. They make it a point to anticipate and understand common problems, issues, concerns, and objections that they may encounter from customers. They have well thought-out strategies and plausible responses (often in scripts) that not only satisfy customers but also exceed their expectations.

Depending on the situation, an effective way to respond to customer issues and especially to complaints is to gain further clarification by asking questions such as these:

- To ensure that I can help you out with this, can you tell me a little more about your concern?

- I think I understand, but do you mind if we talk about that further?
- Do you mind if I ask why you feel that way?
- Do you mind if I ask why that is a specific concern at this point?
- Can you tell me more about why you are thinking along those lines?
- Can you help me gain a better understanding of what you mean?
- What exactly don't you like about...?

Be sure to welcome all customers' issues. One of the biggest mistakes people make is reacting negatively or defensively to a complaint. Avoid confrontation, contention, or debate. Be receptive and welcome the situation. People sense immediately whether you are negative or receptive.

Closing or gaining agreement. It's often necessary to gain commitment from customers, whether it's to buy a product, to begin a service, or to deal with everyday customer issues. *Closing* is the term that describes the process that prompts people to make commitments. Successful businesspeople are masters at closing, so hone your skills.

If you're making a presentation or dealing with a situation that requires closure, accelerate your efforts with a summary of your discussion and a recap of the benefits. Also attempt to uncover any issues or objections that haven't surfaced. The summary is a subtle, logical, and effective way to gain commitment or to ask for the business.

"Isn't it really 'customer helping' rather than customer service? And wouldn't you deliver better service if you thought of it that way?" —Jeffrey Gitomer

Powerful Guidelines for Providing Extraordinary Customer Service

Attitude, commitment to customer service, and an unwavering dedication to train everyone in the organization are the primary determinants of the quality of service that a company delivers.

Jack Welch, the legendary former Chairman and CEO of General Electric and author of numerous business books, said, "You have no right being a leader if you don't have it in you to build others." During his reign over GE's high-octane, performance-based culture he developed the 4E model of leadership: The effective leader has *energy, energizes others*, has a *competitive edge*, and *executes for measurable results*. He increased GE's market value an astonishing 400 billion dollars in just over two decades. We can't go wrong following Jack on this one.

In the following sections we provide a distillation of essential strategies and actionable guidelines to provide extraordinary service which can also serve as the foundation of a basic in-house customer-service training program. We recommend that you continue your pursuit of excellence in this Discipline through further readings, by using customer-service consultants, and by going to professional customer-service seminars.

FROM THE STREET: WHY EXTRAORDINARY SERVICE MATTERS

- It establishes a sustainable differential advantage. Competing products and services (and prices) don't differ much, so providing extraordinary customer sales/ service gives you that needed competitive edge.
- It drives continued growth and increased revenues. It's one thing to have a good reputation for products and services; having a reputation for extraordinary service really sets you apart. It keeps customers loyal and helps you get more business from your customers as referrals.

Create a Customer Service Mission Statement and Set Standards

Have a clearly defined image of exactly what *extraordinary* customer service means for your specific business. If it's really going to be extraordinary, it would be prudent to benchmark the service orientation of not only your competitors but also companies that are standouts in customer service in other industries and see what they're doing. The good news is that today many companies are providing such bad service that it shouldn't be too difficult to elevate yourself above your competitors.

To make your benchmarking efforts less of a task, on page 250 in the Street Smart Workshop we have included a list of ideas that should help you reach an extraordinary level of service.

After you have clearly defined the customer service you will provide, it's time to commit your plan to paper. Everyone needs to know what is expected of them, so you have to create a customer service mission statement. Next, develop standards, which offer a yardstick to measure the quality of service and provide guidelines for everyone to follow and live up to.

"The single most important thing to remember about any enterprise is that there are no results inside its walls. The result of a business is a satisfied customer." —Peter Drucker

Be Proactive in Customer Engagement

Excellent engagement means knowing what your customer needs before he does. As we discussed in Discipline One—Work Smart, change is occurring at a ferocious and profound speed, and customers' needs and views are changing as well. To continue providing ongoing extraordinary service, you must be proactive in your engagement to stay in tune with the changes that are happening or will certainly come.

You may have to rethink and recalibrate your products and services as well as the ways they are marketed, sold, and serviced to adapt to these changes.

Your customer communication can occur through a variety of methods, including personal meetings, emails, letters, newsletters, smartphone apps, social media, and your website. The important thing is to have frequent high-touch customer engagement. Customer contact makes them feel important and appreciated. When you check in with customers, determine how they prefer to be contacted and the frequency of contact they feel is necessary.

Take a close and hard look at yourself and your company from the customer's viewpoint. Are you conveying the right image and impression and not just intending to, but actually delivering extraordinary customer service? All organizations need feedback on how well they are performing. Raise the bar by stimulating and welcoming customer feedback with periodic (at least semi-annually) customer questionnaires and surveys. Keep them short and simple and be clear from the outset as to what you want to achieve. Some important topics to cover should be: quality of products or services, service promptness and courtesy of the staff.

"Be everywhere, do everything, and never fail to astonish the customer."—Macy's motto

Implement customer questionnaires and surveys by having meetings with your customers, mailing and emailing questionnaires, telephone conversations, or online surveys. There are many sample surveys online to help you develop one tailored to your company and business. They can be formal or informal. Whatever methods you choose, develop questions that are well thought-out and invite criticism, comments, and suggestions.

Be sure to act on the results that you compile from questionnaires and surveys, examining those areas where customers have been critical and make the appropriate and necessary changes to improve. You can also look to online survey services that provide a full range of questionnaire capabilities. For example, Surverymonkey.com works with a broad array of large and small organizations and has a menu of survey options that makes it easy to conduct, manage, and analyze your survey results.

Let your customers know in advance about questionnaires and or surveys that you'll be doing and that you appreciate their time to complete them. Be sure to point out that you're submitting the questionnaire or survey because you value their business and are looking for ways to improve and to ensure that they're satisfied customers.

Being proactive in your customer engagement is essential to providing extraordinary customer service. This does not just happen; it must be planned and executed.

FROM THE STREET: CUSTOMER DISSERVICE

Here are some common customer complaints that you should *never* allow to happen. Usually, dissatisfied customers never tell you that they are unhappy with your service. Only about 5 percent of them will. The other 95 percent will move on, some quietly, others not so. In fact, many will tell their business associates, friends, family, neighbors, and others. Raise the customer service and experience bar to "extraordinary," and provide concierge-like service to eliminate these reputation-busting blunders:

- Being kept waiting
- Being ignored
- Being passed around to different people or departments
- Staff that have a poor attitude and just don't care
- Staff not taking responsibility for issues or problems
- Help desks that offer endless automated menus and computerized voice assistance
- Not returning phone calls
- Lack of knowledge of the product/service.
- Call "assistance" that has been outsourced to call centers where the attendant does not have a grasp of the English language
- Not delivering on time as promised
- Arrogance, insincerity

Our business is our customers. See them as individuals and see the world through their eyes. Focus on what they want, and help them get it. Here are a few Street Smart strategies to keep them coming back:

- Never make a promise you can't keep. Be prompt and on time with all delivery dates, appointments, projects, and installations. Keeping all obligations is critical to a successful customer relationship. And if for some reason something goes sideways, communicate, communicate, communicate.

Apologize and explain what happened and what you're going to do about it. It's easy to apologize, and customers like it.

- Expectations become a reality, so stay on top of what customers expect. If you tell customers that they will have a product in two days and you get it in one, you're a hero. However, if you tell a customer it will be a one-day delivery and you can't get it delivered until day two, you're the villain. Think before you promise. Nothing annoys a customer more than a broken one. Always under-promise and over-deliver.

- Understand the power of yes. "Yes, sure we'll take care of that." Giving customers what they ask for may not always be easy, but it's part of providing extraordinary service. Every customer's request should at least be considered and attempted. It may be an exception from your company policy, but even a failed attempt is better than a quick unthoughtful no. Try to look for ways to help your customers get what they want or need and say yes as often as possible. Make doing business with you easy and pleasurable.

- Always give customers the benefit of the doubt. Never get into a situation where you're proving he's wrong and you're right; you don't want to go there.

- Immediately handle complaints and customer problems. Complaints and problems handled promptly and effectively give you the best chance to delight customers and show how much you value them. You can win them over by your care and attentiveness. Actually, it's good to have customers complain to you. If not to you, they'll be complaining to somebody else (maybe even a competitor), embellishing their bad experience.

- Provide training and specific guidelines to help manage potential customer complaints and problems. Offer suggestions on exactly what to say and what to do to help an upset or unsatisfied customer. You can always tell when a person has been adequately trained when they say, "I certainly understand why you would be upset." They have just solved 95 percent of the problem because they have agreed with you. Now the customer is on your side, and you have a much better chance of solving the problem.

- Master the art of dealing with customers on the phone. The phone can be challenging with the face-to face visual element missing. In the Street Smart Workshop on page 252, we have included rules of thumb that will make phone work more successful.

- Are you too busy to deal with customer complaints and problems quickly and professionally? That might have been only detrimental twenty years ago. Today, it can be disastrous with the internet and social media. At the touch of the send button, an upset customer can deal a wide-reaching, potentially devastating blow. Instantaneous and widely read comments and opinions can be very graphic and influential, so pay attention.

- Give customers more than they expect. Think extra, think extraordinary. Demonstrate that you value their business and will go many extra miles to keep it. What can you give them that is totally unexpected? What can you give them that they can't get anywhere else? Figure what "extra" is for your customer, and deliver it.

Do you notice when you enter a store and everyone greets you warmly with a smile? Or when you ask where an item is located and an employee takes you to it? These workers have been trained to give you more than what is expected. And it works. The same goes for any type of business. Customers will not only notice, they will tell other people about their experience too.

Give customers more than is what is expected, give them the unexpected. That's what keeps them coming back again and again.

"Perfection will come through practice. It cannot come by merely reading instructions." —Napoleon Hill

Manage, Motivate, and Monitor Selling and Customer Service Performance

After the Everybody Sells philosophy has been successfully adopted and basic in-house trainings are complete, now what? It's time to manage, motivate, and monitor.

As a leader, you must set the pace and direction for your people. People tend to take their cues not only from what you say but also from what you do; they will tend to treat customers the way you treat them. Make sure you are going in the right direction, because your team will follow you, right or wrong. Try to be the type of boss or employer for whom you would like to work.

To maximize effectiveness and productivity, you need to be persistent, patient, and willing to alter direction and adapt new strategies and trainings as you encounter changing market conditions. This can be accomplished in a variety of ways, including:

- Weekly meetings
- Coaching sessions
- Continuing education
- Staff appraisals

Weekly meetings. We had weekly meetings of usually sixty minutes, covering the topics of sales and service. Each week we introduced new topics and circulated sales and customer-service articles, newsletters, and important tips. We had open discussion of the team's actual selling and customer-service experiences from the field. We motivated. We inspired. And, most importantly, we tried to always have some fun. Remember, keeping everyone's "happy quotient" high is vital to enhancing performance and succeeding.

Coaching sessions. Plan on regularly coaching your people. The frequency and the subject matter will depend on your particular situation.

In managing, motivating, and training, it's easy to assume too much. We assume our people know more than they do. We assume they will intuitively follow our lead. And typically the ones who say they don't need the help are almost always the people who need training the most. Don't assume. Make sure you have communicated clearly. Encourage people to ask questions.

To ensure that you have made your point, ask:

- Did I explain that well enough?
- What questions do you have?
- What could I have explained more clearly?
- What aspects of this topic would you like to know more about?

Part of our coaching, is the use of scripts. Scripts teach and guide people to have positive customer interactions. Many people fear scripts because they think they sound mechanical or disingenuous. But a well-written and rehearsed script gives the person a level of comfort in handling situations. Soon the script evolves into a well-presented, focused, and productive dialogue, a road map for the conversation. Work with your team to identify the most common questions, concerns, and situations they may encounter in their dealings with customers. Work together to write scripts that are comfortable for them yet express exactly what you want conveyed.

Scripts are important power tools for the training process. Simply shooting from the hip usually ends in a dramatically less productive encounter than one that's molded by a script. With a script, your people are more confident about handling situations, especially difficult ones. To reduce resistance, modify the scripts to fit different personality types and styles. A good exercise is to get people to write a draft of how they think the script should go. They might go in the wrong direction, which can be a teaching moment, or you might get some fresh ideas that make the script better.

Remember, without regular coaching, selling and customer service skills atrophy. Don't let that happen.

FROM THE STREET: MONITORING MEANS LISTENING

Listening to your people is one of the most important parts of monitoring. Regularly let them weigh in, and carefully listen to their perceptions and insights on issues. If you listen carefully they will often tell you what you need to do to get their performance on track and better accomplish company goals.

Continuing education. Encourage your team to continually improve their selling and customer-service skills. Have them tap the enormous pool of training resources such as books, audio, websites, and blogs. Make sure they are periodically "going back to basics" to review the fundamentals of selling and customer service as well as revisiting and, when necessary, updating scripts to adapt to changing products, services, or customer and market conditions.

Encourage people to seek out classes, seminars, and professional training sessions in both sales and customer service, and be willing to pay for them. These concentrated and inspiring jump-start classes are an investment in the quality and success of your team, and they will see that you are investing in them, which boosts their confidence and motivation.

Develop and conduct periodic in-house training sessions monthly or quarterly, or whenever necessary. Our sessions are typically once a quarter and two hours in length, covering a specific topic in sales or customer service.

If you don't have a company sales and customer service manual, create an Everybody Sells manual. Here are some of the basics to include:

- A brief overview and history of the company and its mission statement
- A list of the company's products or services and their features and benefits
- Guidelines for providing extraordinary sales and customer service
- Company sales manual
- List of common customer issues, concerns, or problems and how to address them as contained in your scripts

"We are what we repeatedly do. Excellence, therefore, is not an act, but a habit." —Aristotle

Staff appraisals. Use appraisals to help everyone reach their full potential in providing the very best selling and service efforts possible. Review their knowledge of the subject matter and skill set related to their specific job. The evaluations should make clear what each person is doing right and wrong and should include a list of specific steps to help them improve. Share ideas and views to achieve higher levels of performance. Appraisals can be done semi-annually or annually.

Be your company's Chief Enthusiasm Officer. Find something to be enthusiastic about every day. Enthusiasm is contagious. Give everyone a pat on the back and let your people have the spotlight every time you can. Let people know that you have confidence in their abilities and that you are available to help whenever the need may arise.

"A man can succeed at almost anything for which he has unlimited enthusiasm." —Charles Schwab

Reward Excellence

To continually motivate people and ensure the successful adoption of the Everybody Sells philosophy, recognize and reward achievements. Motivate and incentivize everyone. Sales teams always get a compensation plan with commissions and bonuses. What do you give the non-selling people (especially the customer service hero), who make valuable contributions to sales and service?

It is important to know what motivates people, and it's not necessarily a raise and money. Sometimes it is status, being number one on the team, or just being on a team. In many cases it is simply praise and recognition for a job well done. Ask your people what they would like to see included in their incentive plans. Take the time to find out what motivates them, and you'll create a high-octane, performance-driven team.

You don't have to pay everyone in the company a commission to get them actively and productively involved in selling and customer service. After managing hundreds of talented people, we adopted the philosophy to pay people what they need and reward them with what they want.

You can incentivize and reward people in so many ways it could fill a book. In fact, Bob Nelson did just that. His book *1001 Ways to Reward Employees* is a valuable source of creative ideas to reward your people.

Here's a short list of perks you can put in play:
- Recognition awards presented at a company meeting
- Recognition in the company newsletter
- Time off from work
- Cash
- Gift certificates
- A recognition event or party

- Dinner for two at a great restaurant
- Tickets to a sporting event, concert, or cultural event
- Special parking spot for a day, week, or month
- Weekend getaways
- Promotion to a new position
- Stock options
- Upgraded benefits

Any of these incentives can provide the motivation to get people adrenalized and in high gear to help increase sales and provide extraordinary service.

Pay it forward. Take care of your people, and don't overlook the power of small but personal tokens of appreciation. Write people personal thank-you notes for jobs well done. Buy flowers for a staff member or the entire office. Take the time to have coffee, lunch, or dinner with your people; share your time, knowledge, and experience. Let people know they are important to you and your business. Your people are your "internal customers" and should be treated as such. Show them that you truly appreciate their extra efforts. Treat everyone well.

"You can have everything in life you want if you will just help enough other people get what they want." —Zig Ziglar

Developing the Everybody Sells customer service and sales-driven organization doesn't just happen. It must be managed and requires constant attention and fine-tuning to reach the extraordinary level.

STREET SMART WORKSHOP

Create the Blueprint
for Breakout Success

Having an effective goal-setting system and establishing goals are vital for achieving Breakout Success. We have developed a powerful and proven system with detailed exercises to get you started to achieve what you truly want in your life and business.

The process of setting goals helps you understand what you want and why you want it. Goals become a detailed blueprint of where you're going and how to know when you get there. This system will spur you to act and help you stay focused on achieving your goals.

We thoroughly researched the topic of goal setting, but we never found a system that worked effectively for us. Out of necessity, we developed our own system, which enabled us and many of our clients not only to achieve goals but to reach them much quicker. Our system can help you create, focus, take action, and reach your goals.

Goals are very powerful. Once you put them in writing, they take on a life of their own. A goal is a commitment. A commitment creates pressure. Pressure, properly managed, generates activity. Activity, properly directed, leads to accomplishment. Accomplishment leads to the achievement of goals. And the achievement of goals creates success. Goals provide a tractable blueprint for accomplishing your dreams.

Goals need to be specific by answering the who, what, when, where, and why questions for each goal.

Goals need a deadline. Set short-term and long-term goals. As we illustrate in the goal-setting exercises on the next few pages, set one-year, five- year, ten-year and twenty-year goals.

Goals need to be measurable. "Soon" is not a measureable time, and "some" is not a measureable amount. Set specific targets with dates, numbers, and quantities.

Goals should be attainable and realistic. That doesn't mean you can't shoot for the stars, but a goal should not be impossible. No matter how hard you work for the impossible dream, in the end, it is still impossible.

Get Away from It All

With all the distractions and the demands of your everyday life and business, it's essential to set aside high-quality time to hyper-focus on your goal setting. At least once a year, get away by yourself for day or long weekend. Spend the entire time focusing exclusively on your goals and nothing else. If you can't get away, at the very least set aside enough time and go somewhere you won't be interrupted. Be sure to get completely away from your daily routine to make the process productive.

We found that it was impossible to complete our goals in one sitting; your thoughts, dreams, and ultimately your goals need time to gel. Plan for a few days to complete them, such as two to three nights during the week or a couple of weekends.

Six Commandments of Strategic Goal Setting

- Establish both long-range and short-range goals.
- Always put your goals in writing.
- Develop specific goals.
- Set measurable goals, so you will know when they are achieved.
- Set reasonable goals that you have a good chance of attaining.
- Set motivational goals that will inspire you to strive.

How to Set Specific Goals: A Two-Part Plan

Before you can draft your strategic business goals, you must know what you really want out of life. The things you want to accomplish in your lifetime should ultimately shape and dictate your business goals. So begin by creating your Strategic LifePlan—a snapshot of your future, a crystal-clear picture of the goals you want to achieve.

Part One: Create Your Strategic LifePlan

You are probably so busy thinking about today, tomorrow, or next week that you haven't thought about your lifetime goals in ages—if ever. But it is crucial to do your goals once a year, beginning the process by early December and having them completed for January 1 of the following year. It is also important to review your goals quarterly. If you take the time to review them to see where you are, you will have a much better chance of achieving all your personal and business goals.

Start Now

Think about what you really want to accomplish in life. Think about family, recreation, education, spiritual pursuits, travel, material possessions, and community activities.

1. Take five sheets of paper and put the following headings at the top or use the worksheets provided:
- Lifetime goals
- Twenty-year goals
- Ten-year goals
- Five-year goals
- One-year goals

2. Write your name and today's date on each sheet. On all but the lifetime goals worksheet, include a target date and your age on that date. (The target date for your twenty-year goals, for example, would be twenty years from today.) It is important to include target dates and ages, so you can more clearly visualize each period.

3. Put the following seven categories under the heading on each of your five sheets.
- Material possessions
- Recreational goals
- Travel goals
- Family goals
- Spiritual goals
- Educational goals
- Community goals

4. After you have written your lifetime goals, break them down into shorter time frames, listing the things you want to accomplish in twenty years, ten years, five years, and one year. Some of the goals may come from your lifetime list, but others will occur to you as

you fill out the various worksheets. Include them all, but don't get bogged down. Spend only about twenty minutes on each worksheet.

We discovered that by using this system and setting specific target dates and deadlines, we accomplished our goals much faster than we ever thought possible. If you follow all the steps in this two-part plan, we believe you will be surprised how quickly you achieve your goals.

Do Some Blue-Skying

Begin with your lifetime goals. Take a mental journey, visualizing or dreaming of all the things you would like to achieve in your lifetime. Write them down as they come to mind. Don't evaluate them or attempt to figure out how you could make them a reality. Just let your mind wander and come up with your ultimate dreams for the future.

If you're having trouble blue-skying, try asking yourself, "If money, time, aptitude, talent, and capability were no object, what would I really want, do, or hope to achieve?" Give your imagination free rein. Anything goes. Your job right now is simply to identify what you want—not why you want it or how you'll get it. (Those issues will come later.)

"The world stands aside to let anyone pass who knows where he is going." —David Starr Jordan

Okay, it's time to begin. If you want to achieve you goals, you must be committed to some hard work, and be willing to take some risks.

Strategic LifePlan—Lifetime Goals

Name _____ **Today's Date** _____

A. Material Possessions

1. _____
2. _____
3. _____
4. _____
5. _____
6. _____
7. _____
8. _____
9. _____
10. _____

D. Family Goals

1. _____
2. _____
3. _____
4. _____
5. _____
6. _____
7. _____
8. _____
9. _____
10. _____

G. Community Goals

1. _____
2. _____
3. _____
4. _____
5. _____
6. _____
7. _____
8. _____
9. _____
10. _____

B. Recreational Goals

1. _____
2. _____
3. _____
4. _____
5. _____
6. _____
7. _____
8. _____
9. _____
10. _____

E. Spiritual Goals

1. _____
2. _____
3. _____
4. _____
5. _____
6. _____
7. _____
8. _____
9. _____
10. _____

C. Travel Goals

1. _____
2. _____
3. _____
4. _____
5. _____
6. _____
7. _____
8. _____
9. _____
10. _____

F. Educational Goals

1. _____
2. _____
3. _____
4. _____
5. _____
6. _____
7. _____
8. _____
9. _____
10. _____

Need some help identifying goals? Here's a sample worksheet with a few ideas to get you going:

Lifetime Goals

A. Material Possessions
1. Large house with a pool
2. Vacation home
3. Porsche convertible
4. Recreational vehicle
5. Home theater system

B. Recreational Goals
1. Take an annual ski trip
2. Break 80 at golf
3. Plant a rose garden
4. Learn to rollerblade
5. Jog a mile a day

C. Travel Goals
1. Visit Tahiti
2. Take cooking classes in France
3. Go on a photo safari in Africa
4. Bicycle through Tuscany
5. Tour Washington, D.C.

D. Family Goals
1. Send children to college
2. Help parents retire comfortably
3. Take a family vacation once a year
4. Spend more time with spouse and kids
5. Organize a family reunion

E. Spiritual Goals
1. Join a church
2. Go on a retreat
3. Learn to meditate
4. Attend a worship service once a week
5. Achieve "inner peace"

F. Educational Goals
1. Learn Spanish
2. Get an MBA
3. Read one business book per month
4. Take a course in creative writing
5. Get a real estate license

G. Community Goals
1. Volunteer in a local school
2. Run for a city council seat
3. Coach a Little League team
4. Donate 5,000 dollars a year to local charities
5. Participate in a community theater production

Okay, let's continue now with the twenty-year, ten-year, five-year and one-year exercises. Remember the target date for the goals and your age at the target date should be put in each exercise to make this goal system more effective.

For example in the exercise below, Twenty-Year Goals, the target date will be the exact date—day, month, and year—twenty years into the future from the date you complete the exercise. Your age will be how old you are now plus twenty years. Do the same with the ten-year, five-year, and one-year goal exercises.

"Imagination is everything. It is the preview of life's coming attractions."
—Albert Einstein

Twenty-Year Goals

Name _____ **Today's Date** _____

Target Date _____ **Age at Target Date** _____

A. Material Possessions

1. _____
2. _____
3. _____
4. _____
5. _____
6. _____
7. _____
8. _____
9. _____
10. _____

B. Recreational Goals

1. _____
2. _____
3. _____
4. _____
5. _____
6. _____
7. _____
8. _____
9. _____
10. _____

C. Travel Goals

1. _____
2. _____
3. _____
4. _____
5. _____
6. _____
7. _____
8. _____
9. _____
10. _____

D. Family Goals

1. _____
2. _____
3. _____
4. _____
5. _____
6. _____
7. _____
8. _____
9. _____
10. _____

E. Spiritual Goals

1. _____
2. _____
3. _____
4. _____
5. _____
6. _____
7. _____
8. _____
9. _____
10. _____

F. Educational Goals

1. _____
2. _____
3. _____
4. _____
5. _____
6. _____
7. _____
8. _____
9. _____
10. _____

G. Community Goals

1. _____
2. _____
3. _____
4. _____
5. _____
6. _____
7. _____
8. _____
9. _____
10. _____

Ten-Year Goals

Name _____ **Today's Date** _____

Target Date _____ **Age at Target Date** _____

A. Material Possessions

1. _____
2. _____
3. _____
4. _____
5. _____
6. _____
7. _____
8. _____
9. _____
10. _____

B. Recreational Goals

1. _____
2. _____
3. _____
4. _____
5. _____
6. _____
7. _____
8. _____
9. _____
10. _____

C. Travel Goals

1. _____
2. _____
3. _____
4. _____
5. _____
6. _____
7. _____
8. _____
9. _____
10. _____

D. Family Goals

1. _____
2. _____
3. _____
4. _____
5. _____
6. _____
7. _____
8. _____
9. _____
10. _____

E. Spiritual Goals

1. _____
2. _____
3. _____
4. _____
5. _____
6. _____
7. _____
8. _____
9. _____
10. _____

F. Educational Goals

1. _____
2. _____
3. _____
4. _____
5. _____
6. _____
7. _____
8. _____
9. _____
10. _____

G. Community Goals

1. _____
2. _____
3. _____
4. _____
5. _____
6. _____
7. _____
8. _____
9. _____
10. _____

Five-Year Goals

Name _____ **Today's Date** _____

Target Date _____ **Age at Target Date** _____

A. Material Possessions

1. _____
2. _____
3. _____
4. _____
5. _____
6. _____
7. _____
8. _____
9. _____
10. _____

B. Recreational Goals

1. _____
2. _____
3. _____
4. _____
5. _____
6. _____
7. _____
8. _____
9. _____
10. _____

C. Travel Goals

1. _____
2. _____
3. _____
4. _____
5. _____
6. _____
7. _____
8. _____
9. _____
10. _____

D. Family Goals

1. _____
2. _____
3. _____
4. _____
5. _____
6. _____
7. _____
8. _____
9. _____
10. _____

E. Spiritual Goals

1. _____
2. _____
3. _____
4. _____
5. _____
6. _____
7. _____
8. _____
9. _____
10. _____

F. Educational Goals

1. _____
2. _____
3. _____
4. _____
5. _____
6. _____
7. _____
8. _____
9. _____
10. _____

G. Community Goals

1. _____
2. _____
3. _____
4. _____
5. _____
6. _____
7. _____
8. _____
9. _____
10. _____

One-Year Goals

Name _____ **Today's Date** _____

Target Date _____ **Age at Target Date** _____

A. Material Possessions

1. _____
2. _____
3. _____
4. _____
5. _____
6. _____
7. _____
8. _____
9. _____
10. _____

B. Recreational Goals

1. _____
2. _____
3. _____
4. _____
5. _____
6. _____
7. _____
8. _____
9. _____
10. _____

C. Travel Goals

1. _____
2. _____
3. _____
4. _____
5. _____
6. _____
7. _____
8. _____
9. _____
10. _____

D. Family Goals

1. _____
2. _____
3. _____
4. _____
5. _____
6. _____
7. _____
8. _____
9. _____
10. _____

E. Spiritual Goals

1. _____
2. _____
3. _____
4. _____
5. _____
6. _____
7. _____
8. _____
9. _____
10. _____

F. Educational Goals

1. _____
2. _____
3. _____
4. _____
5. _____
6. _____
7. _____
8. _____
9. _____
10. _____

G. Community Goals

1. _____
2. _____
3. _____
4. _____
5. _____
6. _____
7. _____
8. _____
9. _____
10. _____

Now it's time to get very specific with a detailed plan for each of your Strategic LifePlan goals. Set up a separate worksheet for each goal you listed in the exercise above:

1. Write the goal at the top of the page.
2. Rank the importance of the goal, using numbers from 1 to 10.
3. Write the date you would like to start working on the goal.
4. Write the date you would like to achieve the goal.
5. List five reasons you want to accomplish the goal.
6. List the people who can help you achieve the goal.
7. List the obstacles you must overcome to reach the goal.
8. Write down how you will overcome each obstacle.
9. List ten action steps to get started on achieving the goal.

It's important to understand why you want to achieve a certain goal. The "why" provides you with an incentive. Let's say your goal is to take your family on a driving vacation next year. That's a fine goal, but you need to identify what the achievement of this goal will do for you. For example, will it allow you to spend uninterrupted time with your children? See places you have never seen before? Give your family memories of extended time together? Take your family to a place that you visited as a child? Whatever it is, write it down.

Use this sample worksheet as a guide

Strategic LifePlan Goals   **Today's date** _____

1. Goal: _____

2. Importance (1-10): _____

3. Date to begin: _____

4. Date to complete: _____

5. Why you want to achieve the goal:
    a. _____
    b. _____
    c. _____
    d. _____
    e. _____

6. People who can help you achieve the goal:
    a. _____
    b. _____
    c. _____
    d. _____
    e. _____

7. Obstacles to overcome:
    a. _____
    b. _____
    c. _____
    d. _____
    e. _____

8. How to overcome the obstacles:
    a. _____
    b. _____
    c. _____
    d. _____
    e. _____

9. Action steps to get started on achieving the goal:
    a. _____
    b. _____
    c. _____

Here is an example to guide you along:

Strategic LifePlan Goals

1. Goal: Take family on a driving vacation this summer
2. Importance (1-10): 10
3. Date to begin: January 1, ____
4. Date to complete: July 1, ____
5. Why you want to achieve the goal:
   a. Spend uninterrupted time with your children
   b. See ten places you have never seen before
   c. Take family to my childhood home
   d. Create family memories of an extended road trip together
6. People who can help you achieve the goal:
   a. Spouse
   b. Boss
   c. Assistant
7. Obstacles to overcome:
   a. Get the extended time off
   b. Figure out the exact route
   c. Book all the accommodations
8. How to overcome the obstacles:
   a. Plan a meeting with my manager to negotiate and schedule time off
   b. Get maps and information and have a planning session for routing
   c. Plan the distances for each day on the road and book lodging for each night
9. Action steps to get started on achieving the goal:
   a. Coordination of the family schedule and get the dates confirmed
   b. Do the necessary research for planning the trip
   c. Create a list of all the places to see and plan the routing to get there

Part Two: Develop Your Strategic Business Goals

After you have completed your Strategic LifePlan, you are ready to work on your Strategic Business Goals. Set up worksheets similar to those you prepared for your Strategic LifePlan or use the ones provided: Put the following headings at the top.

- Twenty-Year Business Goals
- Ten-Year Business Goals
- Five-Year Business Goals
- One-Year Business Goals

For each time period, write down what you would like to accomplish in your business. Blue-sky. Don't evaluate your goals or try to figure out how you will accomplish them. Just list everything you want to achieve in the next one to twenty years. Your lists might include business goals like these:

- Do five million dollars in sales
- Have my own factory
- Be the largest distributor in the state
- Have four offices nationwide
- Employ twenty-five people
- Take my company public

Ten- or twenty-year goals may seem irrelevant to your current business, but these exercises will help you explore what your company could become. They will give you a vision of your business in the future and provide some valuable insights for the company today.

Twenty-Year Business Goals

Name _____ **Today's Date** _____

Target Date _____ **Age at Target Date**_____

1. _____

2. _____

3. _____

4. _____

5. _____

6. _____

7. _____

8. _____

9. _____

10. _____

11. _____

12. _____

13. _____

14. _____

15. _____

16. _____

17. _____

18. _____

19. _____

20. _____

Ten-Year Business Goals

Name _____   **Today's Date** _____

Target Date _____   **Age at Target Date** _____

1. _____

2. _____

3. _____

4. _____

5. _____

6. _____

7. _____

8. _____

9. _____

10. _____

11. _____

12. _____

13. _____

14. _____

15. _____

16. _____

17. _____

18. _____

19. _____

20. _____

Five-Year Business Goals

Name _____   **Today's Date** _____

Target Date _____   **Age at Target Date**_____

1. _____

2. _____

3. _____

4. _____

5. _____

6. _____

7. _____

8. _____

9. _____

10. _____

11. _____

12. _____

13. _____

14. _____

15. _____

16. _____

17. _____

18. _____

19. _____

20. _____

One-Year Business Goals

Name _____ **Today's Date** _____

Target Date_____ **Age at Target Date**_____

1. _____

2. _____

3. _____

4. _____

5. _____

6. _____

7. _____

8. _____

9. _____

10. _____

11. _____

12. _____

13. _____

14. _____

15. _____

16. _____

17. _____

18. _____

19. _____

20. _____

Again, it's time to get very specific, with a detailed plan for each of your business goals. Set up a separate worksheet for each goal you listed in the exercise above:

1. Write the goal at the top of the page.
2. Rank the importance of the goal, using numbers from 1 to 10.
3. Write the date you would like to start working on the goal.
4. Write the date you would like to achieve the goal.
5. List five reasons you want to accomplish the goal. It's important to understand why you want to achieve a certain goal. The "why" provides you with an incentive. Let's say your goal is to increase profits by 300,000 dollars next year. That's a fine goal, but you need to identify what the extra money will do for you. Allow you to buy a new car? Take a dream vacation? Invest in a new computer? Whatever it is, write it down.
6. List the people who can help you achieve the goal.
7. List the obstacles you must overcome to reach the goal.
8. Write down how you will overcome each obstacle.
9. List ten action steps to get started on achieving the goal.

Use the sample worksheet on the following page as a guide.

Take your time. Don't rush through these exercises. Don't try to complete all the goal worksheets in one evening. Get away for a weekend (as we did once a year to do these) or work on your goals over the course of several evenings or weekends.

Strategic Business Goals   **Today's date** _____

1. Goal: _____

2. Importance (1-10): _____

3. Date to begin: _____

4. Date to complete: _____

5. Why you want to achieve the goal:

    a. _____

    b. _____

    c. _____

    d. _____

    e. _____

6. People who can help you achieve the goal:

    a. _____

    b. _____

    c. _____

    d. _____

    e. _____

7. Obstacles to overcome:

    a. _____

    b. _____

    c. _____

    d. _____

    e. _____

8. How to overcome the obstacles:

    a. _____

    b. _____

    c. _____

    d. _____

    e. _____

9. Action steps to get started on achieving the goal:

    a. _____

    b. _____

    c. _____

    d. _____

    e. _____

    f. _____

    g. _____

Here is an example:

Strategic Business Goals

1. Goal: Open a branch office in Chicago
2. Importance (1-10): 10
3. Date to begin: Today
4. Date to complete: 6 months from now
5. Why you want to achieve the goal:
   a. Increase revenues and profits
   b. Expand the geographic presence of the company
   c. Grow the business
   d. Double distribution capabilities
6. People who can help you achieve the goal:
   a. Staff
   b. Accountant
   c. Real estate agent in Chicago
   d. Sales rep in Chicago
7. Obstacles to overcome:
   a. Don't know the marketplace
   B. Unfamiliar with the competition
   c. Never managed multiple offices
8. How to overcome the obstacles:
   a. Conduct a complete marketplace analysis
   b. Analyze competitors: Who are they, where are they, what do they do?
   c. Get information on "long-distance" management; talk to people who have managed multiple offices
   d. Plan to hire a branch office manager
9. Action steps to get started on achieving the goal:
   a. Do a financial analysis of cost vs. return
   b. Determine staffing and space requirements
   c. Develop an action plan

"There is no meaning to life except the meaning man gives his life by the unfolding of his powers." —Erich Fromm

Your goals are essentially a blueprint, a guiding design for your life and your business. Refer to them often. Review them regularly.

Don't feel that they are set in stone. Adjust and revise them as circumstances change. Ask yourself the following questions:

- What do I need to do right now to achieve my goal?
- What am I not doing that I should be doing?
- What am I doing that is not helping me at all?

Use negative reinforcement. That's right, negative reinforcement. Fear is a powerful motivator, and most people will go to extraordinary lengths to avoid unpleasant consequences. Use the power of negative reinforcement to inspire positive action. List all the bad things that might happen—and all the good things that might not happen—if you don't accomplish your goals. Create a worst-case scenario that you will work very hard to avoid.

Set deadlines. Deadlines are essential. They are your weapon against procrastination. Set real deadlines and stick to them. Set long-range and short-range deadlines; short-range deadlines will keep you from falling behind on long-range projects.

To stick to your deadlines, you may need an external force or an "artificial" motivation. It helps, for example, if you make a commitment to someone else: Set a meeting with customers, suppliers, or employees that will force you to meet a deadline. Most people hate deadlines, but they are a valuable tool for creating what we call progressive stress. Stress can actually be a very positive force; it gets you going and keeps you moving toward a goal.

Review your goals. Visualize your top goals daily; They will remind you of what you really want. Review all your goals on a regular basis, and measure your progress toward achieving your dreams.

Make sure your lists of goals are close at hand. Keep them in a binder on your desk or in the inside cover of your daily planner. Do whatever it takes to ensure that you look at your written goals regularly.

Keep your goals flexible. Review all your goals at regular intervals to make sure they still reflect your ambitions. Ask yourself,

- Has my situation changed?
- Do I still want to pursue this goal?
- Do I still want the rewards that go along with this goal?

Goals must be flexible. They should change as your circumstances, needs or desires change. There were times when we were so fixed on our goals we failed to see that our situation had changed, that certain goals were no longer important to us.

You should be the master of your goals, not a slave to them. Make sure your goals are working for you.

"Most people never run far enough on their first wind to find out they've got a second. Give your dreams all you've got and you'll be amazed at the energy that comes out of you." —William James

Don't stop now. Congratulations! You have just accomplished a tremendous task. You have established business and personal goals, along with a game plan to achieve them. However, setting goals is an ongoing process. Once you have accomplished a goal, it is important to have another one on which to work. Keep preparing and planning for success. Continue to push the envelope to achieve your Breakout Success!

Strategic Multi-Dimensional Analysis-SMDA

Give Your Life and Business a Checkup

There may be more specific questions relevant to your particular situation or business, but we have highlighted common questions regularly used in the analysis of our businesses and those of our consulting clients.

Self-Analysis

Examining your motivations, actions, and goals is very powerful. Focusing inward helps you clarify what you want and why you want it. A comprehensive session with yourself allows you to uncover your true desires and motivations. You may be consciously or subconsciously acting in a particular way in order to take on a particular goal. This self-analysis creates the foundation and blueprint to better prepare you for the analysis of all facets of your business.

1. Have I completed my lifetime goals in the preceding section of the Street Smart Workshop to help me understand where I want to go in my life?
2. What are the five most important things I would like to accomplish in my personal life?
3. What are the five most important things I would like to accomplish in my business career?
4. Why do I want to achieve my goals?
5. Are the goals clearly defined and understandable?
6. What specifically needs to be done to achieve my goals?
7. Do the goals have specific deadlines for achievement?
8. How will I measure my success or the achievement of the goals?
9. Where am I now in relation to achieving my goals?
10. What's holding me back from achieving my goals, and how can I overcome it?
11. Who can help me?

12. Are the goals really important to me, realistic, and stimulating?
13. Can I see myself achieving the goals?
14. What picture/visualization do I have for my goals?
15. What will the cost in people, time, and money be to achieve my goals?
16. Do I have specific strategies developed to attain the goals?
17. Am I willing to invest the time and energy to achieve the goals?
18. Does working toward the goals bring me satisfaction?
19. What makes me happy in life? What do I enjoy? List ten things.
20. What would I like to be doing in my life right now? How can I get there sooner?
21. What do I see when I look in the mirror? Have I taken a close look lately?
22. What are my five greatest strengths?
23. What are my five greatest weaknesses?
24. How can I improve?
25. What am I doing with my capabilities? Am I taking more than I am giving?

"Plan your progress carefully, hour by hour, day by day, month by month. Organized activity and maintained enthusiasm are the wellsprings of your power." —Paul J. Meyer

Company/Organization Analysis

A deep understanding of your company provides a foundation for stronger, more accurate decision making and action planning. Answering these questions will provide a powerful level of comprehension that will enable enlightened, insightful, and progressive future planning.

1. What business are we really in?
2. What is our mission statement?
3. What is our company's overall strategy?
4. Have we defined our long-term and short-term business goals?

5. What makes us successful?
6. What are our company's most crucial assets and how can we increase their value?
7. How are we perceived in the marketplace?
8. How can we better focus on doing those things in which we excel?
9. What is the potential of our company? Where could we be in three, five, ten years?
10. Where do we stand in the marketplace? What is our estimated market share?
11. What are our company's five greatest strengths?
12. What are our company's five greatest weaknesses?
13. Is our pricing competitive?
14. Do we provide high-quality products/services and customer service?
15. How would we define our corporate culture?
16. How do we communicate and support our culture?
17. How will our organization change over the next one, three, five years?
18. In what ways could our company change or evolve for the better?
19. Are we ready to respond to these changes?
20. How can we estimate the difficulty of changing our organization?
21. What is our approach to change?
22. Should we outsource, and where most effectively can we do it?
23. What should we be doing to adapt our organization to future growth?
24. How can our company become more innovative or innovate faster?
25. What are our ten top priorities at this time?

Management/Employees

A company's most precious assets leave the building and go home every day. The workforce and how it's managed are two central components of success. Management that is consistently focused on what matters most will maximize the company's resources, productivity, and profitability.

1. Have we aligned the workforce around our mission statement?
2. Are we effectively communicating our mission statement to the management and employees?
3. Are employee and company goals aligned?
4. Are we regularly motivating our management and employees?
5. What specifically could be done to improve our motivational efforts?
6. Do we have effective and competitive compensation plans in place, and if so, how often are they reviewed?
7. Is everyone adequately incentivized? How do we know? Have we asked?
8. Do we periodically have additional incentive and bonus programs in place to further incentivize people?
9. Do we have adequate training programs in place for the management and employees?
10. Are we effectively evaluating employee performance?
11. Have we provided training in personal management mastery to help our people manage themselves more effectively?
12. Could the management and employees be better trained?
13. How often do we evaluate and improve our training programs?
14. How well do we treat our management and employees? Could this be improved?
15. What possible obstacles exist that could be preventing our people from feeling empowered and performing to the best of their abilities?
16. How often do we create "luminosity" by having Dynamic Immersion Sessions and checking in with management and employees to determine how things are going?
17. Are annual, quarterly, monthly, and weekly goal-oriented action plans established for everyone to ensure maximum productivity?
18. How effectively is management monitoring and reviewing the goals of employees?
19. How often do our supervisors meet with their direct reports to manage, motivate, and reward?
20. Are we consistently challenging management and employees to help the company grow?

21. Are we encouraging management and employees to generate new ideas to stay ahead of changes in the marketplace?
22. Could our managers be more effective? Are they truly leading?
23. Are we prepared and have a process for smooth succession of management?
24. Have we created a learning organization? If not, how can we?
25. Do we have communication programs in place that encourage feedback and ideas?

"Putting off an easy thing makes it hard and putting off a hard one makes it impossible." —Charles W. Wilson

Customer Analysis

Your business success revolves around your customer. A comprehensive understanding of your customers provides the parameters for customer-centric decision making. Understand the who, what, when, where, and why of your customers.

1. What is the profile of our typical customer?
2. Do we know why and how customers are using our products or services?
3. Do we know exactly how, when, and how much they buy from us?
4. Do we fully understand how our products or services benefit our customers?
5. Do we know how our customers perceive our company and products?
6. Have we developed a customer service mission statement?
7. Do we see the world through the eyes of our customer and always put them first?
8. Are we proactive in our customer engagement?
9. Have we set up training programs to adequately teach everyone to provide exceptional customer service?
10. Do we manage, motivate, and monitor everyone to ensure that exceptional service is being provided?
11. Are we providing extraordinary customer service? If not, what can be done to provide it?

12. How can we make our organization more customer service-centric?
13. How often do we implement customer questionnaires and surveys for our customers?
14. How often do we keep in touch with our customers? Should the frequency be increased?
15. How often do we have a heart-to-heart talk with our customers to really understand what is going on?
16. Do we ever share our growth or selected plans with our customers to get their input?
17. Is the way we keep in touch with our customers appropriate and useful? Are we getting the information we need?
18. Who are our best customers, and what are we doing for them?
19. Do our customers enjoy interacting with our sales people and staff?
20. Do we really know if our customers' needs are being met or if our products or services could be improved?
21. Do we always give customers more than they expect?
22. Are customer complaints and problems handled immediately?
23. Have we benchmarked what the companies that are providing extraordinary service are doing?
24. How well do we know our customers' businesses and their future needs?
25. How are customers who are early adopters and ahead of the curve making buying decisions?

Competitive Analysis

Learning about your competitors is as important as learning about your own business. Know who your competitors are. Understand what they do and how they do it. Knowing their products and services and how they market them will provide sound insights.

1. How well do we understand our competitive environment?
2. Who are our top competitors?
3. Do we know everything about our competitors' companies, products, and services?
4. What are our top competitors doing right now that we're not doing? Do we know what they are planning to do?
5. How are we specifically tracking the movement of our competitors? Is it sufficient?

6. Are we using the right tools, technologies, and methods to understand and track the competition?
7. Are we spotting new trends and opportunities before it's too late?
8. What competitive threats exist in our marketplace?
9. How quickly can we respond to a competitive threat?
10. How can we use our strengths to outsmart the moves of our competitors?
11. How do we differentiate our products or services from our competitors' products or services?
12. If we aren't different from our competitors, how could we create a perceived difference?
13. What can we offer our customers that our competitors are not offering or cannot offer?
14. Can we create barriers to entry?
15. Are our competitors competing for the same customers?
16. Are our competitors gaining an advantage, or do we have the advantage?
17. If we have the advantage, are we seeking new ways to maintain it or improve it? If we are not, how can we?
18. What factors could erode our positional advantage?
19. Do we know what strategies our competitors are using against us?
20. Do we know our competitors' pricing strategies?
21. How can we get business from a competitor's customer?
22. Have we seen how a competitor gives a sales presentation?
23. Have we seen our competitors' sales materials and brochures?
24. Can we identify and respond to gaps or niches that our competitors haven't filled?
25. Are there any critical changes that we should make now to be able to withstand competitive turbulence?

Financial Analysis

Financial literacy and fiscal discipline provide a solid platform for developing financial fitness and maximizing profitability.

1. Do we fully understand our accounting processes?
2. Do we know the accounts in which revenue and expenses are booked?

3. Do we have reports that provide the information we need?
4. Do we have income statements and balance sheets that are reliable and accurate?
5. Do we have a specific schedule for receiving those reports—daily, weekly, monthly?
6. Can we access revenue, receivables, payables, and cash total figures anytime?
7. Are all the numbers accurate?
8. Do we completely understand how we generate revenue and profit?
9. What type of cross checking do we perform to maintain accurate numbers?
10. Do we have detailed financial goals and budgets for revenue, profit, and expenses?
11. Do we monitor these goals and budgets for any variance?
12. Have we developed a comprehensive process for cost/expense controls?
13. Do we aggressively manage our receivables with a systematic process?
14. Have we enlisted the help of top accounting/financial advisors?
15. How often do we meet with them?
16. Do we have an established relationship with our bank?
17. Do we have an officer at the bank who knows us personally?
18. How often do we meet with our banker?
19. Do we have or need lines of credit for our business?
20. Do we understand what taxes are owed and have we budgeted for them?
21. If we want to expand, do we have enough capital? If not, how will we get it?
22. If we need financing, how long will it take to get it?
23. Do we know how much the financing will cost?
24. Have we prepared a budget for our growth?
25. Do we know the projected timeline of our expenses and revenues?

Growth/Expansion Analysis

There are many factors that you must consider in developing a successful plan for growth. Strategic goals, viability, tactical, operational, and financial requirements are just a few areas that should be evaluated in depth.

1. Why do we want to grow our business?
2. What specifically are our goals for growth and expansion?
3. Have we prepared a written, detailed business plan for growth?
4. Do we understand what it will take to achieve our growth plan?
5. When do we want to begin expanding, and what is our timetable for growth?
6. How complicated is our growth plan? Is it feasible?
7. Do we have enough experience and knowledge about our current business, industry, and market to go ahead with our growth plan?
8. Have we analyzed the overall strengths and weaknesses of our company to handle the growth?
9. Is the growth beyond our scope of knowledge and/or experience?
10. Does our growth plan fit into the long-term strategic plan of our business?
11. Is our growth plan compatible with our personal long-term goals?
12. Is our growth plan compatible with our current lifestyle?
13. What is the potential stress factor? Can our management team and employees deal with it?
14. Do we have the necessary people, time, and money to invest in our growth plan?
15. Which consultants or advisors can help us assess the soundness of our growth plan?
16. What obstacles do we have to overcome to make our growth plan a success?
17. How long will it take to overcome the obstacles?
18. What are the best-case and worst-case scenarios?
19. What will happen if we are successful? What will the next steps or next phase of growth be?
20. What will happen if our growth plan fails? What impact will it have on the company?

21. Do we have the time and resources to work on the growth plan without jeopardizing existing business?
22. Have we visualized the successful growth of our business?
23. If we run out of cash before we're done with the plan, can we acquire the necessary capital to continue?
24. How much additional office, warehouse, manufacturing, or retail space will we need?
25. What additional requirements in personnel and equipment should we expect and how much will they cost?

Sales Analysis

No matter how well your salespeople are doing, you should never be completely satisfied. Determine how everything in the selling process can be improved to continually increase sales revenues.

1. Why are our customers buying from us?
2. What are the five top reasons they say yes?
3. What are the top five reasons they say no?
4. Why are some prospective customers not buying from us?
5. How can we increase the frequency of our sales?
6. Have we set up sales training programs for everyone in our company?
7. Have we set weekly, monthly, quarterly, and annual sales goals for our salespeople?
8. Are our salespeople meeting the goals? If not, why?
9. If we consistently hit or exceed our target numbers, are we establishing more challenging goals?
10. What can and should we do to optimize sales via our internet and social media usage?
11. How can we optimize our marketing efforts for maximum impact and return?
12. How can we create a greater differential advantage in our sales and marketing efforts?
13. What are the strengths and weaknesses of our sales efforts?
14. Do we need more salespeople? Better salespeople?
15. What sort of training do we need to provide for our salespeople?
16. When was the last time our training program was reviewed, improved, and updated to reflect changes in customer needs and the marketplace?

17. Do we encourage our salespeople to get involved in outside training programs?
18. How often do we hold sales meetings, and are the agendas productive?
19. Do we have a sales training manual? If so, when was the last time it was revised?
20. When was the last time we revised our sales presentation?
21. When was the last time we reviewed common objections and worked on improving responses?
22. How often are our salespeople in touch with our customers?
23. How often do they entertain customers?
24. Are our salespeople asking for referrals?
25. How can we improve the incentives we are providing to further motivate our salespeople?

Product/Service Analysis

Customers see your products and services differently than you do. You are the provider; they are the consumer. Think like your customers. You'll achieve a better awareness and understanding of their perceptions of quality, desirability, and usefulness.

1. Do we know how our customer perceives our products or services?
2. Can we improve the quality of our products or services?
3. Do our products or services offer customers something they really need and want?
4. Do we have our customers rate the quality of our products or services?
5. Are we providing better products or services than our competitors?
6. How and why are our products or services better?
7. Are we anticipating what our customers are going to need in the future?
8. Could our products or services become obsolete?
9. How could further advancements in technology change our products or services?
10. How could technology change the way we market our products or services?

11. How could further automation change our products or services?

12. How could communication and wireless technology further change our products or services or the way they are marketed?

13. How might social networking (Facebook, Twitter, LinkedIn) impact our products or services and our marketing efforts?

14. Do we want to develop and market our products or services on a larger scale, perhaps, internationally?

15. How could our customers change their buying habit enough to affect our products or services?

16. How can we influence their buying habits?

17. How will our customers be shopping and paying for products or services in the future?

18. Do we understand the changes in shopping and paying processes that are happening now?

19. How can we rethink our products or services offerings?

20. Are we always looking for ways to improve the efficiency of our customers' purchasing processes?

21. How can we encourage our employees to further study and better understand our products or services?

22. Are we adequately training our employees to market and sell our products or services effectively?

23. How can we improve the perception of our products or services in the market?

24. What potential objections about our products or services might we encounter from new customers?

25. How will we overcome these objections?

Street Smart Daily Planner

Tips for Daily To-Do Lists

- Work from one list, and stick with it.
- Write down your top ten to twenty business and personal tasks/activities for the day, and rank them in order of importance. Focus on the top ten, beginning with the most important and let the rest go for the time being.
- Throughout the day, ask, "What are the most important tasks I should be working on?"
- If you start to feel overwhelmed, carefully look over the list and ask, "What is the best use of my time right now?" If you get busier than expected or new situations arise, reprioritize your tasks, continuing to focus on the vital ones.

STREET SMART DAILY PLANNER

DailyBusiness	Date:	Emails/Calls
☐ 1.		☐ 1.
☐ 2.		☐ 2.
☐ 3.		☐ 3.
☐ 4		☐ 4.
☐ 5.		☐ 5.
☐ 6.		☐ 6.
☐ 7.		☐ 7.
☐ 8.		☐ 8.
☐ 9.		☐ 9.
☐ 10.		☐ 10.
☐ 11.		☐ 11.
☐ 12.		☐ 12.
☐ 13.		☐ 13.
☐ 14.		☐ 14.
☐ 15.		☐ 15.
☐ 16.		☐ 16.
☐ 17.		☐ 17.
☐ 18.		☐ 18.
☐ 19.		☐ 19.
☐ 20.		☐ 20.

Business Items for Attention	Personal Items for Attention
☐ 1.	☐ 1.
☐ 2.	☐ 2.
☐ 3.	☐ 3.
☐ 4.	☐ 4.
☐ 5.	☐ 5.
☐ 6.	☐ 6.
☐ 7.	☐ 7.
☐ 8.	☐ 8.
☐ 9.	☐ 9.
☐ 10.	☐ 10.

Make Friends with the Future

How to develop a future-focused, change-oriented mentality and culture:

- Repeat this mantra daily: "Relentlessly look for ways to grow, improve, and innovate in absolutely everything I do."
- Frequently test new business assumptions, concepts, and strategies to determine how they fit into the prevailing realities of the business. Is it time for a paradigm shift?
- Aggressively network and enter into partnerships and alliances to put a new spin on your innovation strategies.
- Seek out people who can become your champions of change, and work with them closely to foster innovation throughout the organization.
- Strive to make yours an outwardly focused organization by staying in tune with everything that's going on in the company and with your employees, customers, the industry, and the world at large.
- Foster the mindset that all employees should become creators of change by continually stretching their thinking (actually thinking the unthinkable), by always scanning the landscape for new ideas, and by always engaging in assessment and experimentation.
- Be excited, enthusiastic, and positive about maintaining a strong drive for innovation. Don't sneak back into your comfort zone.
- Frequently check in with your people to better understand day-to-day change issues, foster an innovation mentality, and eliminate any possible fractures that might stymie the company's mission and forward momentum.
- Establish defined roles and responsibilities to execute change and innovation initiatives successfully.
- Incorporate expectations for innovation, and work improvements into job descriptions and performance reviews.
- Reward innovation. Offer incentives or bonuses to employees who come up with forward-thinking ideas despite whether they are implemented or succeed (obviously offer larger

bonuses for those ideas that can be successfully executed). Place a premium on speedy generation of ideas.

- Quarterly, have everyone compile an Innovation Report, which can be as simple as a two- to three-page write-up on all aspects of their jobs, including suggestions for changes and improvements.

- Quarterly or semi-annually have an innovation retreat with your team. Go away for a few days to a mountain or beach resort or even locally—any place conducive to brainstorming sessions to work on change and innovation plans.

Eat Smart

There is a direct correlation between eating well and increased energy, mood level, productivity and keeping your weight in check.

Follow our guidelines below for eating smart.

- Eat lighter: Eating smaller portions at every meal is perhaps the most important technique for losing weight and staying healthy. Cutting down on portion size is the only way to achieve your appropriate daily caloric intake. It's the rare case where someone needs to eat more to achieve optimum health. Put less food on your plate and don't go back for seconds. Also try downsizing plates and bowls, and you'll automatically end up eating less. Healthy people master portion control.
- Eat slower: Make it a habit to take your time when eating. Be conscious of chewing and savoring your food. Slow down and enjoy eating. Studies show that it takes about twenty minutes for chemical signals from your stomach to get to your brain and to tell you that it's full.
- Always stop eating before you are full: This is self-explanatory, but warrants stating.
- Water, water, water: The mind often confuses hunger and thirst; it sends a signal that you're hungry when in fact you're thirsty. At the first pangs of hunger, drink one to two glasses of water—not juice, coffee, or anything else that has empty calories.
  - o A great technique that really helps to prevent overeating is to drink two eight-ounce glasses of water about thirty minutes before eating, which creates a feeling of fullness going into the meal.
  - o Yes, you've heard it a thousand times, but drinking about eight glasses of water throughout the day keeps the body hydrated and also helps keep hunger and weight in check.
  - o Upon waking every morning drink one to two glasses of water before your coffee or food. The body badly needs the hydration after your six to eight hours of sleep.

- o   Liven up water by adding lemon, lime, mint, or cucumber.
- Eat breakfast: It's the most important meal because it refuels your body after sleeping. Forget the muffins, croissants, bagels, or your typical American breakfast of eggs, bacon, sausages, and hash browns. Keep them all away from your mouth and eliminate them from your lexicon. For breakfast, enjoy a protein smoothie, fresh fruit, yogurt, low-fat cereal, toast with some jelly or peanut butter (not butter), or a hard or soft-boiled egg.
- Eat lighter lunches: During the workday, you want your energy and mental clarity at peak levels. Digestion is the most taxing bodily function; that's why we have a sleepy feeling after eating a heavy meal. When you eat light, there's less to digest, and the blood flow isn't all going to your stomach to aid digestion. The idea is to keep the blood flowing to your brain to maximize mental energy and clarity. For lunch, eat fresh fruit, protein shakes, yogurt, broiled/grilled chicken or fish, or green salads topped with strips of chicken or salmon. Eliminate all salad dressings except for olive oil and vinegar or low-calorie ones. Save your bigger lunches for the weekends.
- Snacking: After the breakfast and lunches we just described, you'll probably be hungry often, which is normal. Snacking keeps your body properly fueled, stabilizes blood sugar levels, and maintains optimal energy levels.

So let's snack! Snack after breakfast, after lunch, after dinner. Eat and enjoy, but when you snack, do it intelligently, thinking of snacks more as fuel than as treats or rewards. If you haven't tried the foods listed below, you'll eventually acquire a taste for them and be pleasantly surprised at how they keep your hunger in check.

- o   Grab a handful of almonds, walnuts, seeds such as sunflower and pumpkin, or trail mixes (but avoid the ones with large amounts of sweetened dry fruits or chocolate chips).
- o   Anything that is healthy and especially crunchy is great (the chewing requires work, reduces hunger, and creates

a sense of being full). Try baby carrots, celery, cucumbers, broccoli, cut-up apples, and any other fruits and veggies that you like. Place a bowl of them in the refrigerator, and bring them in a baggie to work.

o Eat power foods, especially during the afternoon when energy levels dip, making you feel tired. Try energy bars (not candy bars, which should be eliminated from your lexicon too), whole-grain crackers with some peanut butter, yogurt, and fresh or unsweetened dried fruits.

- Journal what you eat: Write down everything you eat every day for a week, and you can see all of the empty calories you consume that you chalk up to a reward or just one of those guilty pleasures. When you see how many calories and pounds these little lapses add up to, you'll start to cut back on them and will develop a mindset to ignore these temptations completely.

FROM THE STREET: SLEEP YOUR WAY TO HEALTH

Research shows that a lack of sleep increases levels of the hunger hormone, ghrelin, which can lead to over eating and weight gain.

"To eat is a necessity, but to eat intelligently is an art."
—La Rochefoucauld

What to Reduce or Eliminate
- Sodas and all sugary drinks, such as sweetened iced teas and sports and energy drinks. Replace them with club soda or water with a lemon or lime, natural fruit juices, or if you must, diet soft drinks.
- Foods high in fat and dietary cholesterol including anything from fast-food "restaurants." If you absolutely must satisfy your Mac attack, treat yourself once a month to this admittedly tasty but nutritionally limited food.

- Most bread. Avoid buying it for your home, but occasionally treat yourself to it at restaurants. If you have to eat bread, eat whole-wheat or multi-grain versions.
- All fried and processed foods, including most deli meats.
- Salt, whenever possible. Reduce it significantly when eating at home. Your palate will adjust to it over time, and eventually you'll dislike salty food. There's also far too much salt in restaurant food, so keep that in mind regarding your overall sodium intake. Also, always buy sodium-free or reduced-sodium food products.
- Sugar, wherever possible. Use sugar free or reduced sugar products.
- Potato and all chips. Substitute pretzels, or if you must eat chips, try pita or baked chips.
- Desserts. If you really want to shed weight, make a lifestyle change and completely eliminate desserts from your lunch and dinners, or at least opt for fresh fruits or frozen yogurt.

Beneficial Foods

- Oily fish containing omega-3 fatty acids (salmon, trout, herring) at least two times a week.
- Fat-free or low-fat dairy products such as yogurt, skim milk, and cottage cheese. Consider using them in all recipes instead of traditional ingredients.
- Lots of fruits and vegetables. Research indicates that about three servings a day promotes active brain function. Try tomatoes (which have the anti-oxidant lycopene that fights premature aging), broccoli (packed with antioxidants and also contains sulforaphane, which may help prevent colon cancer) and blueberries (known to boost brain health).
- Lean meats and poultry (without the skin).

Exercise Your Way to Super Productivity

If you're a newcomer to exercising, it's wise to begin by getting a complete physical exam and a doctor's okay to start an exercise program. Then pull the trigger and join a gym. It's well worth it to hire an in-house personal trainer for an hourly session at least two to three times a week for a minimum of a month to get you acquainted with the equipment and different types of exercise programs that suit your needs.

We recommend trying a quick thirty-minute workout first thing in the morning (remember the recommendation to get up a half-hour earlier each day?). Try a brief walk or jog (bring the dog along if you want), or do some calisthenics. If you have a stationary bike at home, jump on it and read the morning paper. Or go to the gym before heading to the office. A morning workout is an ideal way to get a quick jolt of oxygen to your body and brain and to get your blood flowing. It'll help clear the cobwebs of morning mind and increase your energy levels and productivity throughout day.

FROM THE STREET: EXERCISE YOUR WAY TO EUPHORIA

Physical exercise, specifically cardiovascular and aerobics, revs up the brain's production of endorphins, serotonin, adrenaline, and dopamine, the body's natural feel-good chemicals. They help fend off stress-related anxiety, serve as natural pain-killers, and not only eliminate the "blues" but also can be a major mood booster, creating feelings of euphoria.

Research shows that exercise such as light, low-impact walking forty to fifty minutes a day, three times a week, stimulates the production of new synapses, which enhances cognitive skills such as memory, decision making, planning, and multi-tasking.

If you can't exercise in the morning, have your lunch at the gym eating a protein/fruit shake, yogurt, and an energy bar after your work out. Lunchtime workouts are a marvelous way to maintain peak energy levels throughout those normally low-energy periods during the afternoons.

If a lunchtime workout doesn't work for you either, right after leaving the office will have to be the time. You may be saying, "Man, I'm mentally and physically exhausted. I have absolutely no energy and no desire to head to the gym. I just want to go home and collapse." Yes, indeed, we can feel your pain and have been there many times. Those of us who exercise regularly know that occasionally we have to drag ourselves to the gym, but by the time we're finished, we're energized, have a nice mood lift to enjoy the rest of the evening, and get a great night's sleep.

There are many exercise programs and workouts that you can do. The key is finding a program that fulfills your emotional and physical needs. Let's take a moment for some clarification; it's great if you play sports, but what we're talking about in this chapter is the importance of an exercise or workout program in addition to the sports you may play.

"Lack of activity destroys the good condition of every human being, while movement and methodical physical exercise save it and preserve it." —Plato

Tennis and golf are fun, but you don't play these sports to stay in shape. You should be in shape *before* you play them. They also require a lot of mental concentration. Therefore we've long-favored a regimen of aerobic activities during the workweek that allows us to rejuvenate our bodies and clear our minds. Cross-training, or a mix of different types of aerobic exercise, works on various muscle groups and stimulates different parts of the brain. Aerobic activity also has mental and physical benefits such as increasing your energy levels and sense of well-being. Consider doing one or more of these aerobic activities:

Brisk walking	Stationary biking
Jogging	Elliptical trainer
Spinning class	Treadmill
Swimming	Rowing machine
Aerobics class	Zumba
Biking	Bikram yoga
In-line skating	

"The first wealth is health." —Ralph Waldo Emerson

Also consider mixing up your aerobic workouts with muscle-strengthening exercises such as resistance and weight training, which also increase stamina and energy levels.

We're creatures of habit, and we all have our routines (and ruts). If an exercise regimen is not part of your life, it's time to make a life-course correction and work it in. Ask yourself, Why am I not exercising and how can I get out of this rut? It's never too late, and you're never too old. If you really can't find the time to exercise forty-five minutes to an hour a minimum of three times per week, you need to question how seriously you value your health. It takes courage, strength, and commitment, but you must get into a good exercise regimen if you want to be happier and more productive in your business and personal life. Choose whatever exercise suits you at whatever time is best, but get some sort of exercise going in your life. Don't drop the ball on this one!

Stick with It

Make a lifelong commitment to exercise and physical fitness. Once you set up your exercise program, stick with it. Here are a few tips to keep you motivated:

- Know what your exercise goals are. Why are you exercising? To improve your appearance? Lose some weight? Reduce stress? Clear your head?
- Initially try to work out on the same days and at the same time. Get into a comfortable routine.
- Vary your workout routine to stay interested and motivated.

- Keep a daily log, recording how long you exercised and what you did (cycling, lifting weights, running, swimming, etc.). The log gives you a sense of accomplishment and keeps you motivated to reach your exercise goal.
- Work out with a friend occasionally.
- Listen to music, which is a great distraction for many people and can make your exercise session more enjoyable.

Provide Extraordinary Customer Service

Extraordinary customer service can be defined by professionalism, accountability, creditability, honesty, quality, efficiency, and personalized treatment. In every customer encounter, aim to impress and delight your customers by exceeding their expectations. Set yourself apart from competitors and the industry standards. Here are a few ideas:

- Solve problems or complaints immediately.
- Make your products or service easy and convenient to use. Think convenience.
- Provide some value-added service at no charge, like phone consultations or an email follow-up after a project is complete or a service is rendered.
- Offer to get with customers before or after the business day instead of in the middle of the day. They may appreciate your flexibility.
- From time to time, randomly call customers to follow up on their level of satisfaction.
- Send personal thank-you notes in the mail.
- Create a fair and simple return policy.
- If appropriate, set up a customer hotline.
- Send holiday cards to all your customers.
- Send New Year gifts to stand out from the crowd after the Christmas rush and clutter.
- Send gift baskets for any occasion during the year.
- If you like to work early in the morning or late at night, let your customers know they can call you. They may be working too.
- Be open for business when it is convenient for your customer, not you. Open early and stay late if your customers need you to be there when they have the time.
- Offer multiple and easy ways for customers to pay: credit cards, e-bills, online. If you still send bills, include an addressed envelope to make it easy.

- Refer customers to each other.
- Provide a reminder when the customer needs another appointment or more of your products.
- Offer free delivery to the customer's home or business. Every now and then, deliver it yourself. Let the customer know you care.
- Always be looking for any mention of your client in the media, and let them know you saw it.
- Send out articles of interest to your customers.
- Create a high-quality, informative business card that gets your customers' attention.
- Give something away that's cool or useful or fun.
- Practice reliability. Do what you say, when you say you'll do it, and do it well.
- No matter what you do, be consistent. Consistency builds loyal evangelists who will spread the word about you and your business.
- Track customers' birthdays and send them a card or a gift.
- Try to know as many customers as you can by name.
- Personalize mailings or emails that you send.
- Provide a complimentary ride service.
- Offer to pick up the cab fare.
- Occasionally offer free "hotel club floor" refreshments of coffee, soft drinks, wine, beer, and snacks.
- Keep people updated if they are waiting for anything.
- Offer valet parking.
- Promote your services with a money-back guarantee.
- Have everyone in your store ready to ask customers if they need help when they walk in the door.
- Help customers find what they need quickly.
- Never let anyone stand in a long line. Make a policy to keep checkouts quick.
- Make sure someone tells them thank-you, see you soon, and thanks for coming in.

Master the Art of Handling Customers on the Telephone

- First and foremost, answer the phone. Avoid at all costs an automated telephone system. Everyone hates them. A basic tenant of extraordinary service is not to have one of these systems. A live voice that answers promptly within three to five rings starts the positive experience from first contact. If you don't have a staff or an employee to answer the phone, get call forwarding or a professional answering service. Just as important, work with your people or service to determine how you want them to answer the telephone and exactly what you want your customers to hear on the other end of the line.

- The customer is making an initial judgment about your company based on how you sound—your voice and, more importantly, the tone of your voice (people often respond more to the tone of voice than the words). It doesn't matter what you're saying to the customer, your tone will reveal what's really transpiring. The subtleties of tone are far greater than we think.

- "Smile when you speak." Sure it sounds weird, but it works. A customer can feel the energy of a smile and almost see it from the other end of the phone. Smiling helps you be pleasant, positive, and motivated.

- Depending on the circumstances, the tone of your voice may have to run the gamut from being empathic, enthusiastic, kind, reassuring, assertive, and understanding.

- Even if you know a particular customer issue is not your responsibility, it is your responsibility in the Everybody Sells environment to be a helpful bridge for the customer until you can connect him to the right person.

- Avoid at all costs phrases that truly annoy customers: "You have to," "There's nothing I can do," "It's not my job," or the worst, "What's the problem?"

- Ask permission to put a person on hold rather than saying, "I'm going to put you on hold."

- Use the customer's name frequently.
- Demonstrate that you are listening by saying, "I see," "I understand," and so forth. Take notes and read back key points so the customer knows that you were listening and care about what's going on.
- At the end of the conversation, let the customer know exactly what action you or the company will be taking.

Mind Power Affirmations

Here are some affirmations, but create your own that apply specifically to your needs and desires:

- I can attain anything I want in life through extraordinary perseverance. I will always go the extra mile in everything I do.
- I can control the way I feel by controlling the way I think. I can make myself feel good.
- Happiness is really a state of mind, so each day I wake up and find something to be happy about.
- I look for the best in all situations, people, and myself.
- I am talented. I am successful.
- I maintain the image of the person I hope to be.
- I have an incredibly strong belief in myself, my company, and my product or service.
- I make it a habit to act *now*. This eliminates procrastination, which is usually caused by fear.
- I take calculated risks and test my abilities.
- I am resilient, always bouncing back from the obstacles and roadblocks of doing business. There will always be rough times, but I am mentally tough, and I will work through them.
- I don't bother to worry about things. Worrying is a useless activity; there are no benefits in it.
- I will tolerate my imperfections. No one is perfect.
- I will enjoy everything about each day, the good and the bad. Things could always be worse.
- I will maintain a positive outlook when dealing with problems or unpleasant situations.

As you attempt to manage your mind, don't expect miracles. It's not something you can learn overnight, but if you practice, you can master it.

Street Smart Recommended Reading

1001 Ways to Reward Employees
by Bob Nelson

The 7 Habits of Highly Effective People
by Stephen R. Covey

A Business and Its Belief
by Thomas J. Watson Jr.

A New Brand World
by Scott Bedbury with Stephen Fenichel

Accounting for Non-Financial Managers
by Samuel Weaver and J. Weston

Alone Together—Why We Expect More from Technology and Less from Each Other
by Sherry Turkle

The Art of Innovation
by Tom Kelley with Jonathan Littman

The Art of Possibility
by Rosamund Stone Zander and Benjamin Zander

The Art of the Start
by Guy Kawasaki

The Art of War
by Sun Tzu

As a Man Thinketh
by James Allen

Attitude 101
by John C. Maxwell

Awaken the Giant Within
by Tony Robbins

Be Big Somewhere
by Irving Gerson

Chasing Daylight
by Eugene O'Kelly

Choke: What the Secrets of the Brain Reveal About Getting It Right When You Have To
by Sian Beilock

Competing for the Future
by Gary Hamel and C. K. Prahalad

Control Your Destiny or Someone Else Will
by Tichy and Sherman

Crossing the Chasm
by Geoffrey A. Moore

The Definitive Book of Body Language
by Barbara Pease

Disciplined Dreaming
by Josh Linkner

Discovering the Soul of Service
by Leonard Berry

Don't Sweat the Small Stuff
by Richard Carlson

Driven
by Paul R. Lawrence and Nitin Nohria

The E-Myth Revisited
by Michael E. Gerber

The Effective Executive
by Peter Drucker

Emotional Intelligence
By Daniel Goleman

Enchantment
by Guy Kawasaki

Entrepreneuring—The Ten Commandments for Building a Growth Company
by Steven C. Brandt

The Essential Drucker
by Peter Drucker

Execution
by Larry Bossidy and Ram Charan

Extreme Future
by James Canton

Financial Intelligence
by Karen Berman and Joe Knight

The First 90 Days
by Michael Watkins

First, Break All the Rules
by Marcus Buckingham and Curt Coffman

The Five Dysfunctions of a Team
by Patrick Lencioni

The Game
by Neil Strauss

Getting Things Done
by David Allen

The Goal
by Eliyahu M. Goldratt and Jeff
Cox

Good to Great
by Jim Collins

The Great Game of Business
by Jack Stack with Bo
Burlingham

The Greatest Salesman in the World
by Og Mandino

Guerrilla Marketing
by Jay Conrad Levinson

How to Become a Rainmaker
by Jeffrey J. Fox

How to Master the Art of Selling
by Tom Hopkins

*How to Win Friends & Influence
People*
by Dale Carnegie

In Search of Excellence
by Thomas J. Peters and Robert
H. Waterman, Jr.

Influence
by Robert B. Cialdini, PhD

The Innovator's Dilemma
by Clayton M. Christensen

Jack: Straight from the Gut
by Jack Welch

Jump Start Your Business Brain
by Doug Hall

The Knowing-Doing Gap
by Jeffrey Pfeffer and Robert I.
Sutton

The Leadership Challenge
by James M. Kouzes and Barry
Z. Posner

Leadership Is an Art
by Max De Pree

The Leadership Moment
by Michael Useem

Leading Change
by John P. Kotter

The Lexus and the Olive Tree
by Thomas L. Friedman

Little Red Book of Selling
by Jeffrey Gitomer

Losing My Virginity
by Richard Branson

Made to Stick
by Chip Heath and Dan Heath

The Mirror Test
by Jeffrey W. Hayzlett

Networking Like a Pro: Turning Contacts into Connections
by Ivan Misner, David Alexander, and Brian Hillard

Never Give In!
by Winston Churchill

On Becoming a Leader
by Warren Bennis

The One Minute Entrepreneur
by Ken Blanchard, Don Hutson, and Ethan Willis

The One Minute Manager
by Ken Blanchard and Spencer Johnson

The One Minute Sales person
by Spencer Johnson

Only the Paranoid Survive
by Andrew S. Grove

Poke the Box
by Seth Godin

Positioning
by Al Ries and Jack Trout

The Power of Intuition
by Gary Klein

The Power of Patience
by M. J. Ryan

The Power of Positive Thinking
by Norman Vincent Peale

Presentation Zen
by Garr Reynolds

The Psychology of Selling
by Brian Tracy

Purple Cow
by Seth Godin

The Radical Leap
by Steve Farber

Rich Dad, Poor Dad
by Robert Kiyosaki

Sales 2.0 for Dummies
by David Thompson with Elaine Marmel

Secrets of Closing the Sale
by Zig Ziglar

Selling the Invisible
by Harry Beckwith

Social Boom
by Jeff Gitomer

Steve Jobs
by Walter Isaacson

Swim with the Sharks Without Being Eaten Alive
by Harvey B. Mackay

The Tipping Point
by Malcolm Gladwell

*Unfair Advantage: The Power of
Financial Education*
by Robert Kiyosaki

*What They Don't Teach You at
Harvard Business School*
by Mark McCormick

Who Says Elephants Can't Dance?
by Louis V. Gerstner, Jr.

It's Your Biz
by Susan Wilson Solovic

Winning
by Jack Welch

*Words that Sell: More than 6000
Entries to Help You Promote Your
Products, Services, and Ideas*
by Richard Bayan

*The World is Hot, Flat, and
Crowded*
by Thomas L. Friedman

Zag
by Marty Neumeie

Street Smart Thoughts to Live and Work By

Discipline One—Work Smart

"Business is a combination of war and sport." —Andre Maurois

"To be a success in business, be daring, be first, be different." —Marchant

"Most people see what it is, and never see what it can be." —Albert Einstein

"The greatest danger in times of turbulence is not the turbulence; it is to act with yesterday's logic." —Peter Drucker

"Change is the law of life and those who look only to the past or present are certain to miss the future." —John F. Kennedy

"The quality of questions we ask ourselves will determine the quality of our lives." —Tony Robbins

"There is nothing more difficult to take in hand, more perilous to conduct, or more uncertain in its success, than to take the lead in the introduction of a new order of things." —Niccolo Machiavelli

"A prudent question is one half of wisdom." —Francis Bacon

"If you're not listening, you're not learning." —Lyndon Johnson

"Many receive advice, few profit by it." —Publilius Syrus

"Many an object is not seen, though it falls within the range of our visual ray, because it does not come within the range of our intellectual ray" —Henry David Thoreau

"The man who does not read good books has no advantage over the man who can't read them." —Mark Twain

"Thinking will not overcome fear, but action will." —W. Clement Stone

"The greatest treasure is a wealth of information." —Grover Cleveland

"One key to successful leadership is continuous personal change. Personal change is a reflection of our inner growth and empowerment." —Robert E. Quinn

"The only way companies survive is to be miles ahead of the competition. That's what we do." —Sir Richard Branson

"In the long run, men hit only what they aim at." —Henry David Thoreau

"First ponder, then dare." —Helmuth Von Moltk

"The block of granite which was an obstacle in the pathway of the weak becomes a stepping stone for the strong." —Thomas Carlyle

"Courage and perseverance have a magical talisman, before which difficulties disappear and obstacles vanish into air." —John Quincy Adams

Discipline Two—Present Everything
"All the world's a stage." —William Shakespeare

"Before anything else, getting ready is the secret to success." — Henry Ford

"The man who is prepared has his battle half fought." —Cervantes

"There are always three speeches for every one you actually gave. The one you practiced, the one you gave, and the one you wish you gave." —Dale Carnegie

"We rule the world with our words." —Napoleon Bonaparte

"It's not the will to win that matters—everyone has that. It's the will to prepare to win that matters." —Paul "Bear" Bryant

"Talent alone won't make you a success. Neither will being in the right place at the right time, unless you are ready. The most important question is: 'Are you ready?'" —Johnny Carson

"When you are not practicing, remember, someone somewhere is practicing, and when you meet him he will win." —Ed Macauley

"Nothing great was achieved without enthusiasm." —Ralph Waldo Emerson

"There are those who work all day. Those who dream all day. And those who spend an hour dreaming before setting to work to fulfill those dreams. Go into the third category because there's virtually no competition." —*Steven J. Ross*

"The more you say the less people remember." —Francois Fenelon

"Asking the right questions takes as much skill as giving the right answers." —Robert Half

"Nature has given to men one tongue, but two ears, that we may hear from others twice as much as we speak." —Epictetus

Discipline Three—Deal with People
"Success in life, in anything, depends upon the number of persons that one can make himself agreeable to." —Thomas Carlyle

"Our greatest joys and greatest pains come with our relationships with others." —Steven Covey

"Working with people is difficult, but not impossible." —Peter Drucker

"It takes less character to discover the faults of others than it does to tolerate them." —J. Petit Senn

"Everyone thinks of changing the world, but no one thinks of changing himself." —Leo Tolstoy

"Patience and perseverance have a magical effect before which difficulties and obstacles vanish." —John Quincy Adams

"Genius is nothing but a greater aptitude for patience." —Benjamin Franklin

"Fear makes strangers of people who could be friends." —Shirley MacLaine

"For every disciplined effort there is a multiple reward" – Jim Rohn

"You must look into other people as well as at them." —Lord Chesterfield

"You can make more friends in two months by becoming interested in other people than you can in two years trying to get other people interested in you."—Dale Carnegie

"Hear the meaning in the word." —William Shakespeare

"The art of being wise is the art of knowing what to overlook." —William James

"Nobody stands taller than those willing to stand corrected." —William Safire

"The secret of many of man's successes in the world resides in his insights into the moods of man and his tact in dealing with them." —J.G. Holland

"Once you get people laughing, they're listening, and you can tell them almost anything." —Herbert Gardner

"You're either part of the solution or you're part of the problem."
—Eldridge Cleaver

"Our ego is our silent partner, too often with the controlling interest." —Cullen Hightower

"Treat other people as you'd like to be treated by them." —Jesus, in Matthew 7:12

"Never lose a chance to say a kind word." —William Thackeray

Discipline Four—Watch Your Money
"Some of life's greatest enjoyments and most of life's greatest disappointments stem from your decisions about money. Whether you experience great peace of mind or constant anxiety will depend on getting your finances under control." —Robert G. Allen

"The engine which drives enterprise is not thrift but profit." —John Maynard Keynes

"Formal education will make you a living; self-education will make you a fortune." —Jim Rohn

"What gets measured gets managed." —Peter Drucker

"Money is only a tool. It will take you wherever you wish, but it will not replace you as the driver." —Ayn Rand

"Success produces success, just as money produces money."
—Nicolas Chamfort

"Prosperity is the fruit of labor. It begins with saving money."
—Abraham Lincoln

"You don't get what you deserve, you get what you negotiate."
—Charles Karas

"Let us never negotiate out of fear, but let us never fear to negotiate." —John F. Kennedy

"He is well paid that is well satisfied." —William Shakespeare

"If a man empties his purse in his head, no man can take it from him. An investment in knowledge always pays the best dividends." —Benjamin Franklin

"Time is money." —Benjamin Franklin

"Business? It's quite simple; it's other people's money." —Alexandre Dumas the Younger

"Always rub up against money, for if you rub up against money, some of it may rub off on you." —Damon Runyon

"Before borrowing money from a friend it's best to decide which you need most." —Joe Moore

"Those with the gold make the rules." —Old venture-capital adage

Discipline Five—Get More Business
"There are risks and costs to a program of action. But they are far less than the long-range risks and costs of comfortable inaction." —John F. Kennedy

"Business has just two functions and only two. Marketing and innovation. Marketing and innovation make money. Everything else is a cost." —Peter Drucker

"Above all, try something." —Franklin Roosevelt"

"No one knows what he can do till he tries." —Publilius Syrus

"Develop the winning edge; small differences in your performance can lead to large differences in your results." —Brian Tracy

"Only those who dare to fail greatly can achieve greatly." —Robert F. Kennedy

"Once you have a clear picture of your priorities—that is values, goals, and high leverage activities—organize around them." —Steven Covey

"Learning faster than your competitors is the only sustainable competitive advantage in an environment of rapid change and innovation." —Arie de Geus

"There is one thing stronger than all the armies in the world and that is an idea whose time has come."—Victor Hugo

"If the circus is coming to town and you paint a sign saying 'Circus Coming to the Fairground Saturday,' that's advertising. If you put the sign on the back of an elephant and walk it into town, that's promotion. If the elephant walks through the mayor's flower bed, that's publicity. And if you get the mayor to laugh about it, that's public relations. If the town's citizens go the circus, you show them the many entertainment booths, explain how much fun they'll have spending money at the booths, answer their questions and ultimately, they spend a lot at the circus, that's sales. And if you planned the whole thing, that's Marketing!" —P. T. Barnum

"Efficiency is doing things right. Effectiveness is doing the right things." —Peter Drucker

"A path without obstacles probably leads nowhere." —Defalque

"Never give in; never give in, never, never, never, never...never give in." —Winston Churchill

"The person who never objects to anything is a tough person to close." —Tom Hopkins

"One of the best ways to persuade others is with your ears." —Dean Rusk

"Obstacles are things a person sees when he takes his eyes off the goal" —E. Joseph Cossman

"Our greatest weakness lies in giving up. The most certain way to succeed is to always try just one more time." —Thomas A. Edison

"Self confidence is the first requisite to great undertakings." —Samuel Johnson

"Good fortune is what happens when opportunity meets with preparation." —Thomas A. Edison

"You miss 100 percent of the shots you never take." —Wayne Gretzky

Discipline Six—Manage Yourself
"Work is hard. Distractions are plentiful. And time is short." —Adam Hochschild

"Nothing happens, unless first a dream." —Carl Sandburg

"At some point you have to wake up from the dream and start creating the dream." —Larry Page

"People with goals succeed because they know where they are going. It's as simple as that." —Earl Nightingale

"Man is what he believes." —Anton Chekhov

"I'm a great believer in luck, and I find the harder I work, the more I have of it." —Thomas Jefferson

"Never tell people how to do things. Tell them what to do and they will surprise you with their ingenuity." —General George Patton

"Genius is one percent inspiration and 99 percent perspiration." —Thomas Edison

"Nothing is more terrible than activity without insight." —Thomas Carlyle

"I get up every morning determined to both change the world and to have one hell of a good time. Sometimes, this makes planning the day difficult." —E. B. White

"Obsession is the price you pay for perfection." —Warren Buffet

"Procrastination is the thief of time." —Edward Young

"To think too long about doing a thing often becomes its undoing." —Eva Young

"Time is what we want most but what we use worst." —William Penn

"We are drowning in information, but starved for knowledge." —John Naisbitt

"We must learn to balance the material wonders of technology with the spiritual demands of our human race." —John Naisbitt

"The wise man should consider that health is the greatest of human blessings. Let food be your medicine." —Hippocrates

"To eat is a necessity, but to eat intelligently is an art." —La Rochefoucauld

"It is exercise alone that supports the spirits, and keeps the mind in vigor." —Cicero

"Lack of activity destroys the good condition of every human being, while movement and methodical physical exercise save it and preserve it." —Plato

"The first wealth is health." —Ralph Waldo Emerson

"Not a day goes by that I don't have to struggle to overcome negative thinking." —Norman Vincent Peale

"Man's greatness lies in the power of his thoughts." —Blaise Pascal

"Sooner or later, those that win are those that think they can." —Richard Bach

"Change your thoughts and you change your world." —Norman Vincent Peale

"A man is literally what he thinks, his character being the complete sum of all his thoughts." —James Allen

Discipline Seven—Everybody Sells

"People acting together as a group can accomplish things which no individual acting alone could ever hope to bring about." —Franklin D. Roosevelt

"Individual commitment to a group effort—this is what makes a team work, a company work, a society work, a civilization work." —Vince Lombardi

"Setting an example is not the main means of influencing others; it is the only means." —Albert Einstein

"I had to convince my staff that they were in the business of making a difference in the lives of people. I wanted them on board with the idea that everything we did in our company had the potential to change someone's life for the better. There was no task so small that it could be discounted. There were no conversations with customers that were not of monumental importance. Until everyone could see the bigger picture, they couldn't truly understand how vitally important their role in the company really was." —Zig Ziglar

"Treat people as if they were what they ought to be and you help them become what they are capable of being." —Johann W. von Goethe

"Before you can sell yourself successfully to others and thus sell your ideas, your wishes, your needs, your skills, your experience, your products and services you must be absolutely sold on yourself 100 percent." —Joe Girard

"Isn't it really 'customer helping' rather than customer service? And wouldn't you deliver better service if you thought of it that way?" —Jeffrey Gitomer

"You have no right being a leader if you don't have it in you to build others." —Jack Welch

"The single most important thing to remember about any enterprise is that there are no results inside its walls. The result of a business is a satisfied customer." —Peter Drucker

"Be everywhere, do everything, and never fail to astonish the customer." —Macy's motto

"Perfection will come through practice. It cannot come by merely reading instructions." —Napoleon Hill

"We are what we repeatedly do. Excellence, therefore, is not an act, but a habit." —Aristotle

"A man can succeed at almost anything for which he has unlimited enthusiasm." —Charles Schwab

"You can have everything in life you want if you will just help enough other people get what they want." —Zig Ziglar

The Beginning

Congratulations on reaching this point and reading the Street Smart Disciplines.

You've now been introduced to the disciplines that can help you achieve Breakout Success. It's up to you, however, to integrate them into your life and business. If you do, you will see the results—everyone does.

The book is meant to be read more than once and ideally kept as a reference. Because, as you'll see, there is a lot of information within each discipline: street-smart, practical advice.

We have been referring to these disciplines for decades. The underlying key to Breakout Success is to always go back to sound business basics, the fundamentals that these vital disciplines provide. Review and practice them regularly.

For example:

- When we feel we are stagnating, experiencing an innovation deficit, looking for improvement, or want to make changes in our lives or companies, we go to Discipline One—Work Smart. We complete the personal and business checkup using the Strategic Multi-Dimensional Analysis and walk away with a newly defined picture of where we are and exactly what we need to do next.
- For important presentations, it's show time, and we refer to Discipline Two—Present Everything to ensure we are covering the important elements of a winning presentation.
- When we're experiencing roadblocks in dealing with certain people, we do a quick personal audit and refer to the Street Smart strategies for dealing with people.
- We keep ourselves and our companies financially fit by doing a quick review of the Financial Checklist Manifesto in Discipline Four—Watch Your Money at least quarterly.
- To keep us at peak levels of physical and mental performance, a quick review of the Discipline Six—Manage Yourself keeps us on track.

- We're always thinking about getting more business—how to find it, how to secure it, and how to keep it—so periodic reviews of Discipline Five—Get More Business, and Discipline Seven—Everybody Sells help us create a constant source of new business opportunities, new revenue streams, and creative ideas to provide extraordinary service.

This may be the end of the book, but we hope this is just the beginning of your experience with the disciplines that can help you achieve Breakout Success. We've isolated what we feel are seven vital disciplines, but there may be more that you, your colleagues, partners, employees, bosses, or others will find to help you along your way.

Let us know about your discipline, how it became one and how it worked for you. We'll post your discipline and share your success with our online community. Every part of your journey towards Breakout Success is important to us and we welcome any messages, questions and any stories you may have. Please join us at www.streetsmartdisciplines.com. We'd be delighted to hear from you!

John and Mark

Acknowledgments

John A. Kuhn

We started working on this book over ten years ago, but I have spent most of my adult life mining best practices of successful people and companies worldwide, religiously compiling boxes of information that I knew one day would be used for writing this book.

I have been inspired and enriched throughout my life by some extraordinary people and a great network of friends. There are far too many to mention here, but thank you to all of you. You know who you are.

During the last two years while writing this book, I was living in Bangkok, Buenos Aires, and San Francisco, and I have a number of people to thank in these great cities of the world.

In **Bangkok**, I'd like to thank **Ross Blaufarb**, a talented writer, editor, journalist, screenwriter, and publicist who has worked with Universal Studios, HBO Pictures, and Showtime Networks. He is an American I met when he was an editor at Thailand Tatler, part of a prestigious network of luxury lifestyle magazines that are also in Indonesia, Malaysia, Singapore, the Philippines, and Hong Kong. Ross took on our project and completed the first edit of the manuscript. He did a great job and provided valuable guidance and encouragement. Thanks, Ross!

In **Buenos Aires, Eugenia Jaen** is a wonderful person and smart attorney. Your great friendship, love, and support during my years in Argentina meant everything to me. Thanks for your encouragement to get this book published. Te quiero. Besos!

Carolina Barteik, my assistant, is an incredibly resourceful and kind woman who always does a great job on every project she takes on. Special thanks, Caro, for helping with the design and the marketing of the book. Muchísimas gracias!

Dilini Weerasooriya is a bright and energetic management consultant from Austin who lives in Buenos Aires. Thanks for the fabulous job in doing a critical read and providing smart editorial suggestions. Gracias!

In **San Francisco,** a big thanks to **Jon Belzer**, a great friend for many years. I had the good fortune to meet and work with Jon in Honolulu at the 3M Company and then again at American Park Network and Meredith Corporation. We gave Jon our manuscript to read after completing the first draft when we *thought* we were almost done. He helped us realize we had good material but lots of work to do before getting it published (work far beyond our wildest expectations!). Jon did an outstanding review and made great suggestions to improve the book. Thanks J.B.

Ana Le is a fabulously smart and talented businesswoman. We gave her the manuscript and specifically asked for a critical read, underscoring that we didn't want to hear anything good. Her thoughtful insights on the content and format helped shape and significantly make it a better book. Thanks, Ana!

Khorhied Nusratty Samad is an amazingly talented woman who was there at the beginning, over a decade ago, when we first conceived the idea for this book and began to write. Thank you for your great friendship, love, and support.

I'd also like to acknowledge and thank **Judy Lamb** and **Trevor Mullins** for spending time with the manuscript and offering solid suggestions to improve it.

Finally, back to where it all began, my roots in New York. I have had the incredible good fortune of having two "brothers," lifelong friends from childhood: **James "Milo" Melillo** and **Greg Black**. James is an amazing visionary and masterful marketer and was the cofounder with me at the American Park Network. Greg is a smart and talented attorney and businessman and, more importantly, a great friend who always offers his unwavering and enthusiastic support for all my endeavors. Thanks, guys!

Mark K. Mullins

To put your life's business experiences on paper is quite a journey. To help people in the process makes the journey worthwhile. All along the way, many individuals have greatly influenced and enhanced my life. To each and every one of them I am forever grateful.

Loretta, Trevor, and Haley Mullins are my most important inspirations. They support me, encourage me, temper me, challenge me, and help me keep the world in perspective. My greatest love and admiration belongs to them. They provided invaluable input, critique, and perspective to finish this project. You all have a piece of my heart.

Lyla Mullins is an extraordinary mom. She has been an eternal flame of support and guidance. Even when she didn't think I was listening, I never missed a word or message. She is my life editor, keeping me informed yet unspotted from the world. Love you, Mom.

Judy, Sharron, and Mary are the sisters of a lifetime. I was their little brother, and they provided me with unconditional love in our incredibly unique upbringing in a small Midwestern town. They were the perfect role models and outstanding achievers who allowed me to slide through my early years on their coattails. Their insight and experience have given me wisdom beyond my talent and years. My respect and my love to each of you.

The Koch Family provided an incredible in-law network. Since becoming a part of my wife's family in 1978, I have been blessed with inspiration from their hearts, minds and souls and an unwavering support for my efforts throughout the years.

Tom, Sherri, and Dustin Sellers are my second family and my first business partners, whom I met when I lived in Hawaii. They provided an enlightened perspective on life and business that has guided me ever since. They gave me the freedom, confidence, and early disciplines to raise the bar beyond my expectations and achieve my early successes. I am forever grateful. Aloha to my ohana, a hui hou.

Kathy Weeks deserves special thanks for contributing her outstanding proofreading skills and providing insightful editorial guidance during our last critical round of edits.

Finally, very special thanks to **Whitney Parks** and the team at Create Space for doing a fabulous job in editing and designing our book. It was a pleasure working with all of you!

We would both like to thank the following people who contributed in so many ways to our success. They shared their valuable insights and guidance, and also cheered us on along the way, providing the perseverance to carry on. A heartfelt thanks to all of you!

David Arriola

L. D. Brodskey

Dr. Richard Coleman

Tom Dowd

Rod Farrow

Mike Gallagher

Tony Genovese

Dan Jensen

Dave Jones

Kathy Kastler

Steve Kiel

David Kimport

Jerry, John, and Jamie Koch

Jack Litzelfelner

Brian Lorentz

Chris Madison

Donald Mastriano

Earlyn Ebesu Mosher

Doug Murphy

Marty O'Gorman

Richard Pisani

John Poimiroo

Steve Tedder

Greg Valen

Made in the USA
Lexington, KY
29 October 2012